THE MALAYSIAN MALAISE

Also by M. Bakri Musa

Qur'an, Hadith, And Hikayat: Exercises In Critical Thinking (2021)

Race, Religion, And Royalty: The Barnacles On Malay Society (2020)

The Rot In Malaysian Education And Other Essays (2020)

The Plundering Of Malaysia: Najib Razak And 1MDB (2020)

The Son Has Not Returned: A Surgeon In His Native Malaysia (2018)

Cast From The Herd: Memories Of A Matriarchal Malaysia (2016)

Malaysia's Wasted Decade 2004 - 2014: The Toxic Triad Of Abdullah, Najib, And UMNO Leadership (2016)

Liberating The Malay Mind (2013)

Moving Malaysia Forward (2008)

Towards A Competitive Malaysia: Development Challenges Of The 21st Century (2006)

From Malaysia, With Love (2004)
(With Karen E Musa)

Seeing Malaysia My Way (2003)

An Education System Worthy Of Malaysia (2003)

Malaysia In The Era Of Globalization (2002)

The Malay Dilemma Revisited: Race Dynamics In Modern Malaysia (1999; Updated Edition, 2017)

The Malaysian Malaise

*Corrupt Leadership, Failing Institutions,
And Intolerant Islamism*

M. Bakri Musa

Author's website: www.bakrimusa.blogspot.com
Library of Congress Control Number (LCCN):   2023907545
Nine States Press, Morgan Hill, CA, USA 95037

To Our Leaders:

تياد اورڠ يڠ امت چلاک
عاءيب ديريڽ تياد اي سڠک

*(Tiada orang yang amat celaka
Aib dirinya tiada ia sangka.)*

(None more cursed than those blind to their own flaws!)
Raja Ali Haji (*Gurundam Dua Belas – IV*)

Contents

I: MALAYSIA'S 15th GENERAL ELECTION OF NOVEMBER 2022

II: EXEMPLARY LEADERSHIP

III: MALAYSIAN HEROES

IV: CORRUPT, PATHETIC, INCOMPETENT MALAY LEADERSHIP

V: PRISTINE ISLAM

VI: THE PERNICIOUS RISE OF MALAY ISLAMISM

VII: APPALLING MALAYSIAN EDUCATION

VIII: MALAYSIA AND THE WORLD

Malaysian Timeline

April 3, 2009:   Najib Razak sworn in as Malaysia's Sixth Prime Minister

July 31, 2009:   The Trengganu Investment Authority (TIA – a state statutory body) was taken over by the Federal Ministry of Finance to become 1Malaysia Development Berhad (1MDB)

July 20, 2016:   US Department of Justice filed its largest ever civil forfeiture lawsuit under the Kleptocracy Asset Recovery Initiative (KARI) relating to the 1MDB corruption mess

May 9, 2018:   Malaysia's 14th General Election. The long-ruling coalition Barisan Nasional (National Front) was defeated by Pakatan Harapan (National Hope) coalition, ending Najib Razak's tenure as Prime Minister

May 16, 2018:   Anwar Ibrahim released from jail after being pardoned by the Agung

May 19, 2018:   Mahathir sworn in as Prime Minister for the second time; his first was from July 16, 1981 to October 2003

July 3, 2018:   Former Prime Minister Najib Razak arrested related to the 1MDB corruption scandal

Oct 13, 2018:   Anwar Ibrahim won his parliamentary seat at Port Dickson following a by-election

Jan 6, 2019:   Kelantan's Sultan Muhammad V resigned as 15th Agung over his involvement with a Russian beauty queen

Jan 24, 2019:   Pahang's Sultan Abdullah Became 16th Agung

Jan 25, 2020:   Malaysia's first three Covid-19 Cases detected in Malaysia among travelers from Wuhan, China

Feb 5, 2020:   First Covid-19 case of a local resident; he was at an event in Singapore attended by many visitors from China

Feb 23, 2020:   So-called Sheraton Move that led to Muhyiddin becoming Prime Minister *san* parliamentary procedure

Feb 24, 2020:   Mahathir's sudden and unexpected resignation as Prime Minister for the second time; the first on October 31, 2003

March 1, 2020:   Muhyiddin Yassin became Eighth Prime Minister; Anwar Ibrahim became leader of the Opposition

March 20, 2020:   First cluster of Covid-19 cases from the Jemaah Tabligh religious gathering at Sri Petaling, Selangor

March 20, 2020:   Malaysia's First Covid-19 Death

July 28, 2020:   High Court Judge Nazlan Ghazali convicted Najib Razak and jailed him for 12 years and fined RM 210 million. Released on bail pending appeal,
October 25, 2020: The Agung rejected Prime Minister's Muhyiddin request for a declaration of a State of Emergency to deal with the Covid-19 pandemic

December 16, 2020:   PM Muhyiddin, with the Agung's consent, declared a limited State of Emergency thereby cancelling the planned state by-elections in Perak and Sabah

January 12, 2021: Federal State of Emergency declared by Agung using the Covid-19 pandemic as an excuse

Feb 23, 2021:   Covid-19 vaccination (Pfizer) started nationwide

July 21, 2023:   The Federal Government revoked the Emergency Rule. The announcement, however was not made till four days later

Aug 20, 2021: Prime Minister Muhyiddin resigned

August 1, 2021: Ismail Sabri sworn in as Malaysia's Ninth Prime Minister. The Agung was "satisfied" that Ismail had the support of the majority of Members of Parliament through their "sworn affidavits." He was the shortest serving Prime Minister.

Dec 8, 2021:   Court of Appeals unanimously dismissed Najib's Appeal, labelling him a "national embarrassment"

Aug 23, 2022:   Federal (Highest) Court unanimously dismissed Najib's Appeal, characterizing the case "... [A]s straightforward but for the defendant."

Oct 12, 2022:   Ringgit breached lowest ever vis a vis US Dollar at 4.68

Nov 19, 2022:   Malaysia's 15th General Election that resulted in no party or coalition winning a majority

Nov 24, 2022:   Anwar Ibrahim sworn in as Malaysia's Tenth Prime Minister

Dec 19, 2022: Prime Minister Anwar Ibrahim won a supermajority vote of confidence in Parliament and with no dissenting vote.

People, Places, Events, And Acronyms

ABIM: Angkatan Belia Islam Malaysia (Malaysian Islamic Youth Movement) founded and long headed by Anwar Ibrahim

Anwar Ibrahim: Malaysia's Tenth Prime Minister, assumed office on November 24, 2022 following the 15th General Election

Barisan Nasional (National Front): The UMNO-led coalition that has long ruled Malaysia

Biro Tata Negara: National Civic Bureau, the national propaganda arm

Cowgate Scandal: On March 2012 Muhammad Salleh Ismail, husband of a cabinet minister, was charged for criminal misappropriation of funds (MR50 million or US$16M at the then exchange rate) meant to develop the National Feed Lot Corporation. Money was given out to him but no cattle range! He used the money instead to buy personal luxury condos in Singapore.

DAP: Democratic Action Party, now part of the ruling coalition following the 15th General Election

IKIM: Institut Kemajuan Islam Malaysia (Institute for the Development of Islam Malaysia), a government agency

Ismail Sabri: Malaysia's Ninth Prime Minister, appointed by the Agung on August 2021 following a political crisis that resulted in his predecessor's (Muhyiddin Yassin) unceremonious resignation

JAKIM: Jabatan Kemajuan Islam Malaysia (Islamic Development Department), a Federal bureaucracy

JASA: Jabatan Hal Ehwal Khas (Special Affairs Department – the government's propaganda arm)

JPA: Jabatan Perkhidmatan Awam – Civil Service

KSU: Ketua Setua Usaha: Chief Secretary, Malaysia's top civil servant

KTM: Kereta Tanah Melayu (Malayan Railway)

Latheefa Koya: Appointed Chief of the Malaysian Anti-Corruption Commission following the Perikatan Nasional victory in the 14th General Election of May 2018

Malu Apa Boss ku? (What's there to be ashamed of my boss?) Najib's supporters' moniker for him during his many corruption trials

Mahathir Mohamad: Fourth (1981-2003) and Seventh (2018-2020) Prime Minister

MARA (Majlis Amanah Rakyat): Malay acronym for the statutory body tasked with the economic and business advancements of Malays

May 13, 1969: Malaysia's bloodiest race riot that occurred in Kuala Lumpur following the 3rd General Election of May 9, 1969, that took thousands of life, an event that shook the nation. Malaysia' most traumatic civil strife.

May 9, 2018: Malaysia's 14th General Election that saw the ruling Barisan Nasional coalition losing power at the national level for the first time

Muhyiddin Yassin: Eighth Prime Minister. Took office on March 1, 2020 following clandestine scheme concocted at the Sheraton Hotel, Kuala Lumpur, and thus the "Sheraton Move"

November 19, 2022: Malaysia's 15th General Election that led to Anwar Ibrahim-led coalition Pakatan Nasional governing Malaysia

1MDB: (One Malaysia Berhad), a government-linked company Incorporated in 2009

Pakatan Harapan (Coalition of Hope): the PKR-led coalition comprising PKR, DAP and Parti Amanah.

PAS The Malay acronym of the Islamic Party

PKR (Parti Keadilan Rakyat) Citizens Justice Party

Sheraton Move: The February 2020 backdoor political scheming at the Shearon Hotel in Kuala Lumpur that saw Members of Parliament switching their party allegiances leading to the apparent collapse of the Mahathir government and subsequent political instability that saw Malaysia having five Prime Ministers from 2018 to 2022

Tommy Thomas: First non-Malay Attorney General who initiated the successful criminal prosecution for corruption of former Prime Minister Najib Razak

UMNO: United Malay National Organization

Prologue

When the virulent Covid-19 virus broke out beyond Wuhan, China, in January 2020, the entire world was consumed in an unprecedented giant joint effort to contain the outbreak. Not Malaysia, however. As if the pandemic was not serious enough of a threat and burden, Malaysia was one of those self-destructive if not downright dysfunctional countries that brought upon itself additional unneeded and self-inflicted series of political crises. That is part (and a very major one) and consequence of the Malaysian malaise: corrupt, incompetent leadership. The other two components to this triple malaise are failing ineffective institutions and rising intolerant Islamism. Each of the three components would feed on and amplify the corrosive and destructive effects of each other.

If America has its three evils of racism, poverty, and militarism, as per Martin Luther King, Jr., then Malaysia too has her own unique triad of evils. Although Malaysia is not spared poverty or racism, she is thankfully not blighted by militarism. As for racism, Islamism (political Islam) is but a variant and equally virulent form of it. Poverty in Malaysia, as in America, also parallels racial lines.

Malaysia's three strikes of corrupt leadership, failing institutions, and rising Islamism have not yet doomed or condemned the nation to be a perpetual failed state, but there are already many ominous signs pointing in that direction. Consider that between 2018 to 2022 the country had five prime ministers!

There is more. The incumbent Najib Razak, who assumed office in April 2009 upon the forced (more or less) resignation of his predecessor Abdullah Badawi, was booted out in the 14th General Election of May 2018. Two months later he was arrested for corruption, and after lengthy and ultimately unsuccessful appeals, was jailed for 12 years and fined RM210 million (US$45 million) in September 2022. Muhyiddin Yassin, Prime Minister from November 2020 to August 2021, was also arrested together with a number of his top aides for corruption after he was forced to resign. They are all awaiting trials.

Other examples abound of the destructive and reinforcing effects of the triple Malaysian evils. Consider the 15th General Election of November 19, 2022, described by former Prime Minister Mahathir as the most corrupt ever. Even dispensing with the possible sour-grape sentiment (Mahathir and his party were thrashed in that contest, with many of his party's candidates including him losing their deposits, and with not even one being elected), his observation was spot on.

The most obscene scene during that campaign was of Prime Minister Ismail Sabri blatantly distributing cash in a Hindu temple as the worshippers were performing their Deepavali prayers. He did not show even a hint of shame or embarrassment. There was no sense of impropriety for such an outright blasphemous if not criminal act, in a house of worship and at a particularly sacred moment.

Not to be outdone, also during the same campaign, there were those village ulama-cum-PAS (the Islamic Party) politicians handing out crisp cold cash to Malay rural voters. That is, only after making them swear that they would vote for a PAS candidate. "Kerana Allah" (In the name of Allah!), those PAS leaders piously insisted as they grasped tight the recipients' right palm. That people were openly recording the 'transactions' did not disturb the scruples of those ulama. It is hard to dissuade those who have successfully presumed themselves to be doing God's work no matter how hideous (or "un-Islamic") their actions.

The destructive effect of Islamism in Malaysia is amplified and thus particularly virulent as the faith has been co-opted by the state. This Malaysian ulama/state complicity is akin to what President Eisenhower referred to as America's pernicious military-industrial complex in his retirement speech. That evil destructive influence is still being felt not only in America and suffered by her citizens but also globally.

This perversion of Islam where the ulama class has allowed itself to be co-opted by the state for their immediate worldly gains is not unique to Malaysia or only during this era, as recounted by Ahmet Kuru in his *Islam, Authoritarianism, and Underdevelopment: A Global And Historical Comparison*. In ancient times the ulama class has traditionally stood as the vanguard against the excesses of the state, and often at great costs to themselves, as noted by Noah Feldman in his *The Fall And Rise Of The Islamic State*. The teaching (and conviction) of those upright righteous ulama is that the ummah (community) should obey rulers only so long as they obey Allah. When they depart for that "right path," then the ummah is justified – no, obligated – to go against their rulers, the ulama being entrusted by the ummah to be the arbiter.

Corruption is entrenched in Malaysia, Malay culture to be specific. That is also true in the other Malaysian cultures but there is a significant difference. As Malays are the main demographic group and thus form the backbone of the government (by design), Malay corruption directly impacts the country's administrative machinery at all levels, and the corrosive effects thus more profound, widespread, and amplified.

The effects of corruption, whether overt or camouflaged (as commissions or outright campaign donations as in America), are corrosive. The reason that I am more bullish on China than on America today is not because of the brilliance and ingenuity of Chinese scientists and entrepreneurs *vis a vis* their American counterparts, rather that the Chinese authorities are cracking down hard on corruption while the Americans are intent on camouflaging it as lobbying and campaign contributions. In a perversity even harder to fathom, Americans now view such activities as but expressions of their basic rights.

This is also the path Malay leaders are emulating today, treating the loot of corruption as gifts, *sedekah* (charity or donations), or worse, *borkat* (bounty) from Allah. It is this cultural perversion that is the greatest barrier to combatting this blight.

The other cruel irony (and this escapes most Malaysians) is that the man most responsible for Malaysia's current despicable and deplorable state of spiraling excesses of corrupt leaders, failing institutions, and intolerant Islamism is none other than Mahathir Mohamad, Prime Minister from July 1981 to October 2003, and then again from May 2018 to February 2020. In both instances he left trails of massive corruption and a series of both corrupt and incompetent leaders.

First, he burdened Malaysia with the soporific Abdullah Badawi as a successor. He in turn was followed by the insatiably corrupt Najib Razak. He would not have been Prime Minister if not for Mahathir doing the dirty job of bringing down Abdullah and aggressively promoting Najib.

That was not the end. With Najib's downfall, Mahathir again cursed Malaysia with Muhyiddin Yassin and later Ismail Sabri, both corrupt and clueless, a lethal combination. Mahathir has yet to own up to his responsibilities in being instrumental for these despicable incompetent characters to rise so high.

The consequences of the evil perpetrated by these five individuals (I include Mahathir in this lineup) are still ongoing, inflicting needless havoc, destruction, and uncertainty upon Malaysia. This tragic sequence was broken only when Malaysians kicked out Mahathir in the 15th General Election of November 2022, and Anwar Ibrahim became Prime Minister.

Turnaround With The 15th General Election
The Covid-19 pandemic is now manageable, thanks to the better understanding of the virus and consequent development of effective vaccines, improved public health measures, together with new effective therapies.

Not so the terrible consequences of the Malaysian malaise. They are still being felt, and fast deteriorating. The tragedy is that, like Covid-19, the Malaysian malaise is potentially preventable and readily solvable if only Malaysian (in particular Malay) leaders as well as voters were to have a modicum of smarts, sense of dedication, and some minimal integrity.

All these crises are traceable to the inflated personal ego and endless sinister scheming of one conniving character, Mahathir Mohamad. This bears repeating.

The 15th General Election of 2022 was a ray of hope, the defeat of the governing party together with the utter humiliation and total rejection of Mahathir and his new party. Though no coalition won an outright majority, the Agung gave Anwar Ibrahim (his coalition having won the greatest number of seats as well as the highest percentage of the popular votes) the first crack at forming a new government. With his adroit political skills, Anwar crafted a coalition that won a two-third majority in the new Parliament at its first seating, and with no dissenting voices.

Perversely and in an almost psychotic disconnect from reality, old Mahathir still saw himself as the nation's savior. He had the temerity, and without any trace of embarrassment, to proclaim himself ready to assume the nation's leadership once again, and for the third time. In a pean to humility, he did add, "if people were to insist on it and the insistence incessant." Then he would serve for only one year. Such modesty!

The near irreversible degradation of Malaysia today traces back to Mahathir's earlier and much longer tenure of nearly 23 years back in the last two decades of the last century. His second tenure began in a benign way and with all the best intentions. He came out of retirement to help defeat the corrupt Najib Razak and his band of bandits in Barisan Nasional in the 14th General Election of 2018. Mahathir went beyond, however. He claimed the major if not sole credit for that victory and convinced Malaysians that he was indeed the nation's savior, conveniently forgetting or choosing to ignore that he was responsible for Najib's rise in the first place.

The world too was impressed with Mahathir; a nonagenarian making a spectacular political comeback! There was indeed hope for other ageing global leaders; they too became emboldened if not inspired to hang on to their positions. As such Mahathir spent much of his first year this second time around being lauded as a geriatric celebrity of sorts, flying to various major capitals to be interviewed by other oldies in the media, think tank, and global institutions like the International Monetary Fund. Even venerable Oxford University got in the act!

As for domestic problems, he convened a panel of five-member Council of Eminent Persons. Such was Mahathir's newly acquired aura that even his earlier critics like economist K S Jomo and the sugar mogul Robert Kuok gladly agreed to be co-opted into that august body.

At age 93 following the 2018 election, the understanding was that he would retire in two years to make way for Anwar Ibrahim who was then still in prison on some trumped-up charges of sodomy (the second such charge). Unlike the rest of the modern world Malaysia still has such archaic statutes in her books!

With the new coalition's victory in 2018, its acknowledged leader, Anwar Ibrahim, was expected to be pardoned and then return to active politics to assume leadership of the nation, as was agreed upon by leaders of the victorious coalition, Mahathir included.

Then with unexpected suddenness, Mahathir resigned in February 2020. By right then Deputy Prime Minister Wan Azizah should have taken over. Fearful that she would give way to her husband Anwar Ibrahim who by now had been pardoned and subsequently elected to Parliament, Mahathir did what he thought was a shrewd move. He concocted a back door scheme, dubbed the Sheraton Move (named after the hotel where the political horse trading took place), that would lead to the Agung appointing the cancer stricken Muhyiddin Yassin to succeed Mahathir. He himself was not at that infamous conspiratorial meeting, but his fingerprints were very much in evident everywhere.

The Agung was satisfied with that extra-constitutional maneuver, whereby Members of Parliament were summoned to the Palace with their Statutory Declarations in hand purportedly supporting Muhyiddin. The Agung took that to have met the constitutional requirement that the Prime Minister be someone who commanded (or could command) the majority of Parliament. In fact, that crucial statutory requirement had been circumvented, or more correctly, manipulated. There was no formal Parliamentary ratification through open voting.

The Agung was confused, ignorant, or purposely chose to ignore the obvious reality that decisions made in private, statutory declarations in hand notwithstanding, can never replace or be predictable from one taken following open robust parliamentary debates. That should have been the proper procedure. Group dynamics can and do affect decisions quickly and often dramatically right to the last minute.

Like all backroom deals, this Sheraton Move too did not last long. Less than two years later Muhyiddin was outmaneuvered again by another dark backroom scheming, and replaced this time by the clueless character, UMNO's Vice-President Ismail Sabri. Thankfully his Administration too was also short-lived. It was booted out in the election of November 2022. Prime Minister Ismail Sabri retained the record previously held by his immediate predecessor Muhyiddin of having the briefest tenure. The irony was not lost; the election was prematurely called by Ismail himself, instigated by others. The man was incapable of independent thinking.

The Malaysian malaise's downward spiral continues. Using the ringgit as a surrogate indicator, it fell to its lowest level ever vis a vis the US dollar, trading on October 13, 2022, at RM4.70. That is lower than even during the Asian economic crisis of 1998. I wonder what happened to those five "Eminent Council" members tasked with advising Mahathir!

Ever the schemer, Mahathir was still not yet finished. Leading into the 2022 election, Mahathir formed yet another splinter party, Gerakan Tanah Air (lit. Motherland Action Party). Again, not content with the wreckage he had already inflicted upon Malaysia, he offered himself to be a candidate for Prime Minister, without blushing or any trace of embarrassment.

This time and at long last Malaysian voters could no longer be fooled. Mahathir's humiliation at the 2022 election was well deserved. His latest delusion of delivering another promised miracle for Malaysia was punctured, and I hope for Malaysia's sake, for good.

Poster Boy For Term Limits

Leaders like Mahathir, together with his regional ilk like Indonesia's Sukarno and later Suharto, as well as the Philippine's' Marcos, Sr., show the wisdom of having term limits for leaders. America, despite the spectacular successes of Franklin D Roosevelt and his New Deal, adopted presidential term limits in 1947. The angst in China today is that its Chairman Xi, without doubt a far more effective leader than Mahathir could ever hope to be, had amended the Chinese Communist Party's constitution allowing for his serving beyond the mandated limits of two terms. The Chinese memories and evidence of the follies of their Great Helmsman Chairman Mao are still fresh. If Indonesia had not imposed term limits in the immediate post-Suharto period, the republic would not today be blessed with her Jokowi.

The world has seen far too many leaders who have overstayed their welcome, with Islamic nations having a disproportionate glut of them. Mahathir should have resigned, been fired, or be investigated for his role in exposing Malaysia to the 1997 Asian economic contagion. More to the point, had term limits been operative in Malaysia then, she would have been spared at least the worst of that storm. Malaysia punished the wrong leader back in 1998 in jailing Anwar Ibrahim.

As for the obscene greed and egregious corruption of Najib Razak, Malaysia's Sixth Prime Minister, what is not acknowledged is that he is the product of Mahathir's tutelage, his political son. Mahathir was also responsible for the soporific and ineffectual Abdullah Badawi succeeding him in 2003, and five years later, instrumental in Abdullah's resigning and thus making Najib Prime Minister.

Najib learned well from his mentor, but not well enough. The only difference between the two is that Najib lost the election and was pushed out. With that his corruption was exposed and he was jailed. Mahathir won all his elections except this last one in 2022; his many sins thus remain hidden. Consider such debacles during his earlier tenure as the massive foreign exchange loss prior to and thus contributed to the Asian contagion, as well as the earlier equally massive London Tin loss when Mahathir thought that he could outsmart those professional commodity traders. The magnitude of that loss has yet to be accounted for and quantified. Those culprits responsible have yet to be held accountable. Likewise with the Bank Bumiputra collapse, and the many more financial blunders under his watch.

Economist K S Jomo in one of his many books enumerated Mahathir's many earlier economic blunders. Fast forward to three decades later, Jomo was co-opted into Mahathir's Council of Eminent Persons. Thus, we cannot blame ordinary and much less sophisticated Malaysians for having been swooned and taken in by Mahathir's second coming. If Malaysia had term limits, she would have been spared these burdens. Mahathir is the perfect poster boy for the campaign for term limits.

The late Fadzil Noor, President of PAS, made a prescient observation on Mahathir. On one of Mahathir's birthdays in the late 1980s, Fazdil wished him a long healthy life, and then mischievously added, "so he could see the damages he had wreaked upon Malaysia." Fadzil got his wish but was not able to witness it.

The trite, ineffective, and endlessly repeated "explanation" given by Malay leaders in particular Mahathir to the so-called "Malay problem" is that we are "lazy, *mudah lupa* (forget easily), and do not "Look East!" (that is, emulate the successful Japanese, Koreans, and now the Chinese). That reflects these leaders' corruption, ignorance, and incompetence best captured by the wisdom of Raja Ali Haji in his *Gurindam Dua Belas* (IV) as quoted in my epigraph, "*Tiada orang yang amat celaka / ai'b dirinya yang tiada ia sangka.*(None more cursed than those blind to their own flaws). This curse is magnified many times worse when it afflicts leaders.

The failure of Mahathir and other Malay leaders to solve our societal problems is their utter inability to ponder and explore the issues further. Why are Malays lazy if indeed we are. Perhaps we see the futility of our efforts. Canadian farmers are rich and hard working because they see the tangible benefits of their labor, what with their government providing the transport and marketing infrastructures so farmers could sell their wheat abroad. Being rewarded well is a great incentive! In addition, Canadian universities provide various extension courses and services to help farmers improve their yield, mechanize their operations, and plant high-yielding seeds. In short, improve their productivity. Farmers also get "soft" loans.

Back to so-called lazy Malay famers. Getting no rewards for your hard work is a definite disincentive. This is compounded when the rewards of society are heaped upon other the producers and the competitive. Examine Malay society and ponder those reaching the top and being amply rewarded either with wealth or titles. The rent seekers, untalented, and unproductive are overrepresented. That is not unique unto Malay society. Consider India. Her brightest and most entrepreneurial are not there but in the West; likewise with China until recently.

Back to the so-called "lazy Malays." Perhaps there are other reasons not obvious to the non-astute or smart observers. Perhaps these rural folks are anemic infested with worms or chronically afflicted with malaria. We would not know that unless we explore and ask further questions, in short research thoroughly the problem, not repeat the same old imagined causes or using the same old trite "solutions" that have repeatedly been proven ineffective.

In the 1950s Ungku Aziz, the eminent economist, suggested regular deworming of rural primary school children, believing that their malnutrition was a major factor for their under-achievements. Fast forward to four decades later, MIT's Esther Duflo, her husband Abhijit Banerjee, and Harvard's Michael Kramer won the 2019 Nobel Prize in Economics for their studies on deworming of Kenyan students. That was the most significant correlate of their school attendance and thus achievements. Had Malay leaders paid attention to Ungku Aziz in the 1950s, there would be today a Malay Nobel Laureate or two!

To repeat for needed emphasis, my central point is that we must research a problem in depth and not rely on pat explanations of the past that had proven ineffective. Malay underachievement in education, obsession with religion, and general lack of competitiveness reflect as well as are the consequences of Malay leaders' corruption and incompetence, compounded by their lack of smarts and imagination in solving these problems.

To emphasize this last point, consider the leadership of two Asian "tigers" – Singapore and Taiwan. The cabinets of both countries comprised graduates of the world's leading universities. At one time more than half of Taiwan's cabinet members had PhDs, with the President having one form an Ivy League university! Meanwhile in his second reiteration as Prime Minister, Mahathir picked that *semburit* (anal) character Azmin Ali, an "economics education" major from a third-rate American university. He unfortunately is the norm for top Malay appointees in government.

Mahathir, his delusion of grandeur notwithstanding, is no Chairman Deng who endowed China with outstanding successors like the current Chairman Xi. Instead, Mahathir gave Malaysia the sleepy Abdullah Badawi, corrupt Najib Razak, and the unbelievably incompetent pair of Muhyiddin Yassin and Ismail Sabri. Time for a radical change.

Malaysia had a chance of that following the 2018 General Election that saw the long-ruling Barisan coalition led by Najib being booted out. However, leaders of the victorious Pakatan Harapan in their misplaced sense of gratitude asked Mahathir to lead the new government, thinking that the old man still had his mojo. Instead, the wily sneaky Mahathir plunged the nation into an unneeded political crisis that saw her having four Prime Ministers in just over four years, and a time when the nation was stricken by the Covid-19 pandemic!

What those Pakatan leaders should have done was thank Mahathir for his efforts in helping topple Barisan Nasional, humor him by heaping an exalted title like Senior Statesman, and then shunt him aside with a generous stipend. Instead, they made him Prime Minister again, feeding his megalomaniac delusion, or Raja Ali Haji's *celaka* (curse) of a leader unaware of is *aib* (flaws).

It was fortunate that Malaysia had another chance with the 2022 election when Pakatan Harapan, this time led by Anwar Ibrahim. It had won the highest number of parliamentary seats as well garnered the majority of the popular votes and thus rightly given the opportunity by the Agung to form the new government. Anwar's immediate (and continuing focus) was battling corruption. Of even greater significance, his crusade now resonates with the citizenry, more so Malays. As of May 2023, the Anwar's Administration had arrested former Prime Minister Muhyiddin Yassin and his top aides for corruption during the Emergency Rule that he (Muhyiddin) had declared soon after getting into power. They are all (as of May 2023) awaiting trials.

Time Span Of These Commentaries

I wrote these essays from January 2020 to December 2022, covering that dangerous and politically uncertain period which also coincided with the Covid-19 pandemic.

The season began auspicious enough for Malaysia when the long-ruling Barisan Nasional coalition was booted out in the 14th General Election of May 2018. Then in an absurdity hard to comprehend, the new coalition picked the 93-year-old Mahathir to lead. Nobody gave thought to the fact that it was this wily old man who was instrumental for the corrupt Najib Razak becoming Prime Minister in the first place. The old man's many sins were conveniently forgotten what with everyone now praising Mahathir and giving him the full credit for having defeated Najib. Nor did anyone ponder the incredulity that if the man could not achieve what he wanted for Malaysia in his earlier 23 years as Prime Minister and when he was much younger, what hope had he nearly two decades later with his being in his mid-90s and ailing?

Although he indicated that he would not serve the full five-year term (and leaders in the winning coalition would not have agreed to his doing so anyway) nonetheless his early resignation was sudden and unanticipated. In retrospect it is not difficult to discern Mahathir's reason to resign his second term in February 2020. It was for the singular purpose of preventing Anwar Ibrahim becoming Prime Minister even though that was earlier agreed upon by the leaders of the component parties of Perikatan Nasional (National Coalition). That included the man himself.

Mahathir's sin during his first tenure (1981-2003) was both of omission as well as commission. As leader he failed in the most fundamental and elementary responsibility, that is, ensuring a competent successor as well as grooming a stable of capable leaders among the next generation. The abysmal performance of Abdullah Badawi, egregious corruption of Najib, the utter incompetence of Muhyiddin, and the bumbling directionless Ismail Sabri reflect as much on them as on Mahathir.

As for Mahathir's sins of commission, I will enumerate only three, and what a triple whammy! One, he was responsible for the current entrenched culture of corruption among UMNO (meaning, Malay) leaders. Mahathir led the party for over two decades, and it bore all his dark traits, acknowledged as well as unacknowledged, exposed as well as hidden. Two, he encouraged and thus responsible for the rise and assertiveness of political Islam, and with that, not only the dangerous and deepening polarization among Malaysians but also of far greater significance the degradation of the faith among Malays if not paying only lip service to or rejecting it. Three, the rotting Malaysian institutions, in particular educational, especially with his deemphasizing English and the concomitant emphasis on religion in national schools. As Malays are the only ones left in that stream, the burden of both initiatives is borne by them, especially poor rural Malays who have no choice but to enroll their children in these national schools.

Mahathir's failure to groom future honest, competent Malay leaders has resulted in their being consumed in one intrigue after another to grab and retain power, not to serve the nation (they are clueless in matters of statehood) but for personal gains and greed. *Mengambil kesempatan durian runtuh* (lit. taking advantage of the durian season; met. making hay while the sun shines). Both Prime Ministers Muhyiddin Yassin and Ismail Sabri maintained their support among Members of Parliament only through bribing them with ministerial posts, Ambassadorships-At-Large, and chairmanships of various government corporations. Hence their bloated Administrations. No surprise then that the greatest number of my commentaries in this book are subsumed under the heading "Corrupt, Pathetic, And Incompetent Malay Leadership."

The only positive development during this period was the jailing of former Prime Minister Najib Razak for his massive pilfering of One Malaysia Berhad (1MDB – a government-linked company), the greatest such heists. He was sentenced in September 2022 to 12 years in jail and fined RM$240 million after exhausting all avenues of appeals for crimes he began committing over a decade ago. As a parenthesis, the United States Department of Justice first filed its money laundering charges against Najib (then referred to in the indictment papers as "Malaysian Official 1") back in July 2016. It would be unnecessary to add that Najib's own Attorney-General, one Apandi Ali, also an UMNO operative, had earlier cleared Najib of any wrongdoing!

On the surface Najib's incarceration is a positive and encouraging development. However this being Malaysia, the reality is far different. Najib's conviction only feeds and aggravates the already ugly and dangerous Malay/non-Malay divide, with his Malay supporters still considering him a hero, as with their affectionate *Malu Apa Bossku?* (What's there to be ashamed of my boss) moniker.

On My Commentaries

This is my seventh collection of essays. Included are transcripts of my four Malaysian videoconferences in 2021. As these are standalone essays, some of the materials may be repeated as removing them would make each essay not intelligible.

I began writing on Malaysian affairs during my first summer holidays in Canada back in 1964. Freed from the pressure of studies, I had time to reflect and write about my native land during the long holidays, stimulated by my fresh novel experience of studying and living in a more developed country.

My first commentary, not surprisingly, was on education, reflecting on my fresh undergraduate experience, how much more productive I was in my studying in Canada, and how intellectually exhilarating was my freshman year. I attributed the first to the fact that the whole country was cool, conducive to intellectual pursuits, unlike in hot humid Malaysia where I had difficulty concentrating in the stifling heat. Air-conditioned rooms were a scarce commodity then.

I must be on to something, for years later in an interview with the *Wall Street Journal*, Singapore's Prime Minister Lee Kuan Yew attributed the success of his small republic to air-conditioning. It enables those in the stifling tropics to compete physically and far more important intellectually with their counterparts in the temperate zones.

My stimulating first-year courses were initially forced upon me. I remember arguing with my faculty adviser in having to take courses in the humanities, in particular English Literature. My fear was that those would lower my overall GPA, thus jeopardizing my acceptance into medical school, a common anxiety among would-be medical students.

Those non-science courses turned out to be an unparalleled blessing. English Literature and a liberal education opened up my hitherto narrowly focused if not closed mind. I had even considered briefly not becoming a doctor but to pursue the humanities instead.

At the end of that first summer, I wrote an extended article and mailed it to one Dr. Mahathir, then a backbencher Member of Parliament from Kubang Pasu, Kedah, in his capacity as Chairman of the Higher Education Commission. I urged the government to set up a university at cool Cameron Highlands, and to introduce American-style liberal education so others back in Malaysia could benefit from and experience what I had in Canada, the prairie blizzards excepted. Bless the man, he did reply. However, he did not comment on the merits of my ideas. Instead, perhaps concerned about my future, he suggested that I focus on my studies first so I could then return as a physician and be of greater use to the country. He must have seen too many Malay students sent abroad getting distracted and flunking out.

The second summer I worked in a dairy farm operated by a co-operative. Through that I came in close contact with Alberta wheat farmers. That prompted me to write the Chairman of MARA (the Malay acronym for the agency tasked with developing rural Malays) with copies to some big wigs in UMNO, the party purportedly championing Malay causes, describing the cooperative movement (of which Canada was a leader) as well as the Alberta Wheat Pool and similar government-sponsored entities to help farmers. Unlike Mahathir earlier, that head of MARA and those other characters did not even bother to reply or acknowledge my letter.

My lay writing took a hiatus for the next two decades, the first consumed with medical school and preparing to be a surgeon, the second on establishing my professional career.

In the 1980s, prompted by the many government-sponsored Malay students here in America attending third-rate universities, I wrote an extended commentary on advising and preparing our students for top-tier institutions. I sent that to both the Chairman of MARA and the Public Services Commission (JPA, its Malay acronym), the two agencies that sponsored those students. After waiting a suitable time for a response (none came of course), I submitted it to the *New Straits Times*. My gratitude to its then Editor-in-Chief Kadir Jassin for publishing that series and also some of my subsequent essays. He was also kind enough to have had a full-page review of my first book, *The Malay Dilemma Revisited: Race Dynamics In Modern Malaysia* (1999). Later, the newer *The Sun Daily* also carried many of my commentaries.

The late 1990s saw the emergence of the Internet, and with that, on-line media outlets. Stephen Gans of Malaysiakini.com was kind enough to give me a column, "Seeing It My Way." I also had my own blog (bakrimusa.blogspot.com) to serve both as an outlet as well as a repository for my commentaries. I am also indebted to Raja Petra Kamarudin and his popular and controversial Malaysia Today website (mt.m2day.org), and The Honorable Member of Parliament Tan Sri Lim Kit Siang for carrying my essays on his blog. Raja Petra's portal had gone through many name changes to keep ahead of Malaysian censors. I am also thankful to the publishers of "The Malaysian Insight" and "Free Malaysia Today" for publishing some of my writings.

Later in 2013 through the efforts of Umar Zain and his colleagues at Suaris website (now defunct) I started writing in Malay. Writing and thinking out the whole exercise in Malay produces a far different result both in tone as well as meaning than merely translating into Malay my existing essays. However, as the Internet penetration among Malays was not high, I did not receive much feedback from readers to make the effort worthwhile. Besides, no Malay publications would accept my submissions.

Back to my original early 1960s proposal of a university in Cameron Highlands, when Mahathir became Prime Minister in the 1980s, this self-styled champion of Islam and Malay causes instead approved the building of a casino there, the largest in the region and operated by a Chinese who later became a Muslim. I presume that gambling, like intellectual pursuits, is also most conducive in a cool environment.

Apart from Covid-19, my commentaries here focus on the triple whammy burdening Malaysia today. I have only two essays covering education as I have published two earlier books exclusively on that topic: *An Education System Worthy of Malaysia (2003) and The Rot In Malaysian Education* (2020).

On The Title

The phrase "Malaysian Malaise" first appeared as the title of an Op-Ed piece in the *New York Times* September 20, 1999, by its conservative commentator William Safire. He was castigating then Prime Minister Mahathir (as well as other Asian autocrats) for their super sensitivity and intolerance to criticisms. This was soon after Mahathir had jailed his erstwhile deputy Anwar Ibrahim and later, the conviction in Malaysia of long-time Asia correspondent Murray Hiebert of the now defunct *Far Eastern Economic Review.* That was the malaise Safire referred to, not only Malaysians' tolerance of these autocrats but also the acquiescence of their Western enablers in London and Washington. The same title (and theme) was repeated in a subsequent commentary by his colleague, also longtime Asia hand, Philip Bowring on April 12, 2006.

The shift in content but with that same phrase appeared later with Elizabeth Segran's "Letter from Asia" (*Foreign Affairs*, October 2013). She was commenting on the general political malaise following the 13th General Election of May 2013. The Najib-led coalition then won the majority of Parliamentary seats, but the opposition Pakatan coalition garnered the majority of the popular votes. The malaise there was the huge letdown with the unfairness of the electoral process.

On April 22, 2015, *Global Gaming Business Magazine* used the same title for its editorial on Malaysia's affirmative action programs favoring Malays. Why such a topic would appear in such a magazine beats me. Presumably because affirmative action and Malay Special Privileges were a huge and ultimately losing bet. A few more subsequent commentaries amplified on that same theme though with slightly altered titles, such as Kuala Lumpur-based freelance journalist E H Imrantski's "The Malaise of Malaysian Malays" (Newnaratif.com, March 8, 2018), and Chandra Nair's March 4, 2020, in *The Diplomat* ("Malaysia's 'Malay First' Malaise").

Imrantski's piece would be closer in content considering that most of my commentaries deal with Malay leadership and Islam, the Malay version. With the demographic and thus political dominance of Malays, the malaise of Malays is also that of Malaysia, hence my title.

Added Features

My reason for putting these commentaries in a book remains the same as with my earlier six collections. That is, my essays have appeared only in cyberspace as in my blog, social media outlets like Facebook, and various on-line portals.

I have added three new features in this printed edition. One, a brief introductory background material (in parenthesis) to put each essay in perspective with respect to time and content. Two, I have included a sampling of readers' comments, as I did with my first collection, *Seeing Malaysia My Way* (2003).[*] Three, I have graded each essay based on readers' responses. I give one point for "Like," two for each comment, three for sharing my article, four if the essay were to be picked up by other outlets (print or virtual), and five if I were to receive direct individual comments from readers through my e-mail. The five-star articles score over 500 points; one-star, under 100. Unlike in my freshman class, there is no Bell curve distribution to the ratings. The highest-ranking articles were those on corruption; the lowest, religion.

Within each section I have arranged the essays in a sequence that would make the most sense. Thus, with the section on the 15th General Election, I have placed them in chronological order. I have also included the four Malaysian video conferences I was invited to participate, rendering my oral presentations as essays. One was in Malay (*Isu dan Cabaran ke Arah Kesetaraan Dalam Pendidikan*). I have put the English translation ("Issues and Challenges Towards A More Equitable Education") in the main text and the original Malay in the Appendix.

I acknowledge the contributions of and thank my California friend Amir Razelan for introducing me to Dr. Rozhan Othman of LeadUS Malaysia for the invitation to be on a panel with Professor Tajuddin Rasdi on the webinar "Does The Malay Mind Need To Be Liberated?" Both Rozhan and Tajuddin are the beneficiaries of Western (specifically American) liberal education even though both received their doctorates elsewhere (Rozhan from Dublin; Tajuddin, Edinburgh). Tajuddin is

---

[*] Where "None" is noted, that does not mean that there are no comments as I have omitted the usual "I agree!" or "Good one!" responses.

fearless in swimming against the current socio-political trends as reflected in his erudite and contrarian viewpoints on fields far outside his profession, in the finest tradition of a public intellectual.

I am also indebted to another public intellectual, the academic cardiac surgeon Dr. Ahmad Farouk Musa of the Islamic Renaissance Front (IRF), for inviting me to the other three virtual seminars. Though active in his Islamic discourses, Farouk is equally productive in surgical research. He recently obtained his PhD in surgical research from Monash. I treasure the exchanges with my fellow panelists Dr. Sharifah Munirah Alatas of Universiti Kebangsaan Malaysia; Dato Dr. Madeline Berma, Fellow Akademi Sains Malaysia (both American PhDs, Columbia and Wisconsin respectively); and former Fulbright scholar Prof. Zaharom Naim of University of Nottingham Malaysia, together with Shamshir Alam and Nageeb Gounjaria, IRF's Senior Research Fellow as moderators.

Again, a big thank you to husband-and-wife team Jason and Su Pittam for the wonderful cover design. They have created the covers of almost all of my books. To my wife Karen, my first and critical reader, I thank Allah for blessing me with you.

July 2023
Morgan Hill, California, 95037

I: MALAYSIA'S 15th (2022) GENERAL ELECTION

UMNO's Impending Implosion

November 7, 2022

[After the political circus of the past four-and-a-half years that saw Malaysia having four Prime Ministers, each trying to outdo his immediate predecessor in corruption, incompetence, and race taunting, the government finally dissolved parliament, paving the way for a new election on November 19, 2022. Malaysians this time hope that the results of the 14th General Election where the UMNO-led coalition Barisan Nasional (National Front) lost power would be repeated.]

When the United Malay National Organization (UMNO lost power in the 14th General Election of 2018, its leaders deluded themselves into thinking that it was only a temporary setback. This coming 15th General Election on November 19, 2022 will disabuse them of that.

It would be sad to see the end of one of the few (if not the only) Malay entities, be it political, business, or anything else, to have sustained such longevity. Most last slightly longer than the morning dew, or the Malay metaphor, *kupu kupu lepas hujan* (moths after the rain). Beyond that, UMNO successfully spearheaded the nation's peaceful path towards independence. That deserves the gratitude of all.

On the other hand, UMNO is the one entity most responsible for perpetuating and entrenching the collective and destructive Malay submissive feudal mindset and culture. With that, the undue and unquestioning obedience to leaders and others in power. Thus, Malay sultans could cavort with foreign hookers and then burden citizens with the subsequent humongous alimony or grab state land and then sell it to foreign interests. Religious leaders brandish their Qur'an and endlessly quote the hadith while the ummah remains blighted with degrading poverty and crippling social pathologies. In Kelantan, long ruled by the ulama class, *kopi susu* (cafe au lait) refers to the water flowing out of their taps. People of that state (overwhelmingly Malays) are also overrepresented in the socially dysfunctional categories.

The leader of the Islamic Party PAS (its Malay acronym) Hadi Awang once said in a televised press conference in London, complete with simultaneous English translation, that corruption is halal in Islam as both parties agree to the transaction! By his *kitab* (book) and reasoning, then prostitution too is halal. His novel "corruption is halal" justifies his demanding and getting some of the loot of 1MDB, albeit only the crumbs. He sued Clare Rewcastle-Brown of *Sarawak Report* who first exposed that corruption, but ended up paying her to settle the lawsuit as going to trial would risk spilling the whole rotten beans!

At the federal level, again the consequence of UMNO rule, the ulama class has been coopted by the state and reduced to be its handmaidens. They should have instead emulated their counterparts in the early glory days of Islam in forming a formidable bulwark against the excesses of those in power.

As for Malay political leaders, the man who stole billions from Malaysians and then imposed upon them generation-long crippling debt is referred to with great adoration as *Malu Apa Bossku?* (What is there to be ashamed of my boss?) Najib Razak is only one manifestation of the degradation of Malay values. Again, the entity most responsible for that is UMNO, and its longest-serving leader, Mahathir.

It reflects how corrupt and depraved the party is in that four of its seven past leaders have resigned, including Mahathir. He helmed the party and country for over 22 years, the longest of any Malaysian leader. In case you missed it, that matched Muhammad's Prophethood.

Unlike the other three, Mahathir went beyond just quitting. He started his own party to oppose UMNO. Some gratitude! An ugly personification of his *Melayu Mudah Lupa* (Malays easily forget!) mantra, his "repayment" of gratitude to what UMNO had done for him.

Meanwhile UMNO's current (eighth) President, Zahid Hamidi, is facing serious corruption charges. His immediate predecessor, that *Malu Apa Bossku?* character, is now in jail. Bless old Abdullah Badawi; he remains the only one unblemished. One out of eight!

As for Malaysia's (and UMNO's) much revered leader Tun Razak, he died young while in office.

A line from Yeats' poem, "The Second Coming," describes well today's UMNO: "The best lack all convictions, while the worst are full of passionate intensity." And all – leaders as well as members – are hooked on corruption, cronyism, and nepotism.

Back in the 1950s and 60s UMNO members, in particular those in its Youth Wing, were not at all shy in criticizing their leaders. Youth members regarded themselves as the party's ginger group, to spice things up in case UMNO leaders got too comfortable. There was also a time when all UMNO Presidents were challenged at the leadership convention. Again, Mahathir put an end to that, all in the name of party 'unity.'

Today there are no *jantans* (alpha males), young or old, in UMNO, and the party's leadership convention is but a sham. They are all enablers for UMNO's wayward leaders; likewise, leaders of the Barisan coalition parties. These degradations of UMNO and the Barisan coalition it leads happened under Mahathir.

Mahathir exploited Razak's New Economic Policy to the hilt by vastly expanding UMNO's reach into the corporate world. When UMNO was declared illegal in 1988, again during Mahathir's watch, there was a mad scramble for ownership of its vast assets held under various hidden nominees. Likewise with his massive privatization schemes. Both gave rise to instant classic rent-seeking *berlaggak* (ostentatious) UMNO billionaires that included Mahathir's sons. One son's shipping company, near collapse during the 1997 Asian economic tsunami, was "rescued" by yes, the national oil company. Today at age 97, this Geritol politician still feels he has more to give, or more correctly, to take!

Consider corruption; there is no embarrassment among UMNO leaders today to have their workers blatantly handing out cash for votes. My advice to voters is simple. Take the money (it belongs to the rakyat anyway) and boot out those bastards come voting day. Not only do I look forward to UMNO's implosion in November 2022, but also that of its longest-serving leader and the man most responsible for the degradation of this once mighty party – Mahathir.

Readers' Rating: * * *
Sampling of Readers' Reponses:
" ... This is the most pungent and incisive analysis of that rotten party I have ever read! Like you, I will have a party over the demise of this blight on our nation."

"My biggest worry is [that] this would also explode even if UMNO explode first ... to follow countries like Sri Lanka, Pakistan, Greece, or Argentina ... the unsustainability of the country's debt is so obvious, impending implosion ... for those who are familiar with our public finance."

Third (And Final) Chance For Malaysia To Move Forward

November 14, 2022

[After having had three Prime Ministers in about four-and-a-half years since the 14th General Elections of 2018, each trying to outdo his immediate predecessor in the incompetence department, Malaysia has a chance for a redo with the next (prematurely scheduled) general election.]

This Saturday November 19, 2022, Malaysians will have an opportunity to put an end to over forty years of corruption, incompetence, and mismanagement that began in 1981 when Mahathir first became Prime Minister.

For Malay voters, it will also be a chance to expose the cruel fraud of *Ketuanan Melayu* (Malay Special Privileges) that has been perpetrated upon us all these decades. Far from being a scheme to improve the impoverished lot of the Malay masses as envisioned by our earlier enlightened and farsighted leaders, it is but a nefarious scheme to line the pockets of our *Orang Kayangan* (Malay elite). This gluttonous group includes not only the sultans but also hordes of their wannabes, in particular politicians in UMNO and PAS. This perversion of what was once a noble endeavor (Malay Special Privileges) was also the handiwork of Mahathir.

Malaysians had two earlier tries at rectifying Mahathir's colossal errors. The first was the 10th General Election of November 1999, in the wake of the devastating Asian economic tsunami. Mahathir must have had an inkling that he was a major factor to that crisis for he resigned soon after that election.

On superficial analysis, the Mahathir-led coalition had a resounding victory in that election, winning over 75 percent of the parliamentary seats. On closer scrutiny his coalition gained only 55 percent of the popular votes. More telling however was that many prominent UMNO leaders (including later-to-be Prime Minister Najib Razak) would have been eliminated had it not been for the (convenient) "last minute" postal votes from nearby army bases. That election was held in the background of Anwar's massive reformasi movement against KKN (*korupsi, kronism,* and *nepotisma* – corruption, cronyism, and nepotism).

The second try was in May 2018 when the Najib-lead Barisan coalition lost power. In the ensuing euphoria, leaders of the winning Pakatan Harapan were too generous in attributing their victory to Mahathir's efforts. That led to their fatal error in inviting the sly Mahathir to take over as Prime Minister. They should have just expressed their gratitude to the man and then lead him out of the door. Had they done that, there would not have been the subsequent back door "Sheraton Move" where Mahathir schemed to block Anwar Ibrahim's right to succeed him, as was agreed to earlier. Mahathir's "success" burdened Malaysia with her subsequent political instability, with three Prime Ministers in over slightly four years! All equally inept; all Mahathir's handiwork!

Malaysia also missed the chance in having her first woman Prime Minister in May 2018. Wan Azizah would not only have been that but also the best Prime Minister, a Malaysian Angela Markle – quiet, smart, and effective. What an inspiration that would have been for our young girls! Intellectual-wise, Azizah is far above the rest. At the very least she would have spared Malaysia Mahathir's subsequent treachery that burdened the nation with Muhyiddin's embarrassing incompetence and Ismail Sabri's rudderless leadership.

Had Deputy Wan Azizah taken over in February 2020 when Mahathir resigned for the second time, as normal practice would have it, he would at least help rehabilitate his tattered legacy after having cursed Malaysia with Abdullah Badawi and Najib Razak. Instead he further muddied his already tattered legacy by being instrumental for Muhyiddin becoming Prime Minister.

In this 15th General Election, Pakatan's Anwar Ibrahim and Rafizi Ramli are at their political prime, putting the other leaders on the defensive. Consider this poignant scene circulating in "TikTok." The erstwhile formidable Mahathir was about to deliver his campaign speech when a junior police officer told him politely that he (Mahathir) could not do so as he did not have a permit. His body language as he meekly moved away from the microphone and off the stage said it all. A pathetic sight!

Contrast Mahathir to Fahmi Reza, a devastatingly effective political cartoonist but a non-candidate in this election. He too was told to leave a local campus because his "democracy class" did not have a permit. Fahmi however stood his ground and although he finally left with the students cheering him on, he made the authorities look childish if not stupid.

In this election Malay conservative voters, the bulk of the electorate, have not changed, or if so, only marginally, not enough to change the overall electoral dynamics. What has changed is that they are now split between the UMNO-led Barisan coalition and the also Malay-led Perikatan Nasional. This triangulation should work to Pakatan Harapan's advantage.

The other new factor is the expected influx of young first-time voters. The bulk of them too would be Malays but unlike their elders, these young voters are less likely to hew to traditional patterns. I expect them to identify more with the vigorous and inspiring young leaders in Pakatan Harapan.

These young voters are my reasons to be optimistic about this upcoming election. They will usher in a new Malaysia by burying the old, corrupt, and incompetent faces in the Barisan and Perikatan coalitions.

Readers' Rating: * *
Sampling of Readers' Responses:
"I have often thought that Mahathir ... [is] a curse on Malaysia and Malaysians. In fact he is a double curse because of the length of his [leadership] and longevity."

"[Hope] there will be enough Malaysians who will vote for real change."

"Need to trust the young by showing them a better way."

"As long as there is an election there is always a chance for Malaysians to decide [the] direction we want our country to move. Democracy is not neat and easy. Witness the UK with three prime ministers in eight weeks!"

Let Anwar Ibrahim Form The New Government

November 20, 2022

[With the outcome of the 15th General Election not decisive, the Agung took it upon himself to be "kingmaker" instead of letting the politicians solve it among themselves, with Parliament then ratifying the decision. Instead, the Agung decided to rectify what he perceived to be voters' error by resorting to counting the number of "statutory declarations" in support of a particular candidate for Prime Minister. He did that with the two previous Prime Ministers (Muhyiddin Yassin and Ismail Sabri). The consequences were disastrous.]

Malaysia's 15th General Election on November 19th, 2022, saw the implosion of UMNO and the humiliating rejection of its longtime former leader Mahathir together with the new (another!) party he founded. Mahathir and many of his new party's candidates lost their deposits. While my third prediction (an outright victory for the Anwar-led Pakatan Harapan) did not happen, nonetheless it had won the most (81) parliamentary seats as well as garnered highest percentage of the popular votes. As such the Agung should have given Anwar the first crack at forming the new government.

The Agung would be failing in his constitutional duties as well as moral responsibilities to the rakyat if he were to do otherwise. The rakyat have expressed their collective decision. It is now for the Agung to make the call, as constitutionally mandated, to choose from among the leaders of the various contending parties the one who would or could command the confidence of the new Parliament. It is a judgement call reserved only unto him.

It would then be up to the new Parliament to accept the Agung's choice or contest it through an open debate and subsequent formal vote of no-confidence.

The scenario with the outgoing parliament where individual MPs were summoned to the palace with their statutory declarations in hand, *a la* errand schoolkids being called to the headmaster's office, would not do it. It did not work then, and it would not now. The Agung would be well advised not to repeat that charade. There is no constitutional provision for this extra-parliamentary "voting." Those so-called statutory declarations were made following secret inducements, *aka* corruption; hence both Muhyiddin's as well as Ismail Sabri's bloated earlier Administrations with new ministers, ambassadors-at-large, and chairmanships of GLCs galore being appointed. Refined corruption!

There is yet another reason for not relying on those statutory declarations. A decision taken following open robust debate is fluid and dynamic, the outcome often unpredictable right up to the last minute. Not so with backroom deals, whether concocted in a secret hotel room or at the palace. That is scheming, not constitutionally sanctioned, and borders on being illegal if not immoral. The affairs of state should not be handled as if you were haggling at a Middle Eastern souk.

Following the general election that resulted with no entity winning a clear majority, the Agung's Comptroller of the Royal Household issued this statement: "The parties and coalitions will be asked to give a name of one MP who has the confidence of the majority of MPs in the Dewan Rakyat to be the Prime Minister by 2 PM on Monday Nov 21, 2022." Syntax aside, that is misguided. It is for the Agung and not anyone else to make that call, with the House then having the prerogative to affirm or deny his choice. Let's not repeat the "headmaster scenario" of the last Parliament, and the consequent political debacles.

There are other issues with that royal edict. The instructions given to Speaker Azhar Harun was misplaced as he is no longer the Speaker. His Dewan had long been dissolved. It would be the new Parliament's prerogative, after it has been properly constituted with all its members sworn in and a new Speaker elected, whether Anwar could continue as Prime Minister.

This Agung had goofed twice before, including with the outgoing Parliament. Earlier when Mahathir resigned in February 2020, the Agung should have followed standard procedure and appointed Mahathir's then Deputy Wan Azizah to take over. Had that been done, Malaysia would have been spared much of the subsequent unneeded political uncertainties. By "reappointing" Mahathir as "caretaker Prime Minister," an unprecedented practice except when Parliament is dissolved in anticipation of an election or during a declared emergency, the Agung fell for Mahathir's ruse. Or perhaps the two were in cahoots.

Voters rightly saw through that even if the Agung did not; hence Mahathir's utter humiliation by voters during this last 15th General Election of November 2022.

That sneaky and sinister Mahathir's earlier maneuver led to the subsequent so-called "Sheraton Move" and the attendant political uncertainties and backdoor scheming. Reprehensible, as Malaysia was then (still is) facing the Covid-19 pandemic. Mahathir's deception culminated in an unwise general election being called prematurely, and during the treacherous monsoon season and the still ongoing Covid-19 pandemic.

As for picking leaders from the other coalitions, Perikatan Nasional's Muhyiddin had proved his utter ineptness during his brief (fortunately) tenure earlier. His vicious diatribe against Christians and Jews during the last campaign only cemented his unfitness to lead Malaysia. The Agung would have learned nothing if he were to reappoint Muhyiddin.

Barisan Nasional does not even know who its leader is. Zahid Hamidi, its president, is facing serious criminal charges. Ismail Sabri was an abysmal failure earlier on. The Agung would again show his utter lack of capacity to learn if he were to give Ismail another opportunity.

The only and wise option is for the Agung to choose Anwar to lead the new government. Let him then use his political skills and unique talent to craft the necessary coalition to secure Parliament's confidence. Any other option would disrespect the citizen's decision, regardless how eloquent or legalistic the rationale. Forming a new government should not be reduced to the trading and bartering of a souk market, as the Agung's latest edict has already triggered.

Readers' Rating: * *

Sampling of Readers' Responses:

" I agree …. But I fear that we will be disappointed again by the decision of the palace."

"Unfortunately race and religion won the day and people like Hadi was successful in using fear to scare Malays into voting PAS. Muhyiddin magnified the Malay fear of Christians and Jews. The Agung will likely defer to the incompetent Muhyiddin to appease Hadi instead of putting the country in the more competent leadership of Anwar Ibrahim."

"Agree completely on the need for following conventions … and for the King to be above politics. We need greater transparency in the process, but I see 'bartering' as part of the political process."

"Just hope that a certain evil, vindictive twice ex-Prime Minister does not dig up dirt to discredit Anwar."

A Contrived, Unneeded Political Crisis

November 24, 2022

[There was much unneeded delay and contrived drama in announcing a new Prime Minister following the 15th General Election of November 2022 in which no one party or coalition commanded a majority. That uncertainty put the Agung and his fellow rulers in the center of the controversy and decision-making process, resulting in unneeded certainty. It was also an unwise precedent to let the Agung decide. Instead, it should have been left to the elected leaders only.]

At last, five days after the election despite the results having been certified within hours of the closing of the polls, the Agung today (November 24, 2022) finally announced that Anwar Ibrahim will be Malaysia's tenth Prime Minister.

For Malaysia, Anwar's appointment brings a much-needed breath of fresh air after the putrid haze that has suffocated the nation for the past few decades and had threatened to linger forever, becoming thicker and even more stifling. Anwar's selection was as if the windows were now wide open so the crippling incompetence and rotten corruption of the preceding Muhyiddin Yassin and Ismail Sabri Administrations could now be flushed out.

For Anwar, this must be a moment of sweetness and achievement in so many ways, comparable to that felt by the late Nelson Mandela when he was released from prison and later elected President of his country. However, with the many daunting problems ahead, Anwar would have precious few moments to savor his victory and ponder the irony except to express his gratitude to Almighty Allah and to the voters.

The Agung's announcement was no surprise as Anwar's coalition had won the greatest number of parliamentary seats as well as garnered the highest percentage of the popular votes. The obvious question then, why the delay as well as the prolonged negotiations involving leaders of all the other parties, major and minor, as well as the sultans.

This was essentially a federal matter. As such the high-profile involvement of the other sultans leading up to the announcement, though not commented upon, nonetheless begs for explanation. Add to that the non-involvement of the non-royal governors of Melaka, Penang, Sarawak, and Sabah. They were not even invited much less involved. This after all was a decision that would impact the entire nation. Ever wonder why secessionist sentiments are growing in East Malaysia, or that non-Malays feel left out on many important national deliberations?

Back to the delay in the Agung's announcement, what had transpired behind the scenes during the last few days following the election, with the series of breathless last-minute negotiations and slew of press conferences? To the world, all those unseemly activities involving the palace degraded the nation and the royal institution. Those haggling and counter offers as well as the offering and withdrawing of statutory declarations as if they were negotiable checks are what you would expect when buying a ram's head in a Middle Eastern bazaar. Malaysians expect and demand better of their leaders, elected as well as hereditary.

The question that immediately arises is whether all those activities were but a charade, a manufactured crisis to direct citizens' attention elsewhere to conceal something more sinister and consequential.

There is a price to pay for this prolonged political haggling both by the political leaders as well as members of the permanent establishment, including the Agung and his brother sultans. They triggered as well as prolonged this unneeded political crisis and at a time when Malaysians could ill afford it.

Citizens were not apprised and thus did not know what had transpired behind the scenes in the various luxury hotels *a la* Sheraton, together with what had occurred at the palace in the presence of the Agung. Transparency is the essence as well as the demand of democracy.

Had the Agung made the decision he made today (November 23, 2022) four days earlier on the Sunday following the election, then Malaysians would have been spared the ensuing needless political melodrama. Apart from the economic and political costs, this crisis has incited raw racial emotions and ethnic bigotry reminiscent of the dark ugly days following the May 1969 national election. Many in their perversion are still stoking the ambers of that tragedy.

In unnecessarily delaying Anwar's appointment, the Agung must bear a major part of the blame and burden. Had he announced giving Anwar the first crack at forming the government last Sunday, Malaysians would have been spared all the ugly and unnecessary post-election drama. The bitter rivalries and emotions of the campaigns would by now have subsided if not forgotten. In deliberately delaying the announcement, the Agung fanned this unneeded crisis and incited this divisive controversy.

Again, had Anwar been invited to form the government last Sunday, being a polished politician, he would have created the necessary compromises to achieve a workable coalition with like-minded potential partners. He has to; his political survival depends on that. Politicians are by nature and vocation adept at this. Politics is after all, to quote Bismarck, "the art of the possible, the attainable – the art of the next best."

In his misguided quest for a "unity" government, the Agung tried to force a coalition. Forced coalition, like a forced marriage, rarely endures. Sultans by their very nature have minimal to no instinct at negotiations. They are used to having their ways and demands acceded to right away.

This delay in forming a new government carries many unquantifiable costs and possibly irremediable consequences, with the rakyat not the sultans bearing them. This central point must be hammered in, and often, lest this mistake be repeated. The rakyat is paying the Agung and his brother sultans a hefty sum every year. They better earn that by learning to be part of the solution, and not be the problem.

Readers' Rating: * *
Sampling of Readers' Responses:
"Finally, cannot call Anwar's bluff."

"All the wheeling and dealing were unnecessary distraction. I felt the Agung savored the limelight while prolonging a decision that was inevitable."

"Agreed that the Agung could have expedited the process, but I am thankful that the worst-case scenario of the coalition of losers taking over did not materialize."

Agung's Stunning Inability To Learn From Recent Experiences

November 22, 2022

[Following the uncertainties of the 15th General Election in which no party or coalition commanded a majority, the Agung took upon himself to initiate a series of uncalled for negotiations with the various political leaders, each armed with a statutory declaration purporting to show support for a particular leader. In so doing the Agung was about to repeat the same mistakes he did earlier in appointing Muhyiddin Yassin and Ismail Sabri to lead the government.]

Here we go again! In this latest go around in choosing the Prime Minister following the recent 15th General Election, the Agung has again demonstrated his utter inability to learn from the experiences of only just a few years ago. As then, he is again today reduced to being the old headmaster and his errand school kids, summoning newly elected Members of Parliament to the palace with their statutory declarations in their back pockets.

The Agung's earlier maneuvers of only a few years ago had resulted in Malaysia having three failed Prime Ministers (Mahathir, Muhyiddin, and

Ismail Sabri) and a Parliament that shuttered its doors half a year earlier, forcing a premature election upon citizens and during the treacherous monsoon season.

There is only one thing worse than not being able to solve a problem, and that is to add to or complicate it. This is what the Agung has done by not letting Anwar have the first bite at forming the new government. There are severe consequences to that decision.

The Agung's current action has caused the nation to be held in ransom by conniving politicians jockeying for positions. The Agung has also yet to learn that it is never smart to have a "no-action" caretaker government, more so when Malaysia is facing severe economic problems and the Covid-19 pandemic still not under control. The continuing decline of the ringgit is only one and a very visible manifestation of the former.

Worse, and an unquantifiable as well as unnecessary risk is that this dallying by the Agung has unleashed a torrent of ugly vicious racist sentiments that rival those seen in the aftermath of the 1969 election. Perhaps the Agung, just age ten then and cocooned in his parents' palace in Pahang, does not remember that dark period of Malaysian history.

The solution to the current electoral dilemma is as simple as it is obvious. When no political entity has won a clear majority, as with this recent election, the most sensible and logical route would be to let the one entity that has garnered the most seats be given the opportunity at forming the government. Then it would be for the new Parliament whether to reaffirm or reject that decision, and then take it from there.

Anwar's Pakatan Harapan coalition won both the highest number of Parliamentary seats as well as garnered the highest percentage of the popular votes. Eighty-two seats and 37 percent respectively, to Muhyiddin's Perikatan Nasional 73 and 30 percent. Not even close. The decision should have been a no-brainer. One does not need to be a constitutional lawyer or pay undue deference to Westminster practices to adopt that. It is plain common sense. Simple logic also dictates that.

Had that been done last Sunday following the election, Malaysia would today have a functioning government ready to begin tackling the many pressing problems. If any politician were to be stupid enough to call for a vote of no confidence on Anwar, and thus forcing another election so soon, then he and his party must be prepared to face the wrath of the voters. Do so and risk you and your party suffering the fate of Mahathir and his party. Not one of his candidates won and most lost their deposits, including Mahathir. He was far more popular in his time than either Muhyiddin or Ismail Sabri put together.

Instead of taking this most logical as well as common sense step, the Agung wanted to be in the center of things. He was not satisfied in being the King, he wanted to be the kingmaker too. He was hungry for national attention instead of being satisfied to discreetly stay behind the scenes. Let the politicians battle it out where it should be, in Parliament, not at the Palace. Who should be Prime Minister is the choice of the rakyat, and only them, not the Agung.

The Agung should have sworn in Anwar on Sunday following the election and then delivered a general advice to the new Parliament on the need for its members to work together. Remind those new MPs what they had put citizens through recently what with the raging floods, quite apart from the costs of the elections. That should tamper the enthusiasm of any mischievous parliamentarian toying with the idea of an early no-confidence vote on the new government.

There is also more in this case beyond the counting of seats or popular votes. That is, the alternatives to Anwar (Muhyiddin and Ismail Sabri) had proven their inability to lead in the outgoing Parliament. Time for Malaysia to bet on someone else. That someone is Anwar, no matter how you shuffle the cards.

Reader's Rating: * * *
Sampling of Readers' Responses:
"Feels that we are all in a divorce waiting who gets custody of us!"

"In principle the Agung's main job is to ratify, not rectify. The present Agung lacks knowledge and class."

"Experts agree that Anwar's appointment heralded "a good start" in getting [Malaysia] back on her feet again both politically and economically after four years of instability and the impact of Covid-19."

"We got the monarchy involved because we did not cast our votes in unison. It is more correct to say that our education system decided on the new government."

"A simple solution has become utterly complicated because someone ignores conventions and thinks he has to find a solution."

II: EXEMPLARY LEADERSHIP

Anwar Ibrahim's Classy First Press Conference As Prime Minister

November 27, 2022

[Newly elected Prime Minister Anwar Ibrahim's first press conference was a polished performance, far from the usual rambling, muddling, and inarticulate variety that has long been the norm. More heartening was the subsequent Q&A session. The questions were probing and critical, refreshingly different from the usual toadying types.]

Prime Minister Anwar Ibrahim's first press conference shortly after being sworn in was a class act, bar none. He weaved the substantive with the symbolic in an elegant seamless whole. He even handled with remarkable aplomb the congratulatory phone call from Turkey's President Erdogan that had interrupted the beginning of the press conference and threatened to drag on and on.

In that press appearance Anwar first spoke in crisp Malay, followed by his equally flawless English. He had none of the exasperating local habit of jumbling even the simplest sentence in both English and Malay, the latter often the "modern" variety with its glut of bastardized English words. This rojak rambling in bazaar Malay and pidgin English reflects a cluttered and undisciplined mind.

I would have to go back to the 1970s in Canada during Prime Minister Pierre Elliot Trudeau's era to see a comparable polished performance by a bilingual national leader. With Trudeau it was French and English, during a time like Malaysia today, of peak rivalry if not outright hostility between the speakers of the two languages.

Referring to the symbolic, Anwar again reemphasized his central mission. That is, Malay as the national language and Islam the state religion notwithstanding, Malaysia is for all Malaysians regardless of race, region, or religion. That went beyond being symbolic; it was a much-needed balm and necessary reminder following what had been a divisive and polarizing election campaign. Anwar's enlightened message of inclusiveness was in stark contrast to the dark insularity of the other contenders, Muhyiddin Yassin and Hadi Awang in particular.

I was less enamored with Anwar declaring the following Monday a national holiday. The disruption aside, it is expensive, and not just in lost productivity. That gesture is far more expensive than renovating ministers' offices or issuing them with new cars. Anwar rightly rejected those other initiatives.

Anwar reiterated his campaign promise of not accepting a salary. A big deal, symbolically and substantively. The loud applause he received affirmed that. Previous leaders had treated the national treasury as their private bank, and state assets as theirs. Fiscally and operationally however, Anwar not drawing a salary is less significant than his other campaign promises, such as a smaller cabinet. Think of the savings with not just ministerial salaries and perks but also the associated highly paid KSUs (Ketua Setia Usaha – Cabinet Chief Secretaries) and their myriad deputies and assistants.

Anwar reiterated his commitment to tackling corruption and reviving the economy, specifically the escalating cost of living. It spoke volumes that both the ringgit and Kuala Lumpur Stock Exchange Index rebounded on news of Anwar's becoming Prime Minister. I hope he would also commit to a third and equally crucial crusade: repairing the rotting education system. The three are interrelated. You cannot have a robust economy without a well-educated populace, or with corruption corroding the system.

Anwar should not even consider those with pending criminal trials or tainted backgrounds to be in his cabinet. To be specific, I refer to Ahmad Zahid Hamidi because he is head of Barisan (now part of the governing coalition) as well as his close relationship with Anwar. Zahid is responsible for Barisan's post-election support of Anwar, thus enabling him to form the new government. That deed is not to be underestimated and Zahid should be commended for that, but nothing beyond. Anwar should also avoid retreads from the outgoing cabinet; they were part of the problem and thus cannot now be part of the solution.

Bring back Latheefa Koya to head the Malaysian Anti-Corruption Commission and appoint a Special Prosecutor. A Special Prosecutor would be far more effective than forming a Royal Commission, quite apart from pre-empting charges of political reprisals.

Reform education so future Malaysians would be more like Anwar, fluent in Malay and English, of deep faith but not wearing it on the sleeve and be comfortable with the local ambience as well as on the global stage. In short, *glokal* (Malay contraction for global and local) Malaysians.

It reflects Anwar Ibrahim's supreme confidence that his first order of business when the new Parliament convenes on December 19 would be to introduce a vote of confidence on his government.

Back to that press conference, I was gratified by the ensuing questions – probing, pertinent, and perceptive, free from the usual toadying groveling types. It is amazing that when the right signals come from the very top, Malaysian journalists respond.

Anwar can credibly claim aspiring to be Prime Minister not for personal gains but to execute his mission for a better Malaysia. No amount of wealth, glory, or adulation could ever compensate for or be worth the physical and other pains he and his family have endured.

As a coda, since being sworn in as Prime Minister, Anwar Ibrahim has given a number of sermons. It is heartening to see so many non-Muslims listening outside mosques to his message of an inclusive and tolerant Islam, a reassuring as well as refreshing contrast to the divisive venomous variety spouted by the likes of Hadi Awang. That might well be Anwar's most important and enduring contribution.

Readers' Ratings: ✱ ✱ ✱
Sampling of Readers' Responses:
"I am inspired by this post except for the holiday part.... A small gesture and a small price to pay for the journey ahead."

"... [I]t was polished, well-articulated ... and he hit all the right notes with finesse! He displayed a cool, calm, and collected approach. Wish the PM well!"

"Give him a chance to serve the country. It's long overdue. If he can bring glory to our country and serve our people well, then we have made the right choice."

"Parachuting/outsourcing someone from the outside has its liabilities."

"Many senior officers within the system are not there because of meritocracy but political pull. .... Thus there is a need to parachute fearless persons of integrity to clean up the trash."

Anwar Ibrahim's SCRIPT For A New Malaysia

October 19, 2022

[The tradition of aspiring national leaders, at least in America, to pen their biographies is well established. More often than not however, those are ghost-written. So readers are uncertain to what extent they are hearing an authentic author's voice. Not so with Anwar Ibrahim. He dispensed with self-adulating biographies and instead focused on putting his ideas on paper. In 1996 he wrote *The Asian Renaissance*, articulating his aspirations on what a modern Asian state should be. That led to the reformasi movement and two years later, Anwar was arrested and jailed. Pardoned, he is now back in active electoral politics. In October 2022 he launched his *SCRIPT For A Better Malaysia – An Empowering Vision And Policy Framework For Action* in time for the anticipated general election. Let us hope for Anwar's and Malaysia's sake that he will be successful this time, and his enlightened farsighted ideas be implemented for the benefit of Malaysians.]

In terms of output, by word or page count, Mahathir far exceeds any other Malaysian leader. By content or intellectual weightage however, Anwar Ibrahim is in a class of his own. His latest, *SCRIPT For A Better Malaysia – An Empowering Vision And Policy Framework For Action*, published by Institut Darul Ehsan, Selangor, lives up to this billing, the catchy acronym included (Sustainability, Care And Compassion, Respect, Innovation, Prosperity, and Trust).

Buzz words like sustainability, innovation, and prosperity, together with the latest, climate change, are *de rigueur* in today's manifestos, political and otherwise. Less emphasized or never mentioned is trust. At the book's launching on October 2, 2022, Anwar emphasized this, the "T" in SCRIPT. I agree with him that trust is a poor translation of the much broader and deeper meaning of the Malay word of Arabic origin, *amanah*, with its associated profound religious connotations. Fidelity, of being true to one's self-mission, and responsibility, would be a better English equivalent.

Breaches of fidelity (*pecah amanah*) are rampant in Malaysia today, from the highest officials to the lowly traffic constables. It is the root cause of the Malaysian malaise, the genetic core of this virulent destructive social virus now plaguing the nation. By "highest official" I do not mean only former Prime Minister Najib Razak. His recent conviction is but the tip of a huge iceberg. Consider Johor Baru's Forest City, approved sans any environmental studies, or the clear cutting of virgin jungles in Pahang resulting in ravaging floods. No marks for guessing their royal backers. Both instances are gross breaches of fidelity, not only by the rulers but also those entrusted to enforce the rules.

Pecah amanah is the defining issue in the upcoming election. Anwar should be unrelenting and unsparing in pounding this. Targets abound, as with secular leaders in their Armani suits jetting to London to visit their country estates while Malaysia faces devastating floods. Then there are religious leaders in their overflowing robes endlessly quoting the Holy Book while oblivious of their own sins of accepting bribes and *makan gaji buta* (lit. eating a blind salary; met. undeserved or illegal income). They must be exposed for what they are – dangerous and destructive. They are but parasites sucking on the rakyat. Unlike their counterparts in nature, these political blood suckers do not even bother camouflaging themselves or their activities. They are blatant. That is the Malaysian tragedy.

Reformasi, the mass reform movement initiated by Anwar in the late 1990s, is right to focus on building trust among leaders as well as followers, and in institutions as well as personnel. With trust comes respect, and from there, compassion. Trust also encourages innovation, which is key to prosperity.

Related to *amanah* but not its exact antonym is *munafik*, commonly but inadequately translated as hypocrisy. Being of Qur'anic origin, *munafik* too has deep religious connotations. If *pecah amanah* implies your knowing that what you are doing is wrong, *munafik* is your spinning it as otherwise, neigh even beneficial and praiseworthy! To wit, Tun Razak exhorting Malays to enroll their children in Malay schools; meanwhile sending his to England. More sinister, ulama extolling the robbers of 1MDB and labelling the crumbs of the loot these ulama received to fund their Hajj as *borkat* (gift from Allah).

Anwar's reach, intellectual and political, extends far despite his being out of power. His prescient *The Asian Renaissance* released just before the devastating 1997 Asian Contagion caught the attention of global leaders hitherto smitten with the yet to be exposed, flash-in-the-pan Asian Miracle facade. Anwar paid a severe price for his subsequent falling out with Mahathir, as did his then young family and the *reformasi* (reform) movement. If Anwar's coalition were to win the upcoming 15th General Election, then all those pains and setbacks would have been worthwhile, more so for Malaysia.

Anwar's many current critics are trapped by their inability or unwillingness to escape his image as a young, ambitious, and impatient ABIM (Malay acronym for Malaysia Islamic Youth Movement) leader decades ago, ignoring his subsequent and far more consequential experiences and development. Most transformative must surely be his incarcerations, including solitary confinement, not once but twice. Few have been tested as much, and fewer still have emerged stronger and wiser. Nelson Mandela comes to mind when I think of Anwar today. Like Mandela, Anwar has even forgiven his tormentor. That's unmatched magnanimity!

Pardoned following the 14th General Election, Anwar immediately resumed his mission. His reformasi initiatives following that electoral victory were sabotaged by Mahathir. While Anwar did not physically suffer this time, Malaysia did and still does, cursed with Muhyiddin Yasin and later, Ismail Sabri as Prime Ministers. Egregious corruption and blatant cronyism, not to mention gross incompetence, are once again the Malaysian norm.

Malaysians need SCRIPT. It is an effective message and therefore must be messaged effectively. For that, learn from Ronald Reagan. Not gifted intellectually, he knew his limitations and thus corralled accomplished individuals to be on his team. Anwar already attracts many outstanding young talents like Rafizi Ramli, Sim Tze Tzin, and Nurul Izzah. Anwar's greatest challenge is not to repeat his mistake by taking in the likes of that *semburit* (anal) renegade Azmin Ali. He skipped on his bills and cannot even get along with his siblings. Anwar should pay attention to such details before trusting these individuals. Anwar and *reformasi* paid a terrible price for that lapse. I am gratified that for this coming election

Anwar had spurned gestures from Mahathir to join forces. Fool me once, shame on you; fool me twice, shame on me!

The future of Malaysia is with the young, not the has-beens, no matter how great they think they had been. Look forward, not backward in picking your team.

Visuals are integral to messaging effectively. Reagan was ever so conscious of his backdrops and the people he invited to be beside him during "photo-ops." At the recent launching of SCRIPT, there were many foreign diplomats and journalists in the audience, reflecting Anwar's aura. Alas the program, Anwar's superb performance excepted, was subpar. The long introductions and salutations to extraneous personnel, long a Malaysian tradition, were nonetheless unneeded and distracting. People came to hear Anwar, not his publisher or emcee. As for his interviewer, she read from her script. No surprise that she looked scripted. She was! Her fumbling with her microphone was a distraction, with Anwar having to help her. The questions from the floor too were more commentaries.

Anwar should do multiple book discussions with academics and opinion shapers, from the establishment as well as social media, from peninsular as well as East Malaysia, both in Malay and English, but please no rojak jumbling presentations that are now the Malaysian norm.

Malay voters are pivotal in this election. As such I was surprised that the participants, being all Malays, did not use Bahasa at least in the introduction, and then switch to English for the main program out of respect to the many foreigners in the audience. Again, the visuals, as per President Reagan.

Pecah amanah is Malaysia's root problem. That consciousness has to be continually hammered so citizens could then vote out the current corrupt bunch. To that end, Anwar should have a free pdf or e-edition of this book as well as a Malay version, complete with its own cute acronym, thus effecting wider distribution. Anwar did not write SCRIPT anticipating the royalty payments. The rewards for all Malaysians, now and future generations, would be promising if they were to give Anwar and his team the opportunity to execute SCRIPT.

Readers' Rating: * *
Sampling of Readers' Responses:

"No [Malay] edition, which means they are connecting only to their educated supporters .... Totally agree that he should have given away free pdf copies of both English and Malay versions."

"I stop reading when you mentioned Nurul Izzah as an outstanding young talent. Other than being Anwar's daughter, how is she outstanding?"

"She has all the hallmarks of a great leader embracing everything Malaysia needs. Met her once and she was very impressive even then. Respect for diversity, sustained development for the poor, good educational and health systems. Which another young female can compare with her? I see none."

"Appreciate your comments .... The greatest challenge is corruption, especially among the elite. Personnel in enforcement and regulatory agencies find it difficult to investigate or pursue cases involving powerful politicians and senior bureaucrats. These bodies also do not seem to have the independence and strength of resolve when it involves the elite. The system is more efficient with petty cases while the real hemorrhaging and harm come from the millions and billions in misguided ventures and pet projects of politicians. The other challenge is for the peninsular people to embrace their Borneo brothers and sisters in a more inclusive and meaningful way. We are one country but so few Sabahans and Sarawakians are in high positions of authority."

"Indeed the word *'amanah'* is no longer in the vocabulary of the politicians. We have to practice *'amanah'* before we can lead the ummah. It is tempting to accept the contributions from interested parties, and this happens at all levels of society and government service as Malaysians are known for our habit of giving, sometimes too generously.... The older generations expect this. Yes *sedeqah, hidayah*, or giving sincerely may be taken as sincere practices but to induce such activities is not accepted by any religion. This culture has to stop. The giving is as evil as the taking. This breach of trust that follows is also part of the culture. To eradicate it we have to start with the education system. This is where the failure starts. It's time for change."

Anwar Ibrahim: The Right Leader At The Right Time
August 18, 2021

[On August 21, 2021, following the sudden ousting of Prime Minster Muhyiddin Yassin who had earlier usurped power less than eighteen months earlier in the infamous so-called Sheraton Move, Malaysia was again thrown into political turmoil. The Agung now had to choose which Member of Parliament (MP) would command the confidence of the House to be the next Prime Minister. By this time Anwar Ibrahim was already an MP having been elected in a special by-election held on October 2018 soon after he was pardoned and released from prison.]

The conventional wisdom, as well as the constitutional mandate, would have the Agung select from among current Members of Parliament (MPs) the next Prime Minister to replace the hopelessly inept outgoing Muhyiddin Yassin. The only criterion being that the individual must command the confidence of the House.

In the current political circus, where MPs' "Statutory Declarations" (SDs) could be changed on a whim (after suitable "inducements" of course), that would be a tall if not impossible order. One does not have to be an astute observer to realize that no MP today could command majority Parliamentary support. Hence the current mess. The Agung has no special divine powers to ascertain which candidate would command the confidence of Parliament. He goofed once with Muhyiddin. We have no reason to expect that the Agung would be any wiser this second time around. So abandon that wishful thinking or strategy!

Instead, the Agung should heed the counsel of former Law Minister Zaid Ibrahim. He suggested that His Majesty resolve this political impasse by selecting someone "good" to be the next Prime Minister. This "good" leader would then through his display of leadership and management skills command the respect and confidence of Parliament. Zaid is no ordinary statesman. He remains the only cabinet minister to have resigned on principle, and then saw his reputation soar.

To have the Agung first pick a leader who he thinks would command the confidence of the House is putting things backward, the cart before the horse. Picking that "good" leader from among the current MPs, as per Zaid's wise suggestion, is not as difficult a task as it may seem. First eliminate the bad ones. That too would be easy. All those who had served in the outgoing Muhyiddin Administration would by definition fall into this category. That would include ministers, assistant ministers, and other political appointees such as Special Ambassadors together with heads of government-linked companies or statutory bodies. They were all part of the problem and thus they cannot now be part of the solution.

That one criterion alone would eliminate about 70 to 80 of the current MPs. Then exclude those convicted or facing (or had faced) criminal charges. Thus, do not bother with the likes of Zahid, Tengku Adnan, and Najib Razak. That would get rid of a dozen more, leaving about a hundred MPs or so for consideration. From that pick only the leaders of their respective parties, further reducing the field to a handful of candidates.

Once the Agung has picked his choice, then use all his and the citizens' persuasive powers to dissuade MPs from having a parliamentary vote of confidence right away. After all, the Agung's earlier choice (Muhyiddin) did not face any such test despite being in office for nearly 18 months. The new Prime Minister should also be given that same courtesy. If after 18 months he has not proven his ability as with his losing the confidence of Parliament, then the Agung should dissolve it and call for a general election. Hope that the Covid-19 pandemic would have dampened down by then. Calling for an election with many Malaysians not yet fully vaccinated is sheer madness.

Any other measures would risk making the Malaysian Parliament degenerate into the level of the Lebanese one.

By those criteria, there are only three possible candidates to lead Malaysia: Anwar Ibrahim, Shafie Apdal, and Tengku Razali. Tengku's negatives include his not being in any senior leadership position for his party, UMNO. That however could be a plus, what with characters like Tengku Adnan, Najib Razak, and Ahmad Zahid as ready examples. Beyond that, his age does not favor him. Only megalomaniacs like Mahathir think that they could still perform in their 90s. Look at the mess he had created. If only he had stuck to his promise of giving way to Anwar in February 2020, Malaysia would have been spared this unnecessary terrible political crisis. It could not have come at the worst possible time. Yet old Mahathir still thinks he can now be part of the solution. Some chutzpah!

Tengku Razali on the other hand has many positives. He is among the few who dared take on Mahathir when the latter was at the peak of his power and popularity. Tengku nearly toppled Mahathir for UMNO's leadership back in the 1980s but for some last-minute shenanigans by Najib Razak. Tengku's integrity and competence are unchallenged. He remains the only statesman who had sued the venerable *The Financial Times* and prevailed when it implicated him in the Bank Bumiputra debacle. As head of Petronas, he took on the mighty global oil companies and prevailed.

Sabah's Shafie Apdal had once been the Chief Minister of Sabah. Meaning, he has some executive experience. However, his tenure at the federal level in Najib and Badawi's cabinet had been lackluster.

That leaves Anwar Ibrahim. Many Malaysians still remember him from his ABIM (Malay acronym for Muslim Youth Movement) days and during his years as Mahathir's Deputy. As such many still harbor a less-than-favorable view of him. However, the Anwar of today is a far different person. No leader has been tested in adversity, physically and in many other ways more than Anwar. Yet he has emerged stronger, like well-tempered steel. As with Tengku Razali, Anwar dared take on Mahathir in 1997. Unlike Razali however, Anwar suffered all the terrible consequences not only to himself but more significantly, to his young family.

After spending years in prison on trumped-up charges, Anwar, like Nelson Mandela, emerged stronger and his reputation enhanced. Also like Mandela, the fate of the individual who imprisoned Anwar is today tattered. Mahathir's glorified legend of himself remains only in his own small egotistic mind. He does not even acknowledge that this current leadership crisis emanated from his earlier decision to resign and not give way to Anwar Ibrahim.

Anwar is the leader Malaysia needs today. He is committed to Islam and democracy, but his Islam is far different from the variety espoused by the Talibans and their local counterparts in the Islamic Party (PAS, its

Malay acronym). Anwar is also the only Malaysian leader who commands international respect and confidence.

Anwar is the right leader at the right time for Malaysia. The Agung would be doing the nation a great service by naming this exemplary patriot to lead the nation. The Agung cannot afford to goof this second time around. Malaysians pray and hope that he would also be wiser this time.

Readers' Rating * * * * *
Sampling of Readers' Responses:
"Can someone print this in large font and share it with Mahathir!"

"When the bankers pulled the plug from under his feet [during the 1997 economic crisis], Mahathir took a two-month leave. Anwar, then as acting Prime Minister, presented a draft in Parliament to make the Anti-Corruption Agency an independent body answerable only to Parliament. That was when Mahathir had a fit …. The rest is history."

"It's time to give Anwar Ibrahim the chance to show his talent again to help Malaysia during this difficult time."

"... I find it very surprising that you are championing Anwar ...."

"All these political debacles because good people did nothing."

"Wisely said! This weak nation is hoping [for that]."

"Anwar Ibrahim is the leader we have not had for the past two decades. It is about time he is offered the leadership as he has vast experience in government, understands the concerns of the people, and the gumption to make those difficult decisions that have to be made."

Anwar Ibrahim As "Wartime" Prime Minister
October 11, 2020

[Prime Minister Muhyiddin Yassin was forced to resign for lack of parliamentary support in August 2021, less than 18 months after assuming office following Mahathir's sudden devious resignation in February 2020 following the so-called Sheraton Move. The Agung was again faced with having to select a new Prime Minister who could have the confidence of Parliament. Anwar Ibrahim would have been the best candidate. However, his publicly and often-stated mission to tackle corruption caused dyspepsia among many in high places. Instead, the Agung chose the clueless and uninspiring Ismail Sabri. A measure of or trick to Sabri's success can be gauged by the fact his supporters were later co-opted into his bloated cabinet to become among the many newly appointed Ambassadors-at-Large or Chairman of the various Government-linked companies.]

When the Agung meets Anwar Ibrahim on Tuesday, October 13, 2020, he should be treated in the same manner as Muhyiddin Yassin was back in February 2020. Then, recognizing the current public health emergency [the Covid-19 pandemic], the Agung should appoint Anwar as the equivalent of a Wartime Prime Minister.

If Anwar were to be denied the opportunity to lead Malaysia despite his documented majority support in Parliament, then the Agung would risk becoming entangled in the nation's current toxic political bickering by his favoring an incumbent UMNO politician. The Agung would also have to bear the heavy responsibility for unnecessarily exposing Malaysians to Covid-19 should he opt for a general election instead. The recent experience with the state election in Sabah should sober him on that point.

A 'wartime' leader has precedents within and outside Malaysia. Britain had one during both World Wars. Canada invoked its War Measures Act in 1970 following the Quebec riots. Today many countries including such bastions of democracy as Sweden, Australia, and Germany have already adopted special legislative measures in response to the unprecedented challenges of Covid-19.

For Malaysia back in May 1969, the Agung suspended Parliament following the race riots. He appointed Tun Razak as the de facto Wartime Prime Minister with the National Operations Council, also appointed, as his cabinet. The Agung sidelined the leader of the winning coalition Alliance, Tengku Abdul Rahman. Today, unlike in 1969, the Agung need not suspend Parliament. It could continue its oversight functions as with authorizing Bills.

Although the number of deaths from Covid-19 thus far is much lower than with the 1969 riot, nonetheless the uncertainties and number of livelihoods adversely affected already far exceeded that of the 1969 incident, and fast climbing. Make no mistake, this Covid-19 pandemic is war, this time against the smallest and toughest adversary. An effective weapon has yet to be developed. As such, a wartime-type leader is exactly what Malaysia needs now.

As Wartime Prime Minister, Anwar would be spared parochial party considerations and petty political obligations that now plague Parliament and the government. He could pick the best in and outside of Parliament or his party to be in his cabinet without having to worry about the political and other ramifications. Witness the current obscenity of Prime Minister Muhyiddin's bloated cabinet, and his appointing scores of MPs to head Government-Linked Companies or as special envoys. Those are but crude schemes to buy the loyalties of (otherwise known as political bribing) these yahoos in Parliament. The public pays twice, one through their incompetence and two, the associated exorbitant price both in real as well as opportunity costs.

As for Covid-19, Muhyiddin is already but a pathetic figure of an ineffectual *abah* (father) with his schoolteacher cane in hand to enforce his quarantine measures. That is the kampung leadership style of my youth well over sixty years ago! His Health Minister, Adham Baba, is no better. All he could offer is air *suam* (warm water) and *air kosong* (lit. empty water, that is, plain water). And this character is a doctor!

In picking his cabinet, Anwar should exclude those who had served in the Najib Administration. Their allowing the 1MDB debacle to happen is disqualification enough. So out with Mustapa Mohamed, Hishammuddin Hussein, and the rest. Ahmad Zahid Hamidi and Tengku Adnan are both awaiting criminal trials, while Najib Razak is a convicted criminal. He should not even be in Parliament.

Spared the threat of endless charade of "no-confidence" votes in Parliament, the attendant distracting and destructive political jockeying would be gone. The current army of noisy jumping frogs would have their legs cut off, and Malaysians spared their ceaseless croaking. Why jump parties when that would have no effect on the country's leadership, or more precise, your political position and with it, all the attendant goodies? Slimy characters and jumping frogs like Azmin Ali would now have to divert their backroom skills and posterior apertures elsewhere outside of politics and government. Calling for a voluntary political ceasefire or for the Agung and Council of Rulers to have these politicians work together, as a few have suggested, is the height of naivety. These are political animals to their core.

This "wartime" appointment should last till the end of the current parliamentary mandate (September 2023). Imagine, Malaysians spared the threats of jumping frogs, Sheraton moves, Meridien maneuvers, and other yet-to-be-exposed backroom shenanigans! All, including Anwar and his cabinet, could then focus on the necessary work and hard challenges at hand. That would be a welcomed and refreshing relief, quite apart from being productive.

This reprieve would also give the various leaders time to strengthen their parties for the 2023 election. UMNO for example could begin the difficult but much-needed task of ridding the corrupt, racists, and incompetent from within its ranks. Currently those political parties are distracted from undertaking these necessary tasks because of the never-ending drama and uncertainty in Parliament. Clean, strong, and stable political parties are the backbone of a robust democracy.

For Anwar, focus on Covid-19, corruption, improving institutions, in particular educational, and curtailing the rampant rise in intolerant Islamism while grooming the next generation of capable leaders. Execute those well and he would have achieved what Mahathir could not in his nearly a quarter-of-century leadership. For Malaysians, a wartime-like leader would be a welcomed and much-needed reprieve from the current endless scheming and attendant political uncertainties. The burden of Covid-19 is heavy enough.

Readers' Rating: * * * *
Sampling of Readers' Responses:

"What nonsense! There was NO sitting PM when Muhyiddin made his move as Mahathir had resigned. The only way to get rid of a sitting PM is through a vote of no confidence in Parliament. No other way!"

"The idea of a wartime PM free from all the politics of the day is good but the problem is the character of Anwar. [J]ust look at the few things he did recently ...."

"Close enough to [Anwar] to know the skeptics are wrong. [He] is someone blessed with the ability to think clearly and coherently, and able to foresee major issues long before they materialize. Bakri's [writing] is poignant, cogent, and bullseye!!"

Anwar Ibrahim's Comeback And Malaysia's Good Fortune

September 23, 2020

[The 14th General Election of May 2018 saw Mahathir abandoning his long-time UMNO-led national coalition Barisan Nasional to join the opposition Pakatan Harapan. Pakatan gained power, dislodging Barisan that had ruled the country since independence. The plan was for Mahathir to give up his leadership to make way to Anwar Ibrahim who would be expected to be pardoned soon after, and then to win his own Parliamentary seat. To avoid that possibility, on February 2020 Mahathir concocted a scheme dubbed the Sheraton Move where he would resign and the power shift to his old UMNO crony Muhyiddin Yassin. That jury-rigged, hastily crafted coalition did not last long, but not before it threw the nation into an unneeded political crisis that could not have come at the worst possible time with the onslaught of the Covid-19 pandemic. Later in August 2021, through yet another sly closed-door scheming, Muhyiddin himself was ousted. There was much posturing on who would replace Muhyiddin, or whether he could continue. In the end the Agung chose yet another UMNO nincompoop, Ismail Sabri. He remained as Prime Minister until ousted in the 15th General Election of November 2022.]

What next week will bring to Malaysia politics-wise, *Allahu A'alam*! (Only Allah knows!) And He is not telling anyone. We all just have to wait.

Nonetheless it is not difficult to judge and surmise from the respective speeches and body languages of the two protagonists – current Prime Minister Muhyiddin and Reformasi Leader Anwar Ibrahim – who has the upper hand. In his press conference Anwar projected an image of a take-charge leader. He was poised, articulate, and confident, at ease with reporters' questions. Muhyiddin on the other had to remind everyone that he was still in charge.

Let us pray for the Agung to have a speedy recovery from his knee ailment. He should afford Anwar the same reception he gave to Muhyiddin back in February 2020. Meaning, if Anwar could bring documented evidence of support by the majority of Members of Parliament, then he should be Prime Minister.

Should the Agung remain incapacitated and his Deputy, Perak Sultan Raja Nazrin, were to take over, he too should do likewise. For him there was also the precedent set by his father (with Raja Nazrin as Crown Prince) back in 2009 when he accepted the statutory declarations of the three political frogs, thus enabling the erstwhile opposition Barisan to take over the state government from Pakatan.

It would be the height of irresponsibility and serve the nation ill if the Agung were to take a different tack with Anwar and dissolve Parliament instead. That would forever destroy the precious neutrality of the royal institution. It would also be inexcusable to expose the public to unnecessary risks were there to be a general election during this Covid-19 pandemic. Yes, Singapore did it, but that state is known for doing many things right. Malaysians have yet to know and reckon with the possible public health and other consequences of the Sabah State election on Saturday, September 26, 2020, conducted during the height of the epidemic.

I expect Anwar to be Prime Minster next week. Malaysia is more than ready and in desperate need of a new leader of his caliber and the crisp administration he would bring. The challenges for Anwar and his team are many and formidable but he should focus on only three objectives. Manage this Covid-19 pandemic, deal with corruption, and enhance education. Later, deal with the threat of unbridled Islamism. Everything else including reviving the economy should be secondary. As one wise African leader pointed out, you can revive the economy but not a dead citizen. If Malaysia were free of corruption, investments would flow in; likewise, if you have educated, well-trained and healthy citizens. Focus on those major objectives. Dispense with the Ministry for Sports, Tourism, Islamic Affairs, Women's Affairs, and Entrepreneur Development with their massive bureaucracies.

For Covid-19, listen to your professionals. You have in the Director-General of Health Dr. Noor Hisham Abdullah an exceptionally capable man. Support him and his agency. For education, increase the number of hours devoted to science, mathematics, and English. Teach those subjects daily. Make that a condition for any school to receive state funding, including and especially religious schools. Beyond those four subjects and Malay, each school would be free to fill the rest of the school day.

As for tackling corruption, focus on three key personnel: Chief of Police, Head of Anti-Corruption, and the Attorney-General. While there are many competent Malaysians for those positions, recognize that citizens are now deeply polarized. It would be difficult to get a local candidate who would be viewed as impartial. Former Attorney-General Tomas was competent. However being a non-Malay, he was the center point of unjustified racist attacks as most of his targets were longstanding corrupt Malay leaders. As for former Malaysian Anti-Corruption Commission (MACC) Chief Latheefa Koya, she too was effective but her being active in opposition party politics before the 2018 election fueled her many detractors.

Imagine the impact if all three were recruited from such agencies as the FBI or Scotland Yard. At the very least they would be viewed as impartial with respect to race and local politics. For the same consideration with respect to race, I would not recruit someone from India, Singapore, or Hong Kong. The negative impact on Malays of such appointments from those Asian countries would be immediate, dramatic, and negative, distracting your mission.

Those appointments require the Council of Rulers' consent. Lobby and educate them on the wisdom of the proposal. Those expatriate chiefs would then groom capable local subordinates and change the culture as well as integrity of those institutions. With time the scourge of corruption, racism, and mistrust in those institutions would subside.

Anwar pointed out that his government would be Malay-majority. I understand his rationale for doing that, to reassure the restless natives. However, I would not emphasize that fact; it would be obvious soon enough. Besides, Malaysians are now more interested in a clean, competent, and efficient government. There is no joy, much less reflected glory, in having a Malay government but made up of the corrupt and incompetent, as it is now. That would only bring shame to our race and culture.

Anwar aspires to have an inclusive cabinet. So co-opt a few competent non-Malays from the previous Pakatan Administration. Two names prop up immediately, former Transport Minister Anthony Loke and Science Minister Yeo Bee Yin. Yeo would bring both racial and sexual inclusiveness. She would also raise the median IQ of the cabinet! Both are from Democratic Action Party, a party not in the proposed coalition. Anwar should learn from his good friend, former US State Secretary William Cohen, a Republican who was appointed by Democrat President Bill Clinton.

A final piece of unsolicited advice for Anwar. Do not bother giving interviews to BBC and Al Jazeera or addressing august foreign audiences and meeting global leaders. You have your work cut out here at home. There would be plenty of time for that once you are successful. Besides, at our age those jet lags could be quite devastating, taking precious time away from attending pressing domestic issues.

Readers' Rating: * * * *
Sampling of Readers' Responses:

"Most of Malaysia's tension, corruption, and religious extremism started from Dr. Mahathir the [expletive deleted]."

"The whole Malaysian political scene is now nothing but wheeling, dealing, and backstabbing. Wake me up when it's all over!"

"No politician is perfect; all have their flaws. Anwar has gone through the toughest times yet stands strong on his principles. He could have easily walked away a rich man by compromising, but he stood through the times alone in a cell separated from his family. None of us could understand this.... So it is time we should give him the honor...and opportunity to prove his words and promises."

"Yes, I am looking forward to ... a new country with ethics! Alas I am ever the optimist!"

III: MALAYSIAN HEROES

Saluting The Genuine Heroes And Heroines Of 1MDB

September 28, 2022

[That the giant government-linked corporation 1Malaysia Berhad's (1MDB) funds had been criminally siphoned off in mega sums by former Prime Minister Najib Razak is no longer news, locally or globally. It is the biggest heist in the world, and with an equally extensive global reach. The pervasive and thus far persuasive narrative spread (and not just by Najib) is that he and his coterie of corrupt fellow Malay leaders in the United Malay National Organization (UMNO) had been swindled by that moon-faced Jho Lo, a Malaysian Chinese now absconded safely somewhere in China. It is an effective story, a sub-variety of the old "us-versus-them" theme. However not all were taken in as demonstrated by these thus far unsung and unrecognized heroes of 1MDB who smelled the stink much earlier and tried to do something about it and at great risk to themselves, personally and career-wise. I salute them!]

My commentary ("Raja Nazrin Missed A Splendid Opportunity," page 87) on Perak Sultan Nazrin's speech on corruption at the launching of Kamal Hassan's book *Corruption And Hypocrisy In Malay Muslim Politics* on September 22, 2022 elicited many responses. Most were supportive of my views, but a few took exceptions, specifically to my observation that despite the Sultan's strong anti-corruption message he has yet to revoke Najib Razak's Perak royal honorific. Then there were those thinly veiled bigots who saw in Raja Nazrin's "non-action" as reflective of the new norms of a degraded Malay culture and societal values.

Nazrin's non-action on Najib's wrongdoing rightly deserves wide attention and even more scrutiny. First, Nazrin is one of the few Malay rulers who have had the benefit of superior education (Oxford and Harvard), the other ruler being Negri Sembilan's Tunku Muhriz (Law, Wales). Second, Nazrin and his fellow Malay Rulers were apprised of this 1MDB scandal not once but twice and as early as October 2015, months before the United States Department of Justice first filed its own charges.

Third, Nazrin had experienced at a very personal level the ugly effects of political corruption. Who could forget the pathetic image of him (then deputizing for his father, Sultan Azlan Shah) waiting, cooling his heels in the Perak State Assembly Hall antechamber while his Assemblymen and women were literally battling it out as to who was the rightful Speaker. That bizarre May 2009 saga saw Pakatan's Sivakumar being dragged out physically while still clinging onto his Speaker's Chair.

Back to Malay sultans, the Council of Rulers was envisioned to be a third House of Parliament. However, its power had been severely clipped since the constitutional crisis of the 1980s. Nonetheless the collective moral and other sways of the sultans remain. Those would remain and be enhanced only if these sultans were to exhibit exemplary moral, intellectual, and leadership qualities. Attending elite universities reflect the second. As for moral, it would help if these rulers were not to cavort with foreign beaus and then abandon their babies or be accused of keeping slaves in their palaces. That was the serious charge levelled at the Kelantan palace years ago by the family of an Indonesian beauty who caught the eye of one of the princes. As for leadership, sultans must demonstrate that on important national issues. Corruption is the national issue today.

With respect to 1MDB and Najib Razak, then Malaysian Anti-Corruption Commission (MACC) Chairman Shukri Abdull recalled his disappointment at the collective response of the Council of Rulers back in 2015 when they were first apprised of the problem. Nonetheless the Ruler of Negri Sembilan did withdraw Najib's royal title right after he was formally charged in October 2018; Selangor's sultan merely suspended his. Meaning, Raja Nazrin and his brother rulers have had years to ponder this issue. They should now issue a powerful statement and initiate strong actions with respect to Najib and others involved. Non-action is not a viable or acceptable option.

That would be an insult to those brave diligent officers in MACC as well as in the Attorney-General's office who had paid dearly for their early courageous diligent investigations. Shukri had many death threats. When he went to New York City to seek the help of the Americans early in the investigation, he was "tailed" by agents of the Malaysian government and had to seek the protection of the New York City Police! He saw the chilling effects of his colleagues being transferred out, put into administrative "cold storage," or forced into retirement and silence lest their retirement nest egg be taken away. That was the fate of former Attorney-General Gani Patail, former head of MACC Abu Kassim, and others. Aware of the fatal fates of Prosecutor Kevin Morais, model Altantuyaa, and banker Hussain Najadi, it is not a surprise that these brave public servants, Shukri excepted, have remained silent.

Then there were the two government auditors, Nor Salwani Muhammad and Madinah Mohamad, who took great personal and career risks in keeping a copy of the original 1MDB's audit report before it was "sanitized." The original copy proved pivotal at Najib's trial.

Another was Latheefa Koya. Freshly appointed as Chief of MACC following Pakatan Harapan's victory in the 2018 election, in January 2020 released the chilling contents of the phone taps on Najib. In one, he was being tipped off by a prosecutor in the Attorney-General's office of his (Najib's) ongoing criminal investigations. Yes, in characteristic Najib style, he later promoted that prosecutor, Dzulkifli Ahmad, to be MACC Chief! In another instance, Najib was caught groveling to an Arab prince asking to have certain documents pertaining to 1MDB altered and backdated.

There is still yet an unknown and unheralded hero, the individual who tapped Najib's phone. I pray and hope that he is also a Malay. Our culture is very much in need of such brave figures. It was his (or her) action that enabled another heroine, Latheefa Koya, to release the chilling contents of those phone taps. (See: https://youtu.be/7BRgHz1qB-4)

I recall these brave individuals (there are others not mentioned) because one, our culture desperately needs such heroes now to counterbalance such incompetents as former Attorney-General Apandi Ali who cleared Najib of any wrongdoing) and MACC Chief Dzulkifli Ahmad, the prosecutor who earlier tipped Najib. Two, to rebut the thinly veiled bigotry heard these days. "Yes, what do you expect from these corrupt, incompetent Malay public servants."

That aside, my two original queries nonetheless remain: Why are the corrupt so admired in our culture, and the converse, why are the honest, brave, and talented as represented by Shukri and others not honored and rewarded?

Readers' Rating: * *
Sampling of Readers' Responses:

"I am not surprised that Perak has not revoked Najib's royal honorific. Wasn't Najib in office when a legitimate opposition government with Nizar as [Chief Minister] removed? What about the blatant involvement of his sister with Gamuda [a GLC]? Indeed, why have none of them honor the real heroes? Instead, we have the corrupted ones being given one title after another. It's quite disgusting ... that some of these grand looters in office have such long titles ...."

"The Council of Rulers ... represent power from the feudal era. Rulers expect unquestioned loyalty .... Besides, thc current Agung is a close ally of Najib. The Agung himself is not squeaky clean. His son ... is a major owner of a company … that is too willing to accept an Australian mining company's ... toxic wastes."

"When self-serving leaders mislead, a nation and her people will bleed … we are now bleeding to death."

Syabas (Salute) To Our Heroes Fahmi And Zunar!

April 25, 2021

[Political cartoonists in both the English and vernacular media have a long and distinguished tradition in Malaysia, dating back to colonial days. None however could match the courage and sharpness of Fahmi Reza and Anwar Haque (Zunar). Citizens however would have to turn to the social and alternate media to see the creations of these two artistic geniuses as the mainstream press would not dare touch their cutting creations.]

Will Rogers once quipped that everything is changing now, what with comedians taken seriously and politicians a joke. It used to be the other way round.

In Malaysia things go further, much further. Her politicians, besides being a silly joke, are also senile clowns while her cartoonists, virile heroes at their prime. Star cartoonists Fahmi Reza and Zulkiflee Anwar Haque (Zunar) strike fear at the highest levels. In May 2018 CNN described both as "The two cartoonists who helped take down a Malaysian Prime Minister." Their target? Prime Minister Mahathir. After that, who's next? Rest assured that both Zunar and Fahmi Reza have their work cut out. There seems to be no end to jokers who end up in the Prime Minister's seat in Malaysia.

Fahmi and Zunar have been widely lauded by their international peers. Fahmi won the "Most Outstanding Human Rights Film" at the 2007 Freedom Film Festival. His rendition of a red, thick lips Najib as a grotesque clown was the iconic campaign banner during the 2018 General Election. In 2015 Zunar received the coveted International Press Freedom Award. In 2011 he received the Robert Russel "Courage in Political Cartooning" Award, and he won it again in 2020. As for being honored by their local peers, they have none. By that I mean they have no peers among locals.

Fahmi's doodling rattled even the palace. His latest was not a sketch but a playlist on Spotify with the label "*Deng Ki Ke?*" (Are you jealous?) splashed over the portrait of the Queen in her regal yellow. There are titillating subtitles, but we need not go over them. That playlist of songs each with the word "jealous" in the lyrics did not amuse the Queen, prompting her to deactivate her Instagram account. Spotify too was spooked. Undeterred and ever resourceful, Fahmi uploaded his playlist on Apple Music. Having listened to the free preview, I must compliment him for his selection of songs! For that he was detained by the police for — what else in Malaysia? — allegedly insulting those in power, the Queen in this instance. The Queen later reinstated her Instagram but with her earlier posting of "*Dengki Ke?*" deleted.

What was there to be jealous of the Queen? Her wealth? More than a few local tycoons could outmatch her on that front. Her looks? Well, let's not go there!

That jealousy referred to in her earlier Instagram posting had nothing to do with either wealth or beauty, rather over the much sought-after Covid-19 vaccine early in the pandemic. On their recent trip to Saudi Arabia, the royal couple secured (outside regular channels of course) 2,000 doses of the then-scarce vaccine. When someone queried whether palace chefs too had been vaccinated (to justify the large supply), she responded with her now infamous Instagram posting, "*Dengki Ke?*" From there, the ever perceptive and sharply piercing Fahmi struck, and it went viral. Her royal attempt at being "hip" in social media backfired in the worst possible way, one she least expected.

Malay sultans and their families not following the rules are not a novelty for Malaysians. They have long tolerated if not endured that. Thus, the Agung securing those early precious vaccines outside of regular channels would not even raise a yawn in still feudal Malaysia. So why the fuss this time? No one begrudges the King and Queen as well as palace personnel getting top priority. They should, both as a show of confidence for the vaccine as well as for their positions, as having to interact with the public. No need for the haughtiness, much less the secrecy and super-sensitivity. The government could have made special provisions for them and do so openly. That would also be doing the right thing and right way.

It is the unneeded secrecy that is problematic. What other secret deals were being cooked up with the Arabs? With Najib's 1MDB trials now meandering through the courts, citizens cannot be blamed for speculating.

I salute Fahmi's artistic genius and undaunted bravery. What saddens me are his detractors, especially the few prominent Malays. They caricature him as a stooge for the Chinese, the Democratic Action Party (DAP) to be specific. That says more of Fahmi's Malay critics than of him. In effect they are repeating the old Mahathirian refrain: There are no brave, smart, or creative Malays. When there is one, he or she is seen as but a puppet of the Chinese. What a sad commentary, on them – those Malay leaders!

Zunar once famously said that even his pen has a stand. Citizens too must take a stand on this Fahmi versus stupid Malaysian officialdom. When leaders breach their oath of office and abrogate their responsibilities, citizens must act to show their disapproval, and do so in no uncertain terms. Malaysians have had enough with their leaders getting away with impunity, be they politicians looting the public purse in broad daylight or religious leaders groping schoolgirls and taking free junkets to visit abroad.

To Fahmi and Zunar, continue with your brave crusades. We cheer you on! Thanks to his lawyer Nadarajan, Fahmi is now released. As for Zunar, visit his website (zunar.my), buy his books, and be his patrons. His latest collection, *Politik Caca Marba* (Welcomed Lottery of Politics), promises to be another sizzler.

Readers' Rating: * * * *
Sampling of Readers' Responses:
"The people who voted in the 'clowns' and allowed them to run the country like a circus are the real clowns."

"Both are my creative heroes ... salute!"

"Police should never be used as an instrument of terror. It's a slippery slope to authoritarian rule."

"Our next Prime Minister [Muhyiddin Yassin] says that he values loyalty more than intelligence or smart ministers ... so there goes the *bodek* [suck up] and sheep mentality amongst Malaysians."

"The durian is insensitive ... the pickle is being rude. Conclusion: Both are childish. Most of the time, keep 'elegant silence' and avoid needless drama."

"Here we have two very brave, very intelligent and talented Malay artists, yet they are being ostracized by their own Malay community. It's just so sad!"

"This outrageous police action deserves my attention and to pay tribute to a social conscience sadly lacking amongst many Malays. They have a feudalistic mindset to accept the excesses of their leaders."

"Kim" Ahmad Sabian (Aug 9, 1937 – April 17, 2021)
April 17, 2021

[A few days into Ramadan of 2021, our dear friend Mohammad Bin Sabian, affectionately referred to as "Kim" by his many friends here, died after a long illness. We who knew him well were of course saddened and will miss him dearly, but I was overwhelmed by the responses when I posted the announcement of his death on Facebook and other social media.]

Al Fatihah

إِنَّا لِلَّهِ وَإِنَّا إِلَيْهِ رَاجِعُونَ,

"Verily we belong to God, and verily to Him do we return."

It is with a heavy heart that I announce that "Pak Mat" Kim Ahmad Sabian died a few minutes ago at his home in Stockton, California. His wife Rose and his son Hisham were with him. He died a few minutes before the breaking of fast on this fifth day of Ramadan, 1443.

Pak Mat is well known to the Malaysian community here in the Bay Area of Northern California. He is even more well known to the hundreds of Malaysian students who have studied in or visited California during the last many decades. Likewise, the many visitors from Malaysia, including Ambassadors, Ministers, and two Prime Ministers who have been the recipients of his generosities. To be specific, his and his wife Rose's wonderful satay, spicy rendang, and nasi lemak offerings.

Happy And Healthy At Eighty!

Kim had been the unofficial driver and tour guide to many visiting Malaysian dignitaries, as well as being their caterer whenever these visitors long for their home cuisine. It was through Kim that I met many of these important as well as the many more self-important visitors from home.

Once we had a top government official who could not stop bragging about her daughter getting a government "scholarship." Except that the daughter was attending a third-rate institution nearby, not worthy to be supported by the government. Later in the quiet of the moment when the visitors were gone I complimented Kim that his son Hisham had graduated from the University of Southern California, a top-ranked college, and that he (Kim) had one up over those many important Malaysian visitors he had hosted in that he did not have to depend on MARA, Petronas, or JPA (agencies known for their generous support of Bumiputras). Kim and Rose sacrificed much to finance their two children's education.

He beamed to my reminder. He had never thought of it that way. He would never have even considered writing home to those many important visitors whom he had hosted seeking help to secure a scholarship for his son. That was Kim. He lived the true *merdeka* (independent) spirit.

I have known Kim for over four decades. He and his family were frequent visitors to our home, likewise my family and I to theirs. Malaysians in the Bay Area remember him for his wonderful satay and nasi lemak whenever we gathered at our house or his for Hari Raya, or any excuse.

Kim had travelled widely. He came to North America way back in the early 1960s and had lived in Vancouver, Hawaii, Colorado, Washington, DC, before settling in California where we met. He retired many years ago after working with Levitz Furniture. While there he helped a few Malaysian students gain employment with the company.

My family and I will miss Kim very much. He was the kind uncle to my three children and a native buddy for me. He was the only one over here who could appreciate my old kampung jokes.

Our condolences to Rose Mohamad, son Hisham, daughter Rosanna and her husband Kozal, and their son Zayn.

Readers' Rating: * * * * *
Sampling of Reader's Responses:
> "Kim was a wonderful friend, always there for you when you were in need. A very generous man."

> "Both Abang Kim and Kak Rose never miss to meet me whenever my crew and I fly to USA."

> "Abang Kim and Kak Rose were like my big brother and sister while studying in San Jose in 1987-1988."

> "They were there whenever we missed our family back home. No amount of money could repay their kindness to us. We will always remember that deep in our hearts."

> "Not the same without him. Glad we could be there to celebrate and continue his legacy."

Remembering That Special Day, August 31, 1957

September 6, 2020

[After centuries of colonial rule, the last 130 years or so under the British, Malaysia gained her independence on August 31, 1957. Thanks to her enlightened leaders, this was achieved peacefully, through negotiations, an achievement sufficiently rare and unique at the time.]

August 31st, 1957 was a day of ebullient celebrations and unrestrained joy throughout Malaysia (or Malaya as it was then known). Rightly so for on that special day the long oppressive yoke of colonialism was finally lifted off our collective necks. We had our Merdeka! (Freedom!)

I was then in lower secondary school (Form II). In our kampung house however, the mood was anything but jubilant. The day before my father had warned us, my siblings and me, to remain at home. That family curfew would continue till the day after. In contrast to the national celebratory mood, in our house there was only heightened anxiety. The extra supply of food and other necessities my parents had bought days earlier testified and added to that jitteriness.

My parents' paranoia was not unfounded. A decade earlier they had seen ghastly images in the newspapers of the mass madness that had gripped and consumed the Indian subcontinent when it heralded its independence. Next door in Indonesia, the situation was no better. A decade after independence and President Sukarno had to urge his people to trap rats, thus solving the twin blights plaguing his young nation – mass starvation and rodent infestation. At home in the power vacuum at the end of World War II, there was the two-week reign of terror inflicted by the Malayan Communist Party.

More immediate and pertinent, a few days before *merdeka* my father overheard a conversation among his fellow villagers. They were giddy with their plans to seize those elegant bungalows in Kuala Pilah for themselves and drive out those colonials like my school headmaster. My father threw a damper on their ideas. If those houses were to revert to the natives, he cautioned the kampung wannabe heroes, rest assured that they would not be the lucky recipients. Besides, and more practical, who would teach our children if those British teachers were to leave?

Thus on the beginning of that day at midnight, to the delirious chanting of "Merdeka! Merdeka!" on the radio and everywhere, my father would mock, "*Mencakar! Mencakar!*" (Scraping, as in scraping for a living) to remind his listeners of our potential fate, with nearby Indonesia serving as a ready ghastly example.

Fast forward to a decade later, my parents would readily admit to the error of their earlier grim forebodings. Bless them! Malaysia's first Prime Minister Tengku Abdul Rahman had stuck to his words of "building schools instead of barracks, and training teachers instead of soldiers." In the seven-mile drive from my village to my old school in Kuala Pilah for example, no fewer than seven new primary schools were being built. My older brother and sister were among the thousands trained as new teachers.

Malaysians have much to be grateful to the Tengku (as he was affectionately called) beyond his saving the nation from an unnecessary war of independence to achieve freedom Thus on this Merdeka Day, Malaysians have no embellished reenactments of glorious battles and solemn rituals of honoring fallen heroes. Malaysians, unlike Americans, are thankfully spared our Bunker Hills and Paul Reveres.

As Tengku had kept his pledge of building schools and training teachers, young Malaysians like me were able to pursue our dreams. In the final analysis, that is the most precious and enduring gift a leader could bestow upon his nation and people. A grateful nation dubbed Tengku "Bapa Merdeka!" (Father of Freedom!)

This year 2020 was to be Malaysia's "coming-out" party, to mark her entry into the exclusive club of developed nations, the crowning achievement of her long-time Prime Minister Mahathir's Vision 2020 aspiration. Instead, she is today cursed with a government that is bloated, corrupt, and incompetent; her citizens deeply and dangerously polarized. Malaysia is now more known for her 1MDB notoriety, the world's most expensive swindle, perpetrated by former Prime Minister Najib Razak. The price tag of that is humongous and escalating, but at least it is quantifiable. Not so the divisions he had sowed and continues to sow among Malaysians, as well as the culture of egregious corruption that now characterizes Malay leaders.

Mahathir's Vision 2020 proved to be but a cruel hoax. Beyond that, he cannot absolve himself of the responsibility for the rise of the sleepy Abdullah Badawi, the kleptocratic Najib, and now the muddling Muhyiddin, thus turning Malaysia into the sorry state she is in today. What an ugly legacy, obvious to all but Mahathir.

Back in the 1980s on the occasion of one of Mahathir's birthdays, the late PAS leader Fadzil Noor wished for Mahathir to have a long life ... so he could see the follies of his policies. Fadzil Noor got his wish. However, Mahathir still deludes himself as being God's greatest gift to Malaysia. As per the wisdom of Sa'adi's *Gulistan*, "He whose fault is not told him/Ignorantly thinks his defects are virtues!"

Mahathir has surrounded himself with courtiers. They do not dare tell him that their emperor is naked.

Tengku was spot on when he predicted back in 1970 that Mahathir would destroy Malaysia. Mahathir personifies Raja Ali Haji's aphorism in his *Gurindam Dua Belas (IV)*: *"Tiada orang yang amat celaka / Aib dirinya tiada ia sangka."* (None more cursed than those blind to their own flaws.)

Tengku's enlightened vision for Malaysia has been derailed. There is much to be done to put it back on track, as well as build a stronger locomotive and straighten the tracks. That done, then to ensure only the honest, competent, and principled be at the throttle. Only thus could Malaysians savor our Merdeka.

Readers' Rating: * *
Sampling of Readers' Responses:

"The one who derailed Tengku's vision was none other than Razak. Take note of May 13 [1969 riot] and New Economic Policy."

"Sorry chapters of our history. The outlook for the future has become grimmer."

"How about coming home to do national service? We need someone like you here!"

"His mind doesn't belong here where only apple-polishers and lemmings fit in. Chances are he will be persecuted."

"Better remain where he belongs and is appreciated."

IV: CORRUPT, PATHETIC, INCOMPETENT MALAY LEADERSHIP

Get Rid Of Corrupt, Untrustworthy Leaders

October 26, 2022

["Money," to quote California's former Speaker Jesse Unruh, "is the mother's milk of politics." Unlike mother's milk which is nourishing, money politics plagues and corrupts many democratic systems. Malaysia is one. While in America the money is spent on expensive media advertising, in Malaysia it is more retail, with cash handed out directly to voters. Literally buying votes! To add local cultural niceties and enhancements, the giving would be accompanied by such local customs as with the shaking of hands and the utterances of such phrases as "Kerana Allah" (In the name of God). That imparts an almost religious blessing and obligation to vote for the candidate. As your promises then are not to the candidate but to God! Very effective, hence the widespread use.]

Two images circulating on social media recently saddened me. One showed Prime Minister Ismail Sabri grinning from ear to ear and with a blank stare handing out cash to Hindu worshippers celebrating their Deepavali. The second, a video clip showing a Malay Barisan Nasional (BN) campaign worker sticking "Undi BN" (Vote BN) bumper stickers to motorcyclists stopped at a traffic light. In return for their permission to put the stickers on their vehicles, those riders were each given a RM100 Malaysian ringgit note.

Ponder that pathetic first image, Prime Minister 'Mael (as he is known) handing out cash in a House of Worship begging those devotees to vote for his party. Outright vote buying and in plain sight. Those pious Hindus were busy praying and celebrating their Festival of Light. That Light refers to power, virtue, and knowledge, comparable to the Qur'anic *nur*. However, there is minimal power in those ringgit notes given out as that currency is fast depreciating. As for virtue, those worshippers were deep in their spiritual thoughts. We do not need any reminder that no religion considers bribing a virtuous act. As such what 'Mael did was a blasphemy. However, that was not what saddened me about that picture, rather the indelible image it projected to the world — Malay leaders as represented by Ismail Sabri and thus Malay culture as represented by UMNO, being corrupt. In Islam, *pecah amanah* (breaches of fidelity) by leaders are among the greatest sins.

As for knowledge, 'Mael revealed not only his lack of that but also moral sensitivity, quite aside from elementary decorum. He was uncouth as well as desecrating the holy place and occasion. It was an act of utter desperation; vile corruptness personified, your typical slimy third-rate Third World politician. It was gross, with no subtlety or any attempt at hiding his hideous act. Judging from his facial expression, he was proud to be involved in that blatant activity. And this character is a lawyer and a Muslim leader!

The difference between Ismail Sabri and Najib Razak, recently convicted for looting 1MDB, is quantitative not qualitative. Najib looted billions, Ismail, well, for Najib that would be his pocket change. Regardless, both are *pecah amanah*.

Najib at least showed some deference to Hindu culture by dressing himself in proper attire at a similar pre-election campaign in the past. Not this character 'Mael (Ismail). At the minimum he should have donned a *dhoti* (long bright colored overcoat) or one of his gaudy colored open-neck, long over-the-pants shirt that he is so fond of wearing. That temple episode would be comparable to a *kafir* (disbeliever) politician handing out cash in a mosque during Friday prayers and not deferring to our religious sensitivity as with not donning a head cover or keeping his shoes on. What 'Mail did was sacrilegious, if not obscene beyond imagination.

As for that campaign worker, one could be charitable and assume that he was being paid an honest wage for his day's work. As such to him it is work and his earnings would be as halal as that of the roadside *goreng pisang* (fried banana) seller. Or is it?

Imagine the behind-the-scene activities associated with that campaign worker. Assume that he was given 100 stickers for the day and at RM100 each, he would receive 100 pieces of that note, totaling RM 10,000 (100 x RM100), for distribution. Do you think that he would paste the whole one hundred stickers, or would he emulate his superiors Ismail Sabri, Ahmad Zahid Hamidi, and Najib Razak? That is, after pasting the first twenty or so he would throw the rest into the dumpster and pocket the remaining cash. Who would check on him? Then consider the man who gave him that RM10,000. How much was his share of the loot? So be easy on that campaign worker. Besides, he is only emulating them; monkey see, monkey do!

That worker would return to his local BN campaign headquarters at the end of the day and could pose as a hero to party apparatchiks by refusing to be paid for his work as he was doing it for the "love" of the party, and only that!

Likewise, imagine the back scene activities of 'Mael distributing cash in that temple. First, that grinning 'Mael would have his underlings bring in those pellets of cash to his office or home. He would not trust those mountains of ringgit notes to their custody. Remember Najib? He kept his lodes of cash in his condo, discovered only after the police raid following his coalition's loss in the 2018 General Election. He too claimed that those monies were for campaign purposes.

There was only one question with Najib's explanation for the humongous cash found, and nobody has yet posed that. The mountain of seized boxes contained currencies in Euros, pound sterling, and US dollar, all in large denominations. Do you think those big foreign notes would come in handy to those poor villagers in Kemaman? Imagine them buying *ikan bilis* (dried fish) at the local store with their US$100 or Euro 100 bills!

That police raid of Najib's Pavilion Condo was broadcasted live worldwide. That was shameful enough, except of course to Najib and his fellow UMNO leaders. However, there was more! A few days following the raid, more than a few members of the police raiding party (all Malays, I am saddened to state) were soon sporting luxury motorcycles, paid for in cash! At one level it is like that earlier campaign worker, another case of "monkey see, monkey do." More sinister is that it reflected the entrenched and endemic culture of corruption. This is what Malaysia, specifically Malay culture, has degenerated into. This is the culture that not so long ago undertook a mega event attended by our luminaries extolling its supreme values. Remember that Kongress Maruah Melayu (Malay Dignity Congress) of October 2019 attended by then Prime Minister Mahathir? What a mockery!

Again, imagine the scene at Ismail's (and other BN leaders') residence or office during this election time where those huge caches of cash are being kept. The risk of pilfering, not by outsiders as they would have no access, but by his household members would also be high. They would not hesitate to swipe a few bundles before going shopping. Who is there to check or count? Besides, they would not consider that as stealing or swiping but honest wage or commission earned!

What Malaysians should do during this campaign is to take the cash offered and at election time boot out those corrupt and untrustworthy bastards. Remember, the money those UMNO crooked politicians are dishing out belong to the rakyat in the first place.

Readers' Ratings: *
Samples of Readers' Responses:
"Money will do good; money will do evil."
"Somewhat revolting to read about the shameless bribing and cheating but thank you for writing about it."

Perak's Raja Nazrin Missed A Rare Opportunity
September 23, 2022

[When former Prime Minister Najib Razak was finally committed to jail on September 1, 2022, after a long trial and even longer appeal process, the Sultan of Selangor and the Governor of Penang stripped Najib of his state titles. Earlier in 2018 when he had just been charged but not yet convicted, the Ruler of Negri Sembilan did the same. On a recent launching of a book on corruption among Malay leaders, the Perak Sultan who had also awarded Najib a royal title remained conspicuously silent on Najibs's Perak state title.]

The Sultan of Perak recently (September 22, 2022) launched Kamal Hassan's *Corruption And Hypocrisy In Malay Muslim Politics*. The book was published in January 2021, and I reviewed it last July [See page 200]. A Malay version has also been released but this royal launching was for the English edition only. The Malay version was not even mentioned. I wonder how the language nationalists feel about that.

The sultan's speech (about 45 minutes long) and the author's subsequent remarks (over 35) were followed by an hour of panel discussion comprising Johan Jaafar, former journalist, and Chairman of the Anti-Corruption Commission, Tajuddin Rasdi, an academic architect and public intellectual, and Hafiz Saleh Hudin from the International Islamic University. It was moderated by Annuar Zaini, former Chairman of Bernama, the government's news agency.

Halfway into his speech the sultan revealed that his state religious department (of which he is the titular head) had ordered 2,000 copies of the book (not stated whether the English or Malay version, presumably the latter) to be distributed to the state's imams as materials for their *khutba* (sermons). For added measure, at the end of his speech the Sultan ordered two new duas (supplications), condemning corruption, to be recited during Friday sermons. That was his solution to the endemic, entrenched corruption in the country. In short, the sultan echoed Kamal Hassan's thesis in his book that the answer to Malay society's corruption is more religion, Islam to be specific.

The sultan is the head of Islam in his state. Raja Nazrin played that role to the hilt that morning, quoting the Qur'an and hadith more than a dozen times. I ran out of fingers after the tenth. Thankfully he spared us the original Arabic and gave only the Malay translations. For Kamal Hassan's part, he reiterated what he had written in the book, only of necessity more briefly and thus succinctly.

I cannot help but feel how far detached from reality the whole program and the participants were. They all professed to be aware of the grave danger corruption poses to the nation and Malay society in particular, but alas their deliberated solutions were but to resort to homilies and simplistic measures. That is, more dua's, and educate the imams on the evils of corruption!

No one even suggested learning from nations that had successfully tackled the problem, like nearby Singapore, or following the example of China – shoot the bastards. That may be "un-Islamic," but it works. Nor did anyone mention or alluded to the perverse if not pathologic national deification of that *pengkhianat negara* (national traitor) aka Boss Ku Najib Razak. Only the young participant from the International Islamic

University briefly mentioned in the ensuing panel discussion his displeasure to that phenomenon.

What a great pity, and loss of a splendid opportunity. The program could have unfolded very differently and created great national impact.

Imagine if at the end of the ceremony Raja Nazrin had announced that, as an expression of his great displeasure with corrupt leaders and considering the seriousness of the pestilence of corruption, he was withdrawing Najib's and Rosmah's Perak royal titles! That would have captured in an instant the audience's as well as the nation's attention. It would be the next day's blaring headlines! Raja Nazrin should have emulated the Sultan of Selangor, or better yet the Ruler of Negri Sembilan who withdrew the couples' Negri royal awards upon their being charged and not wait for their conviction, as with the Sultan of Selangor.

"Innocent till proven guilty" is the standard in a criminal court. In positions requiring great trust, as with the leadership of the nation, the standard must necessarily be much more stringent, as with not even a hint of impropriety. Yet today UMNO, the party most identified with Malays, is led by a character facing serious criminal charges. Nobody in the party's governing Supreme Council has the gumption to demand that Ahmad Zahid Hamidi resign, at least pending the outcome of his trials. (Yes, trials as he faces more than one.) If these UMNO leaders cannot stand up to this slimy stuttering character, how can we expect them to negotiate with or face foreign leaders?

With the long speeches by both the sultan and the author, there was little time for questions from the audience, the most important part in any discussion or book launching. Noting the number of ex-dignitaries from UMNO in the audience, the moderator gave the floor first to former Deputy Prime Minister Musa Hitam. He took his senior statesman status too seriously as he went on a long monologue, prompting the moderator to interrupt him. As for the other half a dozen or so other speakers, they too were more interested in making their own mini speeches rather than posing probing questions.

If not for Tajuddin Rasdi, the ensuing panel discussion too would have been a dud. Johan Jaafar was asked what greatest pressure he faced when chairing the Anti-Corruption Commission. Political interference! Surprise of surprises! The moderator then asked him to judge the independence from political pressure of his Commission. Johan meekly replied a passable 6 out of 10. Good enough for a general degree, as the moderator commented. If I were the moderator, I would press Johan as to what he did to resist those pressures. I suspect that Johan too was one of those all too common *"Kami menurut perentah"* (I follow orders) type of public servant.

The sparkles in the panel discussion came from Tajuddin Rasdi. He prefaced his remarks by noting that this was the first time he had been invited to address an almost exclusively Malay or Muslim audience. Tajuddin is of course well known to non-Malay or at least English-speaking readers through his trenchant columns in *The Star*.

He made the profound observation that corruption is difficult to eradicate among Malays and Muslims because it enmeshed into the Malay versus non-Malay (or non-Muslim) narrative. It is but a sub-variety of the old "us versus them" divide. We have framed corruption as war against the infidel and thus halal. or can be made so. To make that narrative stick even more easily, to Malays anything coming from the land of the Arabs is halal. It is thus not a surprise that Najib had framed the loot he pilfered from 1MDB as money donated from an Arab prince.

Another astute observation from Tajuddin is that, as in the universities, we are more into the answers without first asking the necessary probing questions. Worse, often the solutions would have been imposed upon us, as with Raja Nazrin ordering those new supplications for Friday sermons. However, we are more likely to find the right solution if we first begin by asking some tough questions. Questioning the answers can be just as revealing as answering the questions.

One simple question is this: Why are the corrupt so admired in our culture? Prime exhibit: Najib Razak. The next complementary question is why are the talented in our midst not rewarded? Instead we reward the duds and those satisfied with a general degree, to paraphrase the moderator. As for expecting Malaysian scholars and academics being more outspoken, you can bet that the likes of Tajuddin would never make it to the National Professors Council!

Malays should learn from our *peladang* (farmers). To ensure a bountiful harvest and a productive orchard, they would prune their fruit trees as well as get rid of the unproductive suckers and water sprouts.

They would also uproot the *lalang* and other weeds that would sap the precious nutrients from the soil. Malay culture today perversely nurtures and rewards those parasites. My late father (himself a part-time *peladang* besides being a teacher) had an apt expression for that stupidity – *membajakan lalang* (providing manure to the weeds).

Readers' Rating: * * * * *
Sampling of Readers' Responses:

"Top class sociological explanation of the conditions breeding corruption or curtailing it, '*membajakan lalang*'! Instead of weeding or spraying *lalang*, we sow and even fertilize it to flourish. I enjoyed the article, raising many pertinent questions."

"A friend remarked that the *kayangan* (aristocratic) class have got their hands in the till too ... from timber, mineral, land, contracts for projects, etc. Can't expect too much from a corrupt and self-serving class...."

"From HADHARI to HARAKIRI nation thru self-greed and self-deception."

"From a non-Malay viewpoint, these scholars and professionals are of no interest at all."

"They only can talk to the wind."

"Thank you for an exceptionally long detailed sharing! Yes, some missed opportunities, but that Sultan Nazrin took the trouble is in and of itself good and well done .... So it was a bold good move, Sultan Nazrin telling the Imams what to read or say."

"Corruption in Malaysia is likely to get worse before it gets better. No matter how bad and corrupt UMNO leaders are, the grassroots, which form the majority of Malays, would still believe they are saints and saviors of the community. This happens because the grassroots are more interested in getting handouts.... There is not even a beam of light at the end of tunnel just yet for this country to get the corruption problem addressed effectively."

"How the Malays are so taken in by Najib and UMNO is akin to Stockholm Syndrome."

"Good observation, but alas you only commented on the receivers of the corrupt practice. No mention of the givers."

"Expecting kings and queens who never work a day in their life to understand the effect of corruption and hardship of rakyat is just plain stupid despite what they say. Monarchy is old, and as with all old stuff, it belongs to a museum."

Investigate Mahathir With The Same Vigor As With Najib

August 29, 2022

[With national as well as global attention now focused on former Prime Minster Najib's conviction for corruption, the far more important element to this sorry saga is conveniently ignored. That is, the man responsible for nurturing and elevating Najib – former Prime Minister Mahathir. They are both of the same mold, their only difference being that the coalition Najib led lost the election and that led to his criminal investigation. Mahathir instead left his old losing coalition and switched to the winning Pakatan Harapan, thus sparing himself tough scrutiny.]

The praises heaped upon Chief Justice Maimun and her fellow Federal Court Judges on their handling of Najib Razak's criminal appeal were not misplaced. Judging by past experiences of the court, they could have easily rendered a very different verdict on August 23, 2022.

As for the Chief Justice, imagine had she been that character who was caught holidaying in New Zealand with a member of the defense bar (I wonder who picked up their tab!), or the former UMNO Legal Advisor who perjured himself in hiding his secret second marriage in Southern Thailand! Worse, remember that infamous lawyer whose VVIP clients at the time included then Prime Minister Mahathir? That attorney was caught on videotape uttering "Correct! Correct! Correct!" on the phone. The party at the other end was a senior judge, later to become Chief Justice; they were trying to fix an upcoming case.

Then consider had the Malaysian Anti-Corruption Commission (MACC) still been under that Dzulkifli Ahmad, the ilk who was caught holidaying in Bali with someone other than his wife. Personal morality aside, this was the same idiot who earlier when he was a nondescript public prosecutor tipped Prime Minister Najib of the then on-going 1MDB criminal investigation. It was unfortunate for both but lucky for Malaysians that their phone conversation was tapped and later released by

Latheefa Koya, Dzulkifli's successor. Dzulkifli was confused on whether he was on the nation's or Najib's private payroll. His reward? Najib made him MACC Chief.

Dzulkifli was not alone in being confused. Witness the many court testimonies of other civil servants. Even Chief Secretary Sidek Hassan admitted that he was being paid more than his official salary to be on the 1MDB Board to "do nothing."

Likewise, had the prosecution been led by career civil servant *"Kami menurut perentah"* (We follow orders!) lawyers, the outcome would also have been very different. There is more! If that third-rate former UMNO lawyer Apandi had remained as Attorney-General, Najib would not even have faced any charges. Apandi had cleared Najib of any charges and told the world that the entire transactions were legal and above board. Thus if not for the new Attorney-General Tommy Thomas, coopted from the private sector, Najib would today be lauded a Wira Negara! (National Hero), with the Agung feting and decorating him on a garish obscene scale as only a Malay sultan could.

There are many honest, dedicated, and competent civil servants, but those are not the ones being promoted. Instead, we have the likes of Dzulkifli, Apandi Ali, and Sidek Hassan reaching the top. I am also aware that there were many brave civil servants who literally paid with their lives for their integrity. Remember the late Deputy Public Prosecutor Kevin Morais whose body was found in a cement drum?

Those aside, the tipping point that led to the unmasking of Najib was voters' denying his UMNO-led Barisan coalition victory in the 2018 national election. Prior to that Barisan and its earlier Alliance coalition had suffered only two major but not power-shifting electoral setbacks.

The first was in 1969 when the Alliance failed to secure a supra-majority of Parliamentary seats and polled less than half of the popular votes. That setback triggered a traumatic race riot that nearly tore the nation apart. The second was in 2008, also with a loss of its supra-majority. That resulted in Abdullah Badawi's resignation and Najib's ascendancy to the top slot.

As for Najib, he had a near-death political experience in the 1999 election when he barely held on to his long-held Pekan seat which he had won with over a 10,000-vote majority in the previous election. In that

1999 contest he scraped through with a threadbare 241-vote majority, rescued at the last minute by "mail ballots" from the nearby army base.

The 2018 national election was a game changer. Unlike the Nigerians and Pakistanis, Malaysians were finally disgusted with their leaders and voted out the corrupt UMNO-led coalition. The new administration, though brief, nonetheless triggered the subsequent cascading events that led to Najib's arrest and later incarceration.

As such, praises for Najib's final conviction should go to the Malaysian electorate. That is the key lesson for the next election. The most powerful instrument in getting rid of corruption in the country is for voters to know where to put the "X" on their ballot.

Had Malaysians been wise in 1999 and booted out the Mahathir-led coalition, they would have uncovered similar egregious corruptions and gross mismanagement in his Administration. Think of the London Tin debacle, massive Forex (foreign exchange) losses, and Bank Bumiputra bankruptcy, among others. Then remember the gruesome murder of the Bank's auditor, Jalil Ibrahim. With Najib, there were the model Altantuyaa, banker Ahmad Najadi, and prosecutor Kevin Morais. Had a similar tough scrutiny been done back then, Malaysia would have been spared the later 1MDB and other boondoggles. Malaysia jailed the wrong leader following the 1999 election.

Najib is Mahathir's political son. Najib would not have risen so early and so fast had it not been for Mahathir. He was also instrumental in Najib replacing Abdullah in 2008. Mahathir greasing Najib's path was in the old Malay tradition of *terhutang budi* (repaying a debt of gratitude). Earlier in the 1970s Najib's father Tun Razak resurrected Mahathir when the latter was in the political wilderness following his expulsion from UMNO.

Come the next election Malaysians must again repeat the 2018 lesson and boot out the Mahathir-controlled coalition as well as the UMNO-led one. Only then could the nation do a similar much needed albeit delayed scrutiny of Mahathir's many outrageous follies. Today the old man is strutting around pontificating on Najib's sins while remaining blissfully ignorant of his own massive ones. Voters must disabuse him of his delusion. There is no statute of limitation to any criminal deed, more so of plundering the nation. Mahathir should be investigated with the same vigor as Najib, for only then would justice be done.

Regardless of whether such investigations are undertaken, one fact remains glaring and indisputable. In being directly responsible for Najib becoming Prime Minister, Mahathir had inflicted the greatest damage on the nation. You cannot put a price tag on that colossal blunder.

Readers' Rating: * * *
Sampling of Readers' Responses:
"There are 191 UMNO Division Heads and one can extrapolate ... how many more billionaires there are in UMNO!"

"It's the crooks not caught that we should be worried about!"

"Mahathir set low standards and bad precedents .... [H]e was a menacing thug to many who opposed him . . . [and] caused national disunity and radicalized Malays. It is even more tragic that his lousy rule lasted so long."

"You nailed it! ... [He] is the forerunner of corruption ... closed one eye to rampant corruption, created cronyism, ... decided on the policy of rewarding mediocrity among Bumiputras ... [and created] so many crutches that have become permanent entitlement."

"When [he] was powerful ... no one dared to voice out all the wrongs that were still there."

"We need evidence .... We just can't accuse or charge without clear and solid evidence."

Single Rotten Apple Versus The Whole Barrel

August 23, 2022.

[On August 23, 2022, Malaysia's highest court unanimously sustained the conviction of former Prime Minister Najib Razak after endless prolonged appeals. He was sentenced to twelve years in jail plus a huge RM 210 million fine for his massive pilfering of a subsidiary of the giant One Malaysia Berhad (1MDB), a government-linked corporation. Far less appreciated is the fact that corruption is now pervasive and entrenched in Malaysia. It would have remained uncovered and be accepted as the norm had it not been for the 14th General

Election of May 2018 that booted out the Najib-led ruling Barisan Nasional coalition.]

There was no joy with that *pengkhianat bangsa* (traitor to our race), *aka* Datuk Sri Al Haj Najib bin Tun Abdul Razak Al Haj, now behind bars. Some relief perhaps, what with the protracted hearings, appeals, and the innumerable requests for adjournments now over. However, this is Malaysia. Hang on and be prepared for the ensuing even more ugly sagas, however difficult that may be to imagine.

More fundamental is this. Is Najib the lone corrupt leader or is corruption now an ingrained trait of modern Malay leadership? A lone rotten apple versus the whole barrel being putrid. Or to resort to a clinical metaphor, is Najib a solitary localized cancer or has the malignancy metastasized throughout the Malay body culture? With the former, the best chance of cure would be to take aggressive action, as with wide radical local excision of the tumor. Meaning, throw Najib in the slammer for a long time to impress upon others who would be similarly tempted. I am against capital punishment, so I do not recommend following China's example. However, even when the cancer has spread, it is still important to gain good local control of the primary lesion, but you would also have to institute additional modalities as with chemo and radiation therapies.

This localized versus disseminated cancer metaphor becomes more relevant what with new scandals like the Littoral Ships Contracts now unfolding and many old ones like the Bank Bumiputra, Forex debacle, and Perwaja Steel Mill still to be fully uncovered.

As for corruption, the narrative of a pious, upright, and not too bright Malay leader being cheated by a slimy cunning Chinaman is an old one. That is but a subvariety of the old recurrent theme of 'us' versus 'them.' Today that still resonates not only among Najib's seemingly urbane lawyers but also by insular Islamist leaders like Hadi Awang. To them, their Najib is honest, only that moonfaced Jho Low had swindled their pious innocent man.

At the practical level, Najib being jailed does not make those massive 1MDB debts disappear. They would still have to be serviced, consuming the nation's scarce resources for the next few decades. Imagine the colossal opportunity costs, with citizens bearing that burden, not Najib.

However, those costs are at least quantifiable. Not so the many more far greater and longer-lasting negative consequences. Already Najib is perceived a hero, and not just among simple kampung folks. Recall that earlier royal invitation to the palace only a few months earlier.

This degradation of our society's norms and values may already be irreparable. In short, the cancer has spread.

Consider Najib's last moments of freedom yesterday (August 23, 2022). He was whisked away to jail not in the usual prison lorry but a dark-tinted luxury SUV, with police outriders fit for the Agung. Those tinted windows notwithstanding, Najib was seen through the clear front windscreen to be still in his Armani suit. Mug shots and orange prison garbs are only for opposition politicians and the common criminals.

Somebody must explain this gross breach of standard protocol. Otherwise, be prepared to see for even more bizarre and offensive scenes, the cancer too having spread to the prison system.

Najib's endless legal maneuverings, fervent multiple appeals, and cheap delaying tactics did not impress the judges. As per Chief Justice Maimun, "Putting aside the personality of the appellant, this [was] ... a simple and straightforward case of abuse of power, criminal breach of trust, and money laundering." Najib was found guilty on all seven charges, reinforcing the earlier decisions of the Trial Judge and Appeals Court Judges. Both appellate decisions were unanimous.

Chief Justice Maimun went further. "[T]he evidence ... points overwhelmingly to guilt ... so much so that it would have been a travesty of justice of the highest order if any reasonable tribunal, faced with such evidence staring it in the face, were to find the appellant not guilty...."

As for spurious delaying tactics, imagine bringing up an issue that allegedly first appeared in social media over four years ago, as the defense attorneys did in trying at the last moment to recuse the Chief Justice. I wished one of the Judges would have asked Najib's smart lawyers whether they had first ascertained the veracity of that alleged Facebook posting by Chief Justice Maimun's husband. Very elementary, my dear! On the other hand, maybe Najib's lawyers should appreciate the judges' kind courtroom gesture of sparing them this embarrassing basic lapse.

Those ugly courtroom spectacles that Malaysians had to endure could all have been prevented if only Judge Nazlan had the courage and used his discretion to deny Najib bail, sending him straight to jail back in July 2020. Considering the gravity of the offense, Najib's brazen manner, and the unprecedented size of the loot, Judge Nazlan would have been more than justified. Had he done so we would all have been spared the ubiquitous hideous displays of his "Malu Apa Bossku!" (What's there to be ashamed of?) placards, with Najib's grinning face dominating the local social and mainstream media. As it turned out, Najib had a lot to be ashamed. For Judge Nazlan, that would have at least spared him Najib's clumsy, belated, and ultimately unsuccessful attempt at smearing his (Nazlan's) integrity.

Those notwithstanding, it did not stop the Agung from inviting Najib, already a convicted criminal, to an official palace dinner. I do not know whether the Chief Justice was also invited to that event. If she was, she did the right thing by not accepting it. The King and his advisors should have known better not to invite a criminal onto the hallowed palace grounds.

Any bets that the Agung, also the current Sultan of Pahang (Najib's home state), would in the coming 65th Anniversary Merdeka Celebration proclaim a new Wira Negara (National Hero) and grant Najib a pardon? Stay tuned! To reiterate, the social cancer of corruption is not only pervasive but has also reached the highest level.

There are many villains in this sorry, sordid 1MDB saga. Some have paid the price. Whether Najib would be included in this group remains to be seen, this latest denial of his appeal notwithstanding. This after all is Malaysia.

There are also many victims, but Najib, his family and cronies, are not among them despite their (as well as those UMNO people) cries of protestations. Instead, there are those millions of Malaysians, the burden disproportionately borne by the poor. Imagine the many decrepit rural schools and underfunded hospitals that would remain so because of 1MDB looting!

While there are many villains in this sad national saga, there are also many heroes. Foremost are ordinary Malaysians. It was their collective courage in throwing out the whole corrupt lot in the 2018 election that made possible the emergence of Latheefa Koya to head MACC, then Attorney-General Tommy Thomas to institute the charges, and most of all the prosecuting team headed by Datuk Sithambaram. The nation owes you much and thank you for what you have done!

Readers' Ratings: * * *
Sampling of Readers' Responses:
"I am proud of her [Chief Justice's] … courage and leadership. Let's support her and others in their efforts to clean house, our house."

"The right [Attorney-General] is key to this case – with integrity in leadership. [H]is officers discharged their duties by framing the charge tightly after studying the evidence and law. Until and unless the wider Malays stop giving UMNO and similar clowns access to positions [of power], the plunder will continue with new actors."

"Wonder if the prison guards bowed and kissed his hand like the [police] did?"

Blame Not The All-Mighty But Our Own Corrupt, Incompetent Leaders

December 26, 2021

[Floods afflict Malaysia with the regularity of well, the monsoon. Yet every season seems to catch the country unprepared and in disarray, resulting in much unnecessary loss of lives and property damages. The memories of those disasters would also be forgotten as fast as the receding waters. As such the country remains woefully unprepared for the next one.]

Last week's devastating floods were heart-wrenching; Malaysian leaders' incompetence only aggravated that. So what's new? A decade and half ago when the southern tip of the peninsula was similarly inundated, then Prime Minister Abdullah saw fit to fly to Australia to open his brother's new restaurant. Today, while Prime Minister Ismail Sabri was at home, he might as well have been in outer space. He was (still is) but a bobbing ping pong ball, visible everywhere but still empty on the inside and just as useless, carrying no weight.

This latest flood could not come at the worst possible time, what with the Covid-19 pandemic. The ulama viewed both as a test from Allah; to me, more a failure of leadership. Quoting the Qur'an, those leaders and ulama reminded us that those are the signs of the end of time. I hope so, for them.

I was enmeshed in two past major Malaysian disasters. First, the May 1969 riot while on holiday at home immediately after graduating from medical school. That tragedy claimed thousands of lives. The second was as a surgeon in Johor Baru responding to the Malaysian Airline System (MAS) hijacking crash in December 1977 that killed all 100 on board, including seven crew members.

Four observations from both experiences that are still relevant today. One, the critical importance of accurate timely information, and the complementary dangers of misleading ones or outright lies. Silence is just as dangerous as vicious rumors would then fill the gaps as quickly as air to a vacuum. Two, the need for adequate preparations, as with having disaster plans and frequent drills. Three, crisp, competent, and empathetic leadership to direct operations and comfort those affected. Last, disasters, more so natural ones, are oblivious of class, race, or other artificial labels we pin on each other. The current Covid-19 pandemic is illustrative. That notwithstanding, rich nations still try to favor their citizens over others in dispensing vaccines while ignoring the needs of poor countries.

Disasters claim far fewer victims and cause much less damage in the West than in the Third World. God is not testing those in poor countries more stringently, as some religious types would have it, rather those in the West have used their God-given *akal* (intellect) to learn from earlier tragedies. California's 1989 Loma Prieta earthquake measured 6.9 on the Richter Scale but took far fewer lives than less powerful ones elsewhere.

I remember that calamity well. After checking on my family's safety, I phoned the hospital. Unable to make contact, I drove there, only to find that nearly all the other off-duty doctors and nurses were already on site. They too had reacted like me. Because we had a disaster plan and frequent drills, we knew what to do, as for example, when the phone system was disrupted, or the power shut off.

With the Johor plane crash, I too rushed to the hospital on hearing the news, as did many of my colleagues. There we waited and waited, with no news or any communication from anyone. Frustrated, I took two carloads of personnel and supplies to where we thought the crash site would be. There we were overwhelmed by the eerie silence, downed trees, and upturned earth amidst the penetrating smell of gasoline fumes and burnt flesh.

The poignant moment of that tragedy was later, at the funeral service the following Friday held on the hospital grounds. Then Prime Minister Hussein Onn had decreed that there would be only one inter-denominational service, with leaders of all the victims' presumed faiths represented. I was never more proud of Hussein Onn's leadership for that one profoundly wise decision. That beautiful and very touching memorial service was a much-needed closure for the victims' loved ones, as well as for the nation. Of even greater significance, no ulama carped about mixing "Islam" versus "non-Islam" remains in one mass grave or having Muslim prayers said alongside Buddhist and Christian ones. The power and influence of enlightened national leadership!

Fast forward to last week, our ulama bemoaned whether those volunteers at the Sikh temple were serving those Muslim flood victims halal vegetarian meals! I applaud former Federal Mufti and Religious Minister Zulkifli Al-Bakri for visiting the temple and thanking those hard-working volunteers of all faith. As for Prime Minister Ismail Sabri, he was irrelevant and useless, missing in action. He was more effective that way!

Following that MAS crash I submitted an unsolicited report outlining an effective mass disaster plan, recommending regular drills, and improving the communication system. My immediate superior was impressed, and he promised to forward my recommendations "higher up." If he had meant to compliment me, he failed. I would have been more satisfied had he responded, "Let's do it!"

As for misleading information during a crisis, despite the gory images on Canadian and Japanese televisions of the May 1969 riots, the Malaysian embassy staff both in Ottawa and Tokyo whom I had earlier contacted for advice kept reassuring me that "everything is fine." Those horrifying scenes were but Western propaganda intent on besmirching "Malaysia's good name," they insisted. The result? I landed at a deserted Subang

Airport and had to be escorted into town in an armed police Land Rover amidst a curfew.

Back to floods. When I lived in Bungsar in 1976, with the slightest rain the sole access road would be flooded, stranding everyone. Intrigued, one day I stationed myself at the entrance at the first sign of the skies becoming cloudy and threatening. Sure enough, with the first rain drop, young men from the neighboring *rumah kilat* (squatter homes) would rush to congregate and throw pellets into the culvert. They would then collect a few ringgit for "helping" the stranded motorists across the flooded access road.

As for those municipal engineers and civil servants, they remained comfortably ensconced in their cozy offices and luxurious homes oblivious of citizens' misery, or what caused the flood. That is still the tragic reality today, and not just in Bungsar or by young men only.

Often the dangers with disasters are the ensuing chaos and panic. Competent leadership, regular drills, and timely accurate information would help reduce that. Malaysia lacks all; that remains her greatest and continuing tragedy.

Readers' Rating: * * *
Sampling of Readers' Responses:
"Your voice of experience is what we need!"

"On point sir ... competent leadership, regular drills, and accurate information."

"Shows how irrelevant our political leaders are. How clueless and incompetent. Alas, come election they will win again!"

"Their motto or bad attitude ... why bother and *tidak apa* [could not care less] attitude."

"Imagine the same attitude and dishonesty that were already ingrained in 1969 as reflected in your experience with the embassies. That is 50 years of dumbing the citizens to where we are today. It's kudos to those who have resisted such systemic organized degradation and persisted in spite of and faced it all."

No Joy, Only A Colossal National Shame

December 7, 2021

[With the Appeals Court upholding Najib's 1MDB-related conviction, we await the next and final level of appeal, the Federal Court. On September 1, 2022 it too reaffirmed Najib's conviction. The decisions at both appellate levels were unanimous.]

Five-and-a-half years after the United States Department of Justice filed (in July 2016) its largest ever money laundering charges relating to the embezzling of One Malaysia Development Berhad (1MDB, a government-linked company), Malaysia's Court of Appeal today (December 8, 2021) unanimously upheld High Court Judge Nazlan Ghazali's earlier (July 2020) conviction of former Prime Minister Najib Razak. He fined Najib RM210 million and sentenced him to 12 years in jail. Judge Ghazali however let Najib out on bail to await his appeal. Najib should not have been granted this privilege considering the scale of his crime and his subsequent behaviors. That the Appeals Court Judges had to admonish his high-priced lawyers and Najib not to treat the courts as *kedai kopi* (coffee shop) was instructive.

Now the Appeals Court is repeating the same mistake made by Judge Ghazali by allowing Najib a stay of execution. He should have been stripped of his expensive Armani suits, put in an orange prison garb, have his mug shot taken, and be driven straight to prison. That smug silly grin must be wiped off his face, to serve as a much-needed antidote for us Malays, especially those in United Malay National Organization (UMNO) still intoxicated with their current revelry of "*Malu apa bossku?*" (What is there to be ashamed of with my boss?)

This being Malaysia, one cannot escape the racial malodor. The only way the Appellate Court's decision could have been more powerful would be had all three judges as well as the prosecuting team (or at least its lead prosecutor) been all Malays. Malays very much are in need of a shock therapy and powerful antidote to our current mass delusion that we are a pristine and innocent lot, only that we had been "cheated" by those crooked Jews at Goldman Sachs and the ever-avaricious Chinese personified by the likes of that moon-faced Jho Low. This mass delusion has been amplified by those government-issued ulama who had been blind to the gross moral lapses of these leaders. That they could be "bought" with the dropped crumbs from the 1MDB loot, as with free Hajj trips, is appalling.

Seeing Najib in orange and his mugshot taken would make global headlines. It would also awaken Malaysians from their collective denial and slumber, as well as disabuse us of our hitherto blind trust in and assumptions of this crooked leader and others like him. Those who still believe in Najib's innocence or that these charges are politically motivated have much to explain. At least three other jurisdictions (US, Singapore, and Switzerland) had much earlier secured guilty pleas or convicted the other principals involved in 1MDB. Goldman Sachs, Najib's premier enabler institution, has already admitted guilt and paid restitutions to Malaysia and elsewhere.

Then there were those obscene images of the piles of boxes stuffed with foreign currencies hauled from Najib's personal residence soon after his arrest following his coalition's defeat in the 2018 election. Najib had used the excuse that those were political "donations" from his friends and admirers abroad, to be used for his and his party's campaign to "uphold the name of Islam." While those learned Appellate Judges could not be persuaded, it was an easy sell to those simple kampung folks. Except for one inconvenient fact. What could those villagers do with those Euros, pound sterling, and US dollars? Those pisang goreng village hawkers would not even recognize those notes much less their value. Beyond that, you would be blind and stupid to think that giving out cash during an election is not plain outright corruption, regardless of whether the country has any specific statutes governing that or vote-buying specifically. Elsewhere such infusion of funds from abroad to influence domestic elections would have been deemed treasonous, and rightly so.

Leading up to as well as during his lengthy trials, numerous legal challenges, and delayed appeals, Najib's supporters clung to the "innocent till proven guilty" mantra. Two observations and clarifications on that point. One, that is a criminal courtroom standard. In positions requiring the highest trust and fidelity, as with the nation's leadership, the criteria must of necessity be much more stringent and higher, as with not even a hint of impropriety. Two, Najib is a convicted criminal since July 2020. That conviction has now been sustained by the Court of Appeal. What would be their excuse now for continuing to support him?

Already we are hearing snippets of this new "truth," as with Najib being responsible for the nation's economic growth. That is a pathetic and poor version of Mussolini making Italian trains run on time. Najib is a crook, plain and simple; nor could he make Malaysian trains or anything else be punctual. For those who still harbor a soft spot for this plunderer, remember Malaysia is still (and for decades to come) being burdened by the humongous debt incurred by 1MDB. Imagine the lost opportunity costs and the good that would accrue had those precious funds been spent on local schools and universities.

While Najib is not at all embarrassed by his many unsavory deeds, Malays (in particular those in UMNO, the party he led for many years) should be. Najib's successor to lead the party, one Ahmad Zahid Hamidi, is himself facing his own series of criminal trials. Mohammad Hassan, a former car salesman from my father's hometown of Rantau, Negri Sembilan, is now helming UMNO. Tok Mat, as he is fondly referred to, is trying to carve an enlightened reformist image but with minimal impact, being overshadowed by both Najib and Zahid. Tok Mat's courageous as well as most meaningful act now would be to summon an emergency meeting of his party's Supreme Council to expel Najib from the party. While he is at it, he should do likewise with its current interim president, Ahmad Zahid.

If Tok Mat does not have the gumption to do that, then UMNO Youth leaders must demand such a meeting. UMNO Youth was once dubbed the party's "ginger group," to spice up leaders who have made themselves too comfortable in their positions. This is the time for the young in UMNO to heed Sukarno's wisdom: "Give me a thousand men and I'll move the mountain. Give me ten young men, and I'll shake the world." I am assuming that those UMNO Youth leaders are *jantan* (alpha males), young men, not pubescent boys or stunted adolescents.

The Sultans as well as the Agung should follow the lead of Negri Sembilan Ruler Tunku Muhriz who much earlier in October 2018 stripped

Najib of the state's royal honor to "safeguard the honor and dignity of the Negri Sembilan royal institution." A short simple statement that spoke volumes. The Sultan of Selangor who had merely "suspended" his on Najib should now rescind the award.

The Oxford and Harvard educated Perak's Sultan Nazrin never tires of pontificating on the evils of corruption. It would be far more effective if he were to retract Perak's honors heaped upon Najib. Most of all the Agung must set the highest example by stripping Najib of his Federal as well as Pahang state honors. That the Agung and those other sultans and heads of states have chosen to remain silent remains the nation's glaring blemish. That speaks volumes on the moral blind spot of Malay leaders.

Kudos to the Johore palace. It saw Najib's dark side early and did not dispense any honors upon him. On the academic side, only one local university saw fit to honor Najib, the now shuttered Limkokwing University. Bravo to our academics and scholars!

Malays must take an unequivocal moral stand against corruption and breaches of faith among our leaders. Time for them to punish this *pengkhianat bang*sa (traitor to the race), Najib Razak. Doing so would not help recover the colossal loss from Najib's embezzlement of 1MDB, but at least it would show the world that our society has a modicum of morals and sense of outrage.

Readers' Rating: * * * * *
Sampling of Readers' Responses:

"Really disappointed although it was expected. How can Malaysia even start to rebuild?"

"Najib is a crook, plain and simple!"

"People who are chanting "*Malu Apa Bossku?*" [What's there to be ashamed of my boss?] ... probably a sign of moral decadence."

"*Menuduh dan membuat fitnah memang sedap lebih2 lagi tak tahu fakta ....*" [To accuse and assassinate characters are fun, more so if you do not know the facts.]

Get Rid Of Our Malim Deman Leaders

August 1, 2021

[When Prime Minister Mahathir resigned suddenly and unexpectedly for no apparent reason (as with health for example) in February 2020, less than two years after assuming power for the second time following the 14th General Election, by right his Deputy Wan Azizah should have taken over. Anticipating that she would later give way to her husband and Mahathir's archnemesis Anwar Ibrahim, the ever-devious Mahathir bypassed her and concocted a back door scheme, dubbed the Sheraton Move, whereby the inept Muhyiddin Yassin would take over. That soon triggered a series of political uncertainties with the expected fierce struggle for power among Mahathir's many far-from-stellar successors. Not unexpectedly, Muhyiddin too later fell following another backdoor conniving, allowing for the equally hapless Ismail Sabri to take over. Malaysia's sorry political saga continues.]

In *Hikayat Malim Deman*, the crown prince and eponymous character caused thousands of his able-bodied subjects to perish in his fanatical pursuit of his literal dream bride, Puteri Bongsu. He conscripted his subjects to escort him on the journey way upriver in search of her. As a result, they all fell victims to the scourges of the fetid Malaysian jungle. Even his beloved pet dog succumbed.

As crown prince, Malim Deman becoming sultan was assured. As such there was little to challenge the young man, hence his fantasy pursuit. As for the horrendous price, well, to Malay sultans their subjects were disposable. Further, in Malay culture to die in the service of your sultan (or crown prince) is martyrdom, secular version. That was true then and still very much the reality today, despite Malaysia's façade of modernity.

Having acquired his trophy wife at humongous human costs, Malim Deman ignored her and returned to his favorite concubine, Si Kembang China (My Chinese Lotus), much like a spoiled rich kid bored with his new toy once the novelty had worn off. On becoming sultan and deprived of his wise father's counsel, Malim Deman soon ignored her and regressed to his old vices – gambling and cock fighting, the avian variety I presume.

With that the state crumbled, and in tandem, his personal life, culminating in his Puteri Bongsu abandoning him, taking with her their young son.

Malaysia is today cursed with her own Malim Deman leaders, each complete with his Si Kembang China. She however had left him long ago after securing her booty. Unlike the young, handsome virile prince in the Hikayat who made virgins wobbly in their knees, the current real life, plebian, scarred-face version, Muhyiddin Yassin, is afflicted with a fatal disease. More accurate to call him Mahiaddin Demam (Mahiaddan The Sick). It matters not with the name, for Malaysia, as with the kingdom in the Hikayat, the results are just as disastrous.

Like the Hikayat's protagonist, our current Mahiaddin Demam is content only with securing his dream trophy, to be Malaysia's Prime Minister, even if it were via the back alley. Ignorant and incompetent, he remains clueless on how to leverage the awesome power of that high office to effect good for the country. Instead, he is back to his old sinister scheming ways of bribing politicians to support him.

Malim Deman caused thousands of deaths in the pursuit of his dream bride. Mahaiddin Demam brought death to thousands and sufferings to millions more after he had secured his dream position, with his negligence in managing the Covid-19 pandemic.

Malim Deman regained his senses when his Puteri Bongsu abandoned him. Meanwhile Mahiaddin Demam surrounds himself with sycophants. Outside of politics, their talents would be valued at best only slightly above that of the hawker. At least hawkers provide much needed services. To these Malim Demans-in-waiting, their sultan is never naked. Court jesters that they are, their job is to humor him in return for the munificence.

Today, Malay leadership is blighted with the Malim Demans, their numbers increasing and spreading to all spheres. That however is not a recent phenomenon.

As a young surgeon in Malaysia back in the 1970s when the number of Malay medical specialists could be counted on one hand, I encountered many of these Malim Deman type leaders in my field. I would have expected them, seeing that Malay specialists then were still very much a novelty, to focus on their professional development so they could contribute to their profession and nation. On the contrary, most were satisfied with *cincai* (perfunctory) professional performances, consumed and obsessed as they were with the pursuit of their dream titles.

One medical Malim Deman was obsessed with being Dean; another eyeing to be Vice-Chancellor; the third, angling to be the next Director-General of Health. Consumed with their pursuits, they "delegated" their clinical responsibilities to their medical officers, delivered the same stale lectures year in and year out, and showed little inclination to undertake much-needed research on the many pressing clinical problems facing the country.

In a chanced conversation with one character aspiring to be Vice-Chancellor, I asked him what innovations he would bring if given the job. He demurred, claiming that the job was not his yet. When I assured him there was not much of a competition seeing that the slot was reserved for a Malay, he admitted that he had not given it any thought. Meaning, he had no idea. His interest was only in the position, like Malim Deman in acquiring his Puteri Bongsu.

Mahaiddin Yassin is thus not an anomaly but the sorry norm of Malay leadership. I salute those brave Lawan (Fight!) protestors, citizens fed up with his empty leadership. However even divine intervention would not save Malaysia as there are many more Malim Demans in the wings.

In the *Hikayat*, Puteri Bongsu knocked some sense back into Malim Deman by abandoning him. With Mahaiddin, his thick skull comes in the way, and there are no brave Puteri Bongsu characters surrounding him.

Do not blame God for this crisis. Sleepyhead Abdullah Badawi, corrupt Najib Razak, and now bungling Mahaiddin Yassin, together with others waiting for his demise share one ugly commonality. They were all tutored by Mahathir Mohamad. Tengku Abdul Rahman, Bapa Merdeka and Malaysia's first Prime Minister, was prescient when he predicted that Mahathir would one day destroy UMNO (United Malay National Organization, the long ruling political party) and Malaysia. In an incomprehensible perversity, many today would prefer Mahathir to lead Malaysia again. Suckers and gluttons for punishment they are!

UMNO's destruction would be good; today it is but a malignancy on Malay society. The other cancer is PAS (Islamic Party, its Malay acronym), and it is spreading fast, like an epidemic of crack addicts, mirroring Marx's celebrated dictum of religion being the opiate of the people.

The divine intervention Malaysians should pray for is that come the next election voters would display their wisdom and displeasure by getting rid of the Malim Demans now blighting the nation. In addition, Malay voters need to excise the twin lethal cancers – UMNO and PAS. As the election is years away, Malaysia's many brave Puteri Bongsus must continue expressing their contempt and disdain for this wretched pretender, Mahaiddin Demam, until he gets the message, be disposed, or Allah intervening, whichever comes first.

Readers' Rating: * * * *
Sampling Of Readers' Responses:
"I read this novel. Thank you, only now I know the story. Will try and reread it."

"Factual parallel events foretold in ancient scriptures."

"Malim Deman as a Malay political archetype as you had conceptualized is very apt and relevant. I have observed political, social, and economic lives and witnessed how they consumed a whole generation which could have been very talented of much national contribution, but for the affliction."

"Gutsy piece and spot on!"

"I am in a constant state of weeping."

"You nailed it! Malaysia is truly doomed unless our Puteri Bongsu comes to the rescue."

"Those in the 50-60 years of age saw how UMNO and PAS [two main Malay political parties] destroy the country, the former with its never-ending battle cry for Malay exclusivity, the latter for its narrow brand of Islam. Even with advancement of education and communication, most Malays are still unable to liberate themselves from the flaws of both ideologies."

Sultans Should Not Interfere With Rakyat's Electoral Decisions

August 20, 2021

[When the Agung picked Muhyiddin Yassin to replace Mahathir who resigned as Prime Minister in February 2020, many questioned the manner or validity of the Agung exercising his judgement. Less than two years later, the Agung would repeat the same mistake in picking Muhyiddin's successor, Ismail Sabri.]

Imagine picking the first officer of a jet that had just crashed to be the new captain! Idiotic would not begin to describe such an action. Yet that is what the Agung, in cahoots with his brother sultans, just did this Friday August 20th in naming Muhyiddin's Deputy, Ismail Sabri, to be Malaysia's new Prime Minister.

When the inept Muhyiddin failed, his whole team should have gone with him if they had any shred of honor. That is collective cabinet responsibility. The Agung and his fellow Malay sultans should have grasped this elementary point. Yet they picked one of those losers to lead Malaysia. The Agung and his brother rulers should have learned a thing or two from their earlier debacle in choosing the dud Muhyiddin to replace Mahathir only 18 months earlier.

Malay sultans' inability to learn from their mistakes and not demonstrating smarts in their judgements on important matters of state (as well as in their personal affairs) is not a novelty. Instead that is the unfortunate sorry and repeated reality. As for personal matters, this Agung's family is involved in some questionable durian land deals in his home state. Earlier his consort was "flamed" for her haughty infamous *"Dengki Ke?"* (You jealous?) Twitter posting. This was her jungle version of "Let them eat cake" response to citizens questioning why her palace cooks received top priority for Covid-19 vaccines which the palace had earlier secured privately through a foreign entity, bypassing the country's laws and public health scrutiny.

The Agung's immediate predecessor, Sultan Muhammad V of Kelantan, was no better. During the night of 2018 General Election, this character managed to make himself unavailable, thus leaving the nation in a state of dangerous and unneeded uncertainty. As for his judgement on personal matters, there were his yet-to-be-released titillating details of his cavorting with a Russian beauty. His subsequent exorbitant alimony payments have yet to be revealed in their full details. As for Sultan Muhammad's actions on state matters, not too long ago there was the sorry picture of his ailing wheelchair-bound father, the then-Sultan, being shoved out of the palace. Despite that unprecedented filial insult, he managed to somehow wow his Kelantan Malays with his put-on piety, as with his fondness for long, white Arabic robes when in public. I wonder if that was the attire that he wowed the Russian beau?

In this latest Agung (Sultan Abdullah of Pahang) debacle, it was pathetic to see otherwise boisterous and obstreperous Members of Parliament (MPs), all spruced up in their Hari Raya best, lining up for a private audience with the Agung at the palace, their latest Statutory Declarations (haggled earlier like a deal as with an Arab carpet dealer) in hand. They were more errant school kids being summoned to the principal's office.

I am appalled that this Agung had deemed it his duty to meet convicted criminals like Najib Razak and others facing serious corruption charges, like Ahmad Zahid Hamidi. He should not have let those renegades set foot in Istana Negara, let alone have a private audience with him. Again, the Agung's poor judgement, quite apart from the permanent ugly stain on the people's palace.

This Agung, like the Sultan of Perak Raja Azlan back in 2009 with his own political problem with his state government, is ignorant or refuses to acknowledge that decisions made in a *tete a tete* private session are not the same as those following open robust debates, as in Parliament. The dynamics of the latter while unpredictable would at least be transparent. I blame this Agung and his fellow rulers in not learning from that earlier Perak State Assembly fiasco. What assurance does the rakyat have that the Agung did not coerce those MPs?

This inability of Malay sultans to learn from their mistakes and thus continue making awful decisions is the norm. In my lifetime I have witnessed Malay sultans repeatedly misbehaving badly both in their personal capacity as well as in important matters of state. In my state of Negri Sembilan, more than a few have been enmeshed in personal bankruptcies as well as struck by maladies caused by what we would euphemistically call "bad" lifestyle choices. Another sultan was convicted of murder. No problem with that either as he later became Agung.

On substantive matters of state, Tengku Abdul Rahman once rued that the biggest obstacle he faced when negotiating for Malaysia's independence came not from the colonial office but the Malay sultans. They were against independence, at least initially.

The greatest blunder of Malay sultans in recent history remains their collective decision made in the immediate post-war period (1946) when they willingly gave away the nation's sovereignty with their signing the Malayan Union Treaty. If Datuk Onn had not been successful in having that reversed by mobilizing the rakyat, Malay sultans would today be reduced to the status of the Sultan of Sulu. Onn was hailed a hero for that singular feat. However, seeing how these sultans have degenerated today with their state-sanctioned excesses, I wonder if he would have any regrets for having saved those Malay sultans.

Malaysians too need to ponder this important question on whether it is worth keeping these expensive sultans. Their costs may be tolerable but not their interference (twice now) to reverse the rakyat's collective decision of the 2018 election.

Readers' Rating: * * * * *
Sampling of Readers' Responses:
"We are rich in natural resources, by right we should be much better than Singapore. Those ... [leaders] except for Tunku stole much from the rakyat to enrich themselves and their cronies. [Where's]. . . Malaysia now?"

"If this was written by a non-Malay, all hell would have broken loose … to oppose this write up."

"The Tunku who helped draft the country's constitution had nothing to depend on. But he did have his caveat, that is, the government must keep tight control on the Malay sultans who are naturally given to excesses."

"We are all aware of these mishaps, unfortunately our hands are tied in anger and frustration. Thanks for the write up; hope it can open the eyes and mind of the *rakyat*."

"…[L]ooks like people never learn; still praising these kleptocrats. The current turmoil, a bit unfair to squarely blame the Agung, but the buck should stop at the one who always claimed to have formidable support …. Still wondering where went wrong and who is being bluffed big time?"

"Many desperate to see the end of PN/UMNO thought with the Palace's intervention, they would get to see 'justice'. Me thinks they forgot about the danger of relying on royal intervention and that the royals are also humans after all. People expected the King to advise a vote in Parliament as the ultimate decision-maker while his position is as the [titular] Supreme Head of the Federation. Let's hope citizens learn to rely on their own power to make change happen."

"Brother, I feel the Malay rulers have done the right thing: they choose Malay leaders who are loyal and will look after royal interests. Their majesties are all smart; they know who will look after their strategic interests."

"Wind of change must commence. There shall be no turning back after that. That reminds me of the rock band the Scorpions."

"… We need a Malaysia Unity government and not one based on race or religion anymore. How much longer do we need to suffer due to this lack of insight amongst our politicians? They clearly only care about themselves as shown over the last few decades."

"… The destruction of Malaysia was initiated by Mahathir when he first stepped in as PM, and following PMs who adopted his ideology continued this culture of corruption, theft, racism, etc., that have brought our country to its knees. Malaysia was the most aspiring country in SE Asia but we went down the drain with all these idiots with UMNO DNA. Malaysia is already at the bottom of the pit, now it will start digging the hole deeper and deeper with another UMNO donkey helming the country. This Agung will be remembered for his incapability to assume his duty as Ruler. He made a huge mistake by allowing Muhyiddin to become PM although he did not have majority support then. Now he appointed this racist donkey to take over …."

"It's not about UMNO. It's a Malay thing …. *Ini namanya politik Melayu yang masih mengamalkan Politik Kampung.*" [This is Malay politics kampung-style!]

Corrupt, Inept, And Unimaginative Leaders Fancying Themselves As Otherwise

July 31, 2021

[The need for honest, competent, and accountable leadership is never more acute than during a crisis. It is a cruel perversity for Malaysia that during this dangerous Covid-19 pandemic she is cursed with corrupt, inept, and dishonest leaders who fancy themselves as otherwise. This blight afflicts leaders at all levels and in all spheres, from the Agung and his fellow sultans to Prime Minister Muhyiddin (or whatever his real name) and his cabinet to the callous nurse at a government clinic giving blank vaccine shots, reflects this systemic rot. More stunning is the Health Minister's reaction and advice that those affected by that nurse's willful if not criminal negligence just be revaccinated, reflecting a shocking ignorance of the underlying major systemic problem.]

Pandemics are an integral part of human history. As such there is much that we can learn from the past. First, a much-needed reality check: all pandemics will end, with or without enlightened leadership. The challenge is how to accelerate the process, minimize the damage, and anticipate as well as respond to the ensuing inevitable social and physical turmoil as well as upheavals. That is where leadership is critical; it would make all the difference.

It is also worth reminding that unlike the Spanish flu which occurred in the backdrop of the already horrific World War I, this Covid-19 pandemic is not burdened with unneeded global conflicts. Regional wars there are, and many. For those caught in them, their pain and sufferings are magnified that much more. Also unlike the Spanish flu, we now have effective vaccines while medical care is a quantum leap more advanced.

For Malaysians, yet another timely reminder and much needed reassurance. This pandemic is not another horrible May 13, 1969 "incident," much less the Japanese Occupation or the Great Depression. Just to be reminded of those past horrors would inject a much-needed dose of realism if not optimism. Even if current Covid-19 fatalities were to exceed that of the Occupation, there would be no associated infrastructure damages. Our schools, bridges, and factories would remain intact, ready to re-serve the community once the pandemic is over, as surely it will.

Effective leaders as well as ordinary citizens can do much to alter the trajectory of this pandemic. Even within America the course is very different in Alabama as compared to California, a difference that has all to do with leadership as well as citizens. In any epidemic there are those who for a variety of reasons would be spared. Herd as well as personal immunity is a factor. Another is the instinct for survival. Somehow humans learn intuitively how to avoid getting infected. As for those who fail to heed sound advice and thus fall victim, the kindest view would be to view that as letting evolutionary forces play their full merciless role. May Allah lighten the load of their surviving kin.

Pandemics are democratic or "equal opportunity" wreckers in that they do not differentiate between natives versus *pendatangs*, legal versus illegal residents, or leaders versus followers. Both Boris Johnson and Donald Trump fell victims, their braggadocio notwithstanding. The damages wreaked however, are not unselective. As in the past, this pandemic affects disproportionately the poor, marginalized, and disenfranchised. The significance for Malaysia, as in America, is that those are also surrogate indicators of race. Whenever race is injected in a crisis, that adds yet another volatile mix.

In America, apart from the visible poor minorities, another subset of Covid-19 victims are white evangelical Trump conservatives disdainful of and hostile to vaccines and other public health measures. They view face masks and social distancing as infringements on their personal liberties. They forget that the greatest, irreversible, and ultimate loss of one's personal liberty is death. In Malaysia the victims of Covid-19 are disproportionately Malays. The associated socio-economic correlates aside, these Malays have much in common with American white evangelicals with their dangerous "fear God (or Allah) more than the virus" mindset.

Unlike those Christian evangelicals, Malays have the wisdom of our Holy Prophet to guide us. Mindful of the Islamic precept on the sanctity of life as Allah's most precious gift, the Prophet advised us that when we hear of a plague in a land, do not go there. If you are already there, do not leave. There is no equivocation in that ahadith, as with except for Hajj, funerals, Hari Raya, or Friday prayers. The Prophet, *s.a.w.*, went further and declared victims of pandemics as *syaheeds* (martyrs), dying in the cause of Allah. As such they have an express ticket to Heaven, or so is the belief, and we could dispense with the usual funeral rites. Besides having a sound scientific rationale for that exemption (to prevent contagion), that belief would also be a much-needed salve for those who feel they have not done their final duties to their loved ones in their last hour.

Malaysia's corrupt, inept, and irresponsible leaders notwithstanding, that should not be the excuse for Malaysians as individuals not to do their part to protect themselves and their families. With or without the vaccines, continue wearing masks, maintain social and physical distancing, and wash your hands frequently. Only then pray to Allah that He would protect us.

According to Stanford's Walter Scheidel in his *The Great Leveler: Violence and the History of Inequality from the Stone Age to the Twent-First Century*, pandemics, like wars and revolutions, are great equalizers of society. Malay society today is at its most unequal, and the current abysmal failure of Malay leadership will have severe consequences. If this pandemic were to destroy those leaders and our feudal culture, then those sacrifices of the *syaheeds* would indeed be not for nothing.

As for the current crop of corrupt and clueless Malay leaders in UMNO, remember them come the next election. To modify an oft-quoted Qur'anic *ayat*, Allah will not change our leaders unless we do it ourselves.

Readers' Rating: * * * *
Sampling of Readers' Responses:
"It is all about leadership. Sad that this is happening in our beloved country. [Every man] for himself, referring to our so-called leaders."

"Changing voters' mindset is an uphill battle. This pandemic hopefully would play its part as a catalyst."

"Only doctors are the ones who never care about the consequences of prolonged lockdowns. How to finance subsidized healthcare when tax revenues are obliterated due to the destruction of the economy? ...."

"You nailed it ...; honest, competent, and accountable leadership is the crying need. Too many cases of national leaders much too full of themselves, doing whatever pleases them and getting away with it!"

"If only those who are entrusted to head positions of authority...put on their wise thinking cap ...!"

Malaysia's Grand Delusion 2020

December 6, 2020

[In 1991 Then Prime Minister Mahathir unveiled his Vision 2020 that would have Malaysia enter the league of developed nations by Year 2020. An ambitious plan that would require the country to have a sustained annual growth of 7 percent annually over a thirty-year period. A few years into it, the Asian economic contagion of 1996 derailed that. By coincidence Mahathir was again Prime Minister for the second time by 2020. Alas not a word from him or anyone else about Vision 2020. No surprise as the nation was behind in all parameters, with Malaysia stuck in Third World status in all spheres.]

This year 2020 was supposed to be a "coming out" celebration of sorts for Malaysia, akin to South Korea's glittering 1988 Olympics Game that heralded the nation's entry into the developed world. Had everything gone right for Malaysia during the past three decades, this year would have been the realization of her Vision 2020 aspiration of joining that exclusive club.

Alas that was not to be. Instead of Vision 2020, Malaysia endured Delusion 2020. The country is now fast slipping irreversibly into the ranks of failed states and chronic Third World status *a la* Haiti and Zimbabwe, with political instability and entrenched corruption the sorry reality. Malaysia tops the world where companies feel that they have lost business because of their competitors' bribery. Meanwhile Najib's 1MDB heist remains the headlines worldwide.

That reference to South Korea is both ironic as well as painful. Back in 1966 South Korea's General Park visited Malaysia to study her rural development scheme. Oh, how the trajectories of the two nations have shifted!

There are three grand Malaysian 2020 delusions. One is not really a delusion but the very real and devastating Covid-19 pandemic that is fast raging out of control. I am confident that modern science will handle that, despite the preoccupation of medieval-minded Malaysian ulama trivializing the halal issue with respect to the forthcoming vaccine. They forgot that Malaysia's first and major super-spreader event was the Tabligi Jamaat gathering in Sri Petaling back in February 2020. That mass ostentatious display of piety breached the very tenet of our faith – to first protect human lives. The vaccine would do that, and thus halal.

As for the other two, first is the still unpunctured delusion of a nonagenarian who fancies himself as Allah's greatest gift to Malays and Malaysia. Mahathir deludes himself, and increasingly many, that he could achieve in his remaining ageing few years what he could not for nearly 23 years in power earlier in the 1980s and 90s when he was much younger. Second is the equally bizarre fantasy of a sixty-something Najib, convicted of criminally looting a Government-Linked Company (1MDB) on an unprecedented scale, parading himself as the nation's savior.

There is no cure in sight, scientific or otherwise, for those two delusions. The problem goes far beyond the two flawed characters to the very essence of *Maruah Melayu* (Malay dignity). Large numbers of Malays adulate Najib as their *bossku* (my boss), while Mahathir is still viewed as a grand savior despite the mess he has created and continues to wreak. Malaysia not achieving Vision 2020 is only one of the many sorry examples that is now conveniently forgotten.

Consider the overtly racist Malay Dignity Congress of last October 2019, launched by Mahathir. The attendees were not simple villagers but highly educated and seemingly sophisticated Malays, with the event organized by leaders of universities!

Even if Najib and Mahathir were gone, the pair currently running the country are no sparkles either. The ailing Muhyiddin Yassin, like Najib, has the same corrupt political tutelage from and the blighted political genes of Mahathir. Najib and Muhyiddin are not aberrations but the predictable and inevitable outcome of Mahathirism.

As for that *semburit* (anal) character positioning himself as Number Two, he could not even manage his family's finances. Azmin Ali stiffed a small Bumiputra travel agency with his humungous vacation bills. There's more. This third-rate politician is Malaysia's economic czar! So far his talent has been with backroom and other backside maneuvers. As a needless reminder, Mahathir was instrumental in Muhyiddin's as well as Azmin's ascent, just as he was with Abdullah and Najib. Malaysia wasted a decade and a half with that second pair.

The greatest endorsement for Anwar Ibrahim as leader is precisely this: Mahathir is dead set against him. Anwar is the antithesis of Mahathir's ideal of an effective leader. If the old man has any sense of self-introspection, he will have by now realized that all his previous picks had been duds. He has zero talent in identifying potential leaders. Malaysians should have by now recognize this destructive deficiency in the man. Far from being the Energizer Bunny that keeps going and going and going, Mahathir's continued political presence is more the stink of a skunk that just would not go away.

To add to Anwar's credibility, his Parti Keadilan Rakyat has been the most successful, the Democratic Action Party excepted, in inspiring talented young Malaysians to enter politics.

Mahathir's morbid obsession with denying Anwar his right to lead Malaysia is not to save Malaysia as he (Mahathir) often expressed, but to save his hide and kin. Mahathir knows that if Anwar Ibrahim were to assume power, with his commitment to transparency and honest government, he would investigate all past shenanigans. You can bet that Mahathir's many hideous warts (London Tin, Perwaja Steel, forex debacle – the list is long) would be exposed. With that, his hollow sanctimonious condemnations of Najib's plundering. Therein lies Mahathir's pathological preoccupation with denying Anwar's ascent.

Mahathir's stand reveals more on him. Mahathir's visible anguish is a telling contrast to Anwar's confident equanimity.

Short of the actuarial tables doing Malaysia a favor, Malaysians must shatter these 2020 delusions by ridding the nation of this poisonous political virus that began with Mahathir and is now showing up in all its ugliness and virulence with Muhyiddin Yassin and Azmin Ali. Let Anwar

Ibrahim and his fresh young talents take over. Save Malaysia from becoming another Zimbabwe.

Readers' Rating: * *
Sampling of Readers' Responses:
"We need young leaders with integrity, and there are many, but none has stepped up yet!"
"It looks like you do not have a better solution."
"Time for these old leaders to retire gracefully."
"He [Mahathir] did not pick him [Anwar]. This 'clever' man was so worried about Anwar joining PAS thus threatening UMNO's position. He rather had Anwar 'pissing' in the UMNO tent rather than from the outside into the UMNO tent. Being a shrewd Machiavellian politician, he knew when to arrange for the slaughter time of the 'goose.'"
"You are right. We have many other knowledgeable and talented younger people with experience. We should not get caught into this old-timer's prison of thinking. Think outside the box!"
"Whatever anyone says about Anwar is all theoretical. He has never been given a chance to prove himself so far."

2021 Budget – Lessons Not Learned!

November 8, 2020

[The 2021 Malaysian Budget presented to Parliament on the last working day of October 2020, barely a couple of months after Ismail Sabri becoming Prime Minister, was the biggest. It repeats the same old mistake – the belief that throwing money at a problem would solve it. As in the past, billions are again being allocated to Bumiputra institutions like JAKIM (Malay acronym for Islamic Development Agency) and JASA (Special Affairs Agency, a government propaganda arm), as well as to MARA (Malay acronym for the Agency entrusted to help Bumiputras) and UiTM (MARA's university). Despite such generosity, now and in the past, there has been no appreciable improvement in Bumiputra competitiveness *vis a vis* non-Bumiputras.]

Stripped of their fancy acronyms, JAKIM, JASA, and other fancy alphabet governmental agencies are but massive public works programs for otherwise unemployable Bumiputras. Those institutions go beyond. They are responsible for Malays not being competitive. There is little incentive to do so for the likes of JAKIM and JASA are ready to employ you. If you want Malays to contribute to the socioeconomic development of the nation, as is the aspiration of all Malay leaders, then get rid of those institutions.

MARA continues to squander billions by still sending Malays to third-rate universities abroad, though thankfully not in the same massive numbers as in the 1980s and 90s when they sent them abroad even for Sixth Form! When cash-strapped you become prudent in your spending. As for UiTM's bountiful windfall, none will be used to recruit English or Philosophy lecturers. Then we wonder why our students have abysmal English fluency or are incapable of critical thinking.

The "help" Malays are getting from their government reminds me of an old Reagan advice to ranchers in the west. "When you hear, 'I am from the government, and I am here to help,' run for the hills fast!"

With JAKIM and its government-paid ulama are distracting Malays to be obsessed with getting into Paradise, there would be that much fewer left to ensure that we do not suffer our own collective Hell right here and now in Tanah Melayu. For every Malay consumed with revealed knowledge or prophetic traditions, that would be one fewer to do research on Covid-19 or clean the environment. It is that simple. Yet Malay leaders cannot grasp the elementary zero-sum dynamics.

What Malays need are better engineers and architects, not more exquisite Qur'an reciters and mesmerizing ulama with their fire-and-brimstone sermons. Consider Malaysian masjids. One showpiece mosque in Kuala Lumpur (recently built) has acres of open marble floors that are unwalkable during the sunny day. You would be walking on a furnace. I suppose to be charitable, that was part of the design — a preview of how hell would be like! Even with more recently completed masjids, there are extension cords everywhere as the designers did not anticipate the electrical outlet needs. In Kelantan, the most "Islamic" state, you cannot get clean water to do your ablution.

When we do get those few Malays away from this obsession with religion, we do not let them practice their craft. Instead, we seduce them into doing something else, like administrative chores.

It breaks my heart to see those few Malays of my generation who were trained in the sciences being seduced into becoming pseudo-ulama. I would have thought they would have served as much-needed role models for the young in the kampungs by being productive in their respective fields. It is sad to see the first Malay PhD in mathematics (Mat Rofa Ismail) now touring village mosques giving *khutba* (sermons) on the supposed past glory of Islam in the Malay world. A more worthy legacy would have been for him to establish an Institute of Mathematics to encourage the young to pursue the subject. Another, also of my vintage, abandoned his doctoral work in mathematics at a prestigious university to go into religion.

I am also saddened to see the few precious Malay scientists and professionals not being rewarded and honored, not for their sake but as a societal statement to inspire the young. The honor of Emeritus Professorship is being heaped not upon those few precious Malay pioneers in the sciences and professions, but in Malay and Islamic Studies. We already have a glut of the latter. Meanwhile we keep harping on the lack of Malays in the sciences! My late father had an apt observation on that misplaced priority: *Membajakan lalang* (adding fertilizer to *lalang* – a particularly tenacious weed).

A Christian cobbler would best show his faith, wrote Martin Luther, not by carving crucifixes on the shoes he makes but by making them durable and cheap so the poor could afford them. Likewise Muslim engineers would best demonstrate their faith in Allah not by carving intricate Qur'anic verses on the bridges they build but making sure that during floods more water would flow under than over them, and that there are no unexpected right angle turns at mid-point.

Islam is a great faith. It has withstood the hordes of Mongol invaders as well as Stalin's brutal suppression. The faith does not need defenders, least of all from these characters in IKIM and JAKIM. Islam cannot advance in Malaysia if Malays are overrepresented in the socially dysfunctional categories. Getting rid of JAKIM and JASA, as well as MARA and BTN (Bureau Tata Negara – National Civic Bureau) would be a great first step. Thus far that reality has not even registered on Malay leaders.

Non-Malays should relax; quit worrying about all those goodies showered on Bumiputras. Heed the wisdom of Plutarch: The man who first brought ruin upon the Roman people was he who pampered them by largesses and amusements.

Remember, when Malays holler *"Tanah Melayu Untuk* Melayu!"* (Malay Land for Malays!) that is not a threat, it is more a desperate cry from those betrayed by their own leaders.

Readers' Rating: * * * * *
Sampling of Readers' Responses:

"Sorry sir, I am not comfortable on the part you wrote that non-Bumi should relax to see the ruin forthcoming …."

"Besides brotherly love, a part of the body ruined would not bring any good to the other part."

"Your Roman example is exquisite! The first step in solving problems is to admit that there is a problem. It's the denial that spirals downwards to the depths of sun-soaked marbles."

"It really worries me to see young boys learning Tahfiz. How productive could they be for the nation?"

No "Guided" Constitutional Monarchy For Malaysia

November 1, 2020

[When Muhyiddin Yassin became Prime Minister in February 2020, there was no formal vote of confidence on him made in Parliament. It was only an assumption on the part of the Agung that Muhyiddin had majority parliamentary support. Thus, when his government presented the following year's budget, speculations and anxiety were high that it could serve as a surrogate vote of confidence on him, thus resulting in the dissolution of Parliament and fresh elections.]

Alas the accolades heaped upon the Agung for not acceding to Prime Minister Muhyiddin's earlier request for Emergency Rule had not yet ebbed when the Agung startled Malaysians with his unprecedented "advice" for Members of Parliament to pass Muhyiddin's forthcoming 2021 budget.

This royal "advice," or "guided" constitutional monarchy from the palace if you will, has all the stink of an overripe durian. At least with that you could salvage it into *tompoyak* paste, a delicacy if you can get past the malodor.

The Agung issued that *menasihat* (advice) only a few hours after Muhyiddin had presented his proposed budget to him. The Agung had barely enough time to skim the headings and he already had his advice for the rakyat.

Something about Malay language. You and I *menasihat* each other, but sultans decree. Therein lies the danger. Already those in UMNO and Muhyiddin's camp are making this point of the *menasihit* being a *titah* (royal decree), and thus to be obeyed as such, to suit their political expediency. Indeed, a few paragraphs into the palace statement, it used the word *titah* to describe it, just in case you missed the message. Little subtlety there.

Those who think that this was merely an advice from a concerned monarch are ignorant of Malay language, culture, or norms. To go against a *titah* is *derkaha* (treasonous). That would make those who would vote against the budget traitors.

It is not coincidental that the palace issued the statement in Malay and with no accompanying English translation, as is the practice. I would like to see palace officials (or anyone else) translate the first few words of the fifth paragraph of the October 28 Palace Statement: "Al Sultan Abdullah *bertitah* [my emphasis] *demikian selepas menerima menghadap* YAB Perdana Menteri ...." (The Agung decreed this following an audience with the Right Honorable Prime Minister ....)

Back in 1957 the incompetent but egotistic President Sukarno, unable to perform the basic tasks of governance, introduced "guided democracy," with him being the "guider" of course. With that as a beginning, a decade later he was replaced by a brutal dictator, Suharto. That reign of terror would not end till 1996.

Malaysians be warned! Do not go down this well-trodden path of "guided" or "*menasihat*" of anything from anyone. The path to Hell is paved with good intentions.

Members of Parliament should do their job they were sent to do. They are paid by the rakyat. MPs must listen to those who sent them there and paid their salary, not anyone else even if he were to heap upon you exalted titles of some ancient supposedly glorious Mashuri Dynasty.

An earlier Agung said it best. "Democracy as a political system does not become a democracy because it is given that appellation. The true meaning of democracy can be summed up by the phrase 'government by the people.'"

Now that is sound *nasihat* (advice)! That earlier Agung, Raja Azlan Shah, had also served as the nation's Chief Justice.

He went further. "Any form of pressure or arbitrary limits imposed on the people in their free exercise of the right to choose their own government will be a clear abrogation of any parliamentary system of government. Similarly, major bills must not be rushed through Parliament. The people should have an opportunity to express their views."

An annual budget is a major if not the bill for the government. This Agung wants it *diluluskan tanpa sebarang gangguan* (passed without any interference).

That is a very dangerous mindset, to equate robust parliamentary debates as *gangguan* (interference). Palace advisors must be disabused early and in no uncertain terms of this treacherous path that they have chosen to follow. If this Agung believes that the current Covid-19 pandemic presents such a clear and present danger to the nation such that parliamentary bills must be passed without *gangguan*, he should have approved that earlier request for Emergency Rule.

By giving this *titah* to support Muhyiddin, the Agung has implicitly endorsed him as the legitimate Prime Minister. As such, his earlier denial of the advice from the "Prime Minister" for an Emergency Rule set a very dangerous precedent. The King reigns but does not rule.

The Agung's *titah* to the rakyat was misplaced. He should have directed it instead to Muhyiddin. That advice is the same one Malaysians have bombarded on Muhyiddin during the last few months, that is, get Parliamentary endorsement of your leadership. If you do not or cannot, then get out! This manufactured political crisis is Muhyiddin's, not Malaysia's.

Malaysia's system of constitutional monarchy is unique in many ways but it is still in its infancy. Malays have just emerged from the old ugly days of feudalism. Many still yearn for those days. As such our system of constitutional monarchy should be strengthened and not breached under some misplaced pretext of loyalty or stability. To repeat for emphasis, our constitutional monarchy is still new and fragile.

It was not so long ago following the 2008 state election when the Menteri Besar of Perak said this to his sultan: *"Patek memohon derhaka ….!"* (I, your slave, beg to commit treason …!) Imagine the people's representative being a slave to the sultan! In a constitutional monarchy, sovereignty lies with the rakyat, not the raja.

To switch my earlier metaphor of an overripe durian, this attempt at breaching the clear lines in a constitutional monarchy and parliamentary democracy must be plugged before the entire edifice crumbles. Do not let the nation be swamped. Malaysian MPs should be like the brave Dutch boy: stick your finger in the dyke and do it now with the budget session next week.

Readers' Rating: ★ ★ ★ ★ ★
Sampling of Readers' Responses:
"Sovereignty lies with the rakyat [citizens]. Members of Parliament should read Article 43 of our Constitution and follow it in letter and spirit."

"The rakyat still yearn for the past – feudalism – because like cats and dogs many of them like to be fed, domiciled, and tamed."

"The Malay elite likes to think the rakyat are stupid."

"Kehebatan Melayu bodohkan Cina." [The obsession of Malays is to belittle the Chinese.]

Parliament Must Reject Muhyiddin Yassin

October 25, 2020

[News Item: After Mahathir's resignation as Prime Minister in February 2020, Muhyiddin Yassin assumed the post without getting the necessary parliamentary vote of confidence. To avoid being rejected by Parliament, he tried to bypass the process by urging the Agung declare a National State of Emergency, using the ongoing Covid-19 pandemic as an excuse.]

The Agung's rebuff to Prime Minister Muhyiddin's request for the declaration of a State of Emergency is but an expression of his lack of confidence in Muhyiddin's leadership. If he has any sense of responsibility, Muhyiddin should resign. However, in his over 40 years in politics, Muhyiddin had never shown any sense of public accountability. Do not expect him to have any or show it now.

It is Parliament's turn to drive home the Agung's message (shared by the people) by rejecting Muhyiddin's upcoming budget, if not through the adoption of a formal "no confidence" vote, thus forcing him to resign. The Agung would then be free to select a Member of Parliament who in his opinion would command the confidence of the House. Meaning, he would have to accept Anwar's candidacy of October 13, 2020, and appoint him as Prime Minister. If as the Agung indicated, protecting people from this Covid-19 is his highest priority, then the alternative, calling for a general election, would not be a wise option.

On thing is crystal clear. The Agung rejecting the advice of an elected Prime Minister is no small thing and could be a dangerous precedent. Muhyiddin however is far from one. He is but an illegitimate "backdoor" Prime Minister; Parliament had never ratified his leadership.

If Muhyiddin were to prevail in Parliament, as with bribing every UMNO MP with a cabinet position or directorships of the multitude of government-linked corporations, he would have won his battle, but the nation would lose the war. It would forever be established that the King could dispense with his Prime Minister's advice. There would be no turning back once that bridge is crossed. This should weigh heavily on those inclined to vote for Muhyiddin.

Muhyiddin should take no comfort with the Agung's proforma expression of confidence hidden deep in the Council of Rulers' statement. To be noted, Muhyiddin's name was not mentioned, only the office. The message from the Agung and the Council of Rulers was not even subtle. As a distracting aside, but one not missed, is that the four Governors were not in the decision. Ever wonder why the secessionist movement in East Malaysia is gaining traction, or that citizens in Penang and Malacca feel left out?

Muhyiddin never indicated or even hinted on why he would need the sweeping powers of the Emergency Ordinance to fight Covid-19. If he did, then the Agung, like the rest of Malaysia, was not impressed. The most egregious violators of the current public health measures during this Covid-19 pandemic are Muhyiddin's ministers and party officials. Emergency Rule would not change his ability to deal with that.

The obvious but unacknowledged fact is that Muhyiddin is an ineffectual leader; he could not lead even his ministers. All he knows is how to buy their loyalty through bribery, with public money. His cabinet is bloated for a reason.

Being weak is bad enough but Muhyiddin is also incompetent. He is not even the Peter Principle personified (being promoted beyond one's competence). Muhyiddin has been incompetent all along.

Muhyiddin faces two choices: Resign with grace or face the prospect of an ugly and highly divisive "no-confidence" vote in Parliament and then be hauled out. No Malaysian Prime Minister, save perhaps the first, has ever gone out with any sense of class.

Meanwhile former Prime Minister Mahathir deluded himself as being indispensable. He thought he had performed a class act back in February 2020 by resigning. He had expected an outpouring of support, a reprise of his June 2001 decision when he first tried to resign during his first go around as Prime Minister. Instead, he plunged Malaysia into her present unneeded, distracting, and divisive crisis. Welcome to his Vision 2020!

Mahathir's predecessor Najib tried to escape to Indonesia in a private jet on the night of his May 2018 election mauling. Vigilant citizens mobilized through social media thwarted his "planned vacation." Before him was sleepyhead Abdullah; he woke up and found himself out of office. Before him was Mahathir, Version 2001, with his staged melodrama that succeeded in delaying his departure for two years. We know what happened to Hussein Onn (ill health) and Tun Razak (death).

Only the first Prime Minister exited with a modicum of grace. As Tunku Abdul Rahman wrote in his memoir, had he known his Deputy, Razak, was desperate for the job, he (Tunku) would have resigned sooner. There was no need for Razak's behind-the-back scheming that triggered the May 1969 riot. That was the first and only time Parliament was suspended and emergency rule by decree instituted.

Going by history, Muhyiddin would have to be pushed out. On the other hand, as per Muslims' belief, everything is in Allah's hands. We propose; He disposes. Malaysia might yet get that divine intervention with the ailing Muhyiddin.

Readers' Rating: * * *
Sampling of Readers' Responses:
"Zero leadership qualities and definitely a non-performer."

"…[T]he writer is someone living overseas. [As such he is] able to make very logical comments from afar. It is very easy for him to do that. Say whatever he wants to say."

"There was no meeting of the Conference of Rulers. But there was a discussion with brother-rulers who were able to attend despite a very short notice. Attendance was not compulsory like that of a Conference (Majlis Raja Raja) involving all State Heads and their official advisors."

"Very true, sir. Every head of state should be consulted. Their views are of equal importance too."

Muhyiddin Yassin – Resign Or Recall Parliament

October 14, 2020

[Since becoming Prime Minister via the backdoor (*aka* "The Sheraton Move"), Muhyiddin Yassin has been avoiding recalling and thus facing Parliament for fear of not gaining its vote of confidence. He has resorted to all tricks including threatening to declare a National State of Emergency.]

Anwar Ibrahim has given the Agung the assurance of his (Anwar's) majority support in Parliament. The ball is now not at the palace but with Prime Minister Muhyiddin Yassin. He has to prove that he has the people's support by securing a parliamentary vote of confidence. Failing that, he must resign. That is the only right and honorable course, for him and the nation. Amateurish press conference with put-on bonhomie is no substitute. With the Covid-19 threat and the tanking economy, the nation does not need this added leadership crisis.

Parliament can meet virtually within days and end this divisive, unnecessary, and distracting issue. Parliament should not be allowed to drag this crisis on like a debilitating cancer upon the nation. In a democracy, sovereignty lies with the people, meaning parliament, not the palace. Parliament was scheduled to meet last August to pass the 2021 Budget but was postponed many times. Malaysia is now well into her new fiscal year and without a budget. What a way to run a country in crisis!

Had that Budget been approved as scheduled, Muhyiddin's legitimacy would not have been questioned, and there would be no leadership issues. Member of Parliament Tengku Razali had sought that vote of confidence back in August but was denied. Speaker Azhar Harun's excuse was that it did not have a minister's consent! Typical civil service mindset of *Kami menunggu arahan*! (I await instructions!) This character may have a law degree but functionally he is but a minister's peon.

If there is one critical factor in a leadership crisis, it is this: Citizens want certainty and assurance now, not weeks or months later. Anything that does not help that or worse, muddles it and thus delays its resolution only aggravates the problem.

The bland palace statement issued following Anwar's visit falls into this category. Far from clarifying the matter, it muddled it even more. If the Agung was not satisfied with what Anwar had presented, as the palace statement implied, then he (Agung) should have raised it with Anwar right there and then, not issue a useless press statement hours later. Anwar's meeting with the Agung was a business one, and very serious one at that, not the usual ceremonial *sembah menyembah* (ceremonial genuflecting) bit with everyone obsequiously bowing and grinning, with nothing accomplished.

That meeting lasted over 30 minutes. Was Agung not prepared to ask tough questions of Anwar at the time? That did not reflect well on the palace advisors.

In that statement the Agung expressed concerns over the Covid-19 pandemic. Had he resolved the leadership matter there and then he would have made his greatest contribution towards controlling this pandemic. Anything else, no matter how heartfelt the message, depth of concern, or eloquent the prose, pales in comparison.

Now the Agung is reduced to being a Director of Human Resources seeking references for his top hire. Quit the parade of MPs to the palace. While the constitution is clear on the Agung's function to appoint the nation's top executive (the individual must or believe to have the confidence of parliament), less clear is his power to dismiss. That should be the prerogative of and only of Parliament, if Muhyiddin Yassin refuses to resign.

It is praiseworthy for Agung to have met Tengku Razali. As the longest serving MP, he is the repository of that body's history, wisdom, and tradition. As for meeting UMNO leader Ahmad Zahid Hamidi, those facing criminal charges should have no privileges of a royal audience. Innocent till proven guilty is fine in the court of law, but not at the palace. It must demand a much higher standard, as without even a hint of impropriety. As for Mahathir, he started this mess; dispense with him.

In meeting every Member of Parliament, the Agung reduces himself to a royal interviewer-in-chief. The crucial point here is not the individual MP's decision expressed in private to him but the MPs' collective resolution after deliberating in Parliament where the proceedings are open. Democracy demands such transparency.

Meanwhile Anwar should set up his team, ready to go. Let us pray for Malaysia's sake that day will be soon. Malaysia has had enough of decades of corrupt and incompetent leadership. Malays have a special reason for wanting this to end now. We are fed up with our race and culture being equated with those loathsome traits and detestable characters now running the country.

Readers' Rating: * *
Sampling of Readers' Responses:
"Clear and lucid … and the truth, … the way forward. Let Parliament decide…. Let's do this … hurry up … once and for all … the right thing to do. Are we saying the Agung is shirking his duty?"

"You are assuming that Muhyiddin wants to do the 'right and honorable' thing."

"There was nothing "right and honorable" about the way he hijacked the people's mandate in the first place."

"Bringing UMNO crooks and PAS hypocrites into power was definitely the 'right and honorable' thing to do."

Prove Us Wrong, Muhyiddin

March 7, 2020

[News item: On Sunday March 1, 2020, following a week of political intrigue triggered by Prime Minister Mahathir's unexpected sudden resignation, Muhyiddin Yassin was sworn in as Malaysia's 8th Prime Minister. The Agung was satisfied, through individual interviews with MPs, that Muhyiddin Yassin had the majority support in Parliament. That assumption has yet to be ascertained.]

To assert that new Prime Minister Muhyiddin is an underwhelming leader would be a severe understatement, his successful machination to the top slot notwithstanding. Despite his long years in politics, it is hard to gauge his legacy. One that comes to mind was the notorious "Cowgate Scandal." He approved that project as Minister of Agriculture way back in 2006.

Muhyiddin may take inspiration from world leaders who despite their initial underrated status would later shine. President Reagan was one. Like Muhyiddin, Reagan too reached the top at an old age, and was initially dismissed as just a third-rate actor. There is no shortage of books about Reagan. Muhyiddin however, is not the reading type, and there are no Readers' Digest editions of those books. Instead I suggest that he ponders some of Reagan's memorable quotes.

Like Reagan, Muhyiddin had made a good start in stating his objectives. He wants a government that is *bersih, berintegriti*, dan *berkaliber* (clean, with integrity, and of caliber). Reagan went further and surrounded himself with smart competent people who shared his worldview, as well as commitment to freedom and free enterprise.

So too should Muhyiddin. Bersih means that those now facing criminal charges should be excluded. That would eliminate a dozen aspirants. Former Deputy Prime Minister Ahmad Zahid Hamidi has removed himself. That he was even considered should be the big question. Innocent till proven guilty is fine in a criminal court, but in appointing individuals to positions of high trust and responsibility, the standard must be much more stringent, as with not even a hint of impropriety. As for *berintegriti*, (with integrity) that would eliminate that *semburit* (anal) Azmin Ali character. This is the slimy character who stiffed his travel agent. Deadbeats lack integrity. Likewise, those who squandered public funds, as with buying helicopters but not delivering them. That would disqualify the likes of Hishammuddin Hussein. *Berkaliber* would eliminate that *latah* (echolalia) lady Zuraida Kamarudin who fudged her academic qualifications, as well as a few other items.

Acknowledging his uncertain health, Muhyiddin should select young blood. Eliminate tired old characters like Mustapha Mohamad. If Muhyiddin were to pick UMNO's has-beens, retreads, and turncoats, then he would merely be returning favors, not creating an A-team.

There is no shortage of local talent. If Muhyiddin wants a Malay-centric cabinet, at least pick smart Malays, like outgoing Minister Dzulkefli Ahmad, as well as young MPs like Nik Nazmi and Nurul Izzah. They would be more effective in furthering the Malay agenda by improving national schools over those who forever holler "Ketuanan Melayu" (Malay hegemony). Also, entice that shining star Rafizi Ramli.

If Muhyiddin fears unnecessary "politicking" among his appointees, then have them commit to not running in the next election. That would discourage the career politicians and party hoppers. Most of all Muhyiddin must acknowledge the limits of government. Disabuse Malays on our misguided notion that the answers must always come from there. As Reagan once quipped, the most terrifying words in the English language are: "I am from the government, and I am here to help!" Malaysians, Malays in particular, must now question the answers they get from the government, and not be passive as in the past by seeking answers for their myriad problems only from the government.

Malays have been getting "help" from their government for decades. Look at the good that does. Special privileges did not improve Malay competitiveness, instead they bred corrupt ersatz entrepreneurs like that billion-ringgit UMNO stalwart "Tengku" Adnan. Name a product, enterprise, or service associated with him. The government's first duty is to protect the people, not run their lives, as Reagan asserted. A timely reminder should Muhyiddin ponder working with the likes of Hadi Awang, President of the Islamic Party (PAS).

The needless drama of the past two weeks reminded me of yet another Reagan quote. "Politics," he said, "was the second oldest profession, but I have learned that it bears a striking resemblance to the first." Look at those politicians whoring themselves, utterly without shame or morals.

It is well over a week and Muhyiddin has yet to select his ministers. If the delay is due to his seeking the most qualified, then by all means take all the time he needs. However, if it is due to ongoing backroom horse trading, then beware. Plunderers are rarely satisfied with their loot. There is no honor among thieves. Expect more betrayals.

Muhyiddin may not turn out to be a Malaysian Reagan. Nonetheless if he were to have *bersih, berintegriti, berkaliber* Administration, then

Malaysians, more so Malays, would be the beneficiary. And America might just resume repatriating more of the recovered 1MDB loot.

Readers' Rating: * *
Sampling of Readers' Responses:

"I regard this opinion as a guiding principle for Muhyiddin to observe in appointing his cabinet. The best guide, and that is not an overstatement. It would take him longer if he were to avoid those of low moral integrity, the corrupt and dubious dealers of power. If he fails to come up with clean candidates, he and the country would be heading south towards a failed state."

"Anyone with a modicum of integrity and an ounce of *kebolehan* [ability] will avoid being part of a government that would implode soon."

Pathetic Malay Leadership – Recycling The Turncoats

March 2, 2020

[News item: On February 29, amidst a week of unneeded political crisis triggered by his resigning unexpectedly on his own accord, Mahathir was promptly appointed Interim Prime Minister by the Agung. After the MPs (each armed with their "Statutory Declarations") as well as the Attorney-General and Chief Justice paraded themselves through Istana Negara, the King then announced Muhyiddin Yassin as Prime Minister.]

The Agung's process in appointing Muhyiddin as Prime Minister merits scrutiny. Granted, Malaysia has never faced a similar challenge before, which makes the decision-making process critical. If unchallenged it could be precedential. Dispensing with the constitutional propriety of the Agung consulting the Attorney-General (a political appointee) and the Chief Justice (who may have to adjudicate the matter later), I would have been more reassured had the Agung sought independent legal counsel. Malaysia has no shortage of such luminaries. Even if they were to charge their customary fees, that would still have been worth it. One good solid advice is worth thousands of free ones, especially when those freebies have a stake in the Agung's decision.

The Agung did consult his brother rulers. One of them skipped the meeting, perhaps busy cavorting with yet another Russian beauty. Significantly, the Agung bypassed the four governors. Ever wonder at the increasing chatter for secession in East Malaysia?

I do not blame the Agung for this major oversight. He is new at his job. Instead, I put the blunder straight on his advisors, specifically the Keeper of the Rulers Seal and the government's Chief Secretary. They are but glorified overpaid clerks. This pair and the sultans collectively also demonstrate the pathetic state of Malay leadership.

Earlier we saw Malay political leaders in action. They triggered this mess. As for Malay intellectuals on campus and pundits in the media, they remain uncharacteristically silent. Their wet finger has yet to tell them from which direction this new wind would blow. Malay religious leaders are no better. The usually vociferous former Mufti of Perlis, Dr. Asri (he goes by his acronym Dr. MAZA), is curiously mute, likewise the establishment Federal Mufti. None of his usual sterile pontifications.

It used to be that Malays could comfort ourselves that while non-Malays control the economy, we were adroit in matters political. The hope was that we would leverage that to improve the lot of our community. Instead, Malay leaders exploit that to enrich themselves, their cronies, and fellow kleptocrats.

While there are more and more Malays, including former UMNO stalwarts who had long been apologists for the party and the establishment generally, now coming out against current Malay leaders. However, their efforts are a tad too little and too late. Where were they when Anwar Ibrahim and his reformasi movement needed support? How long can Malays continue blaming DAP specifically and the *pendatangs* (immigrants) generally? It must hurt Malays deeply to acknowledge that two of the most effective ministers in the outgoing cabinet — Transport Minister Anthony Loke and Energy, Science, and Technology Minister Yeo Bee Yin — are from DAP. You cannot credit their education, for while Yeo is Cambridge-educated, Loke had his from Universiti Kebangsaan.

Malays too have capable ones like Health Minister Dzulkifli Ahmad (Imperial College PhD) but they are vastly overshadowed by the likes of that *latah* (echolalia) lady, Housing Minister Zuraida Kamarudin, who has an uncontrolled urge to blabber on reporters' microphones, and that *semburit* (anal) Minister of Economic Affairs. Don't blame them. Blame the character who appointed them – Mahathir.

After the Agung had bypassed him, all Mahathir could brag was, "My number is bigger than yours!" referring to the MPs' Statutory Declarations, reminiscent of my adolescent days, except we were then not referring to numbers, rather our anatomical member! He lamented that the Agung did not want to see him anymore. The Agung is not the only one. As for Muhyiddin, he may have been expelled from UMNO, but he still retains its core political genes. He still has UMNO's sense of integrity (meaning, none), Abdullah Badawi's competence (a tad less sleepy), and Najib's morality (Muhyiddin's salacious extracurricular activities had previously been exposed).

Unless his Singapore surgeons goofed their diagnosis (pancreatic cancer), Muhyiddin would have minimal impact on Malaysia's future based on his clinical prognosis. More ominous would be his choice of a Deputy, and thus potential successor, as well as his cabinet.

In his first address Muhyiddin promised to appoint ministers from among those who are *"bersih, berintegriti, berkaliber* (clean, have integrity, and of caliber). I was amused that he felt compelled to assert *a la* Nixon, "Saya *bukan pengkhianat*!" (I am not a traitor!)

Nonetheless if he were to appoint those facing criminal charges (like Ahmad Zahid Hamidi) or who have skipped their bills (Azmin Ali), then Muhyiddin's lofty promise would ring hollow; likewise if Muhyiddin were to appoint those political turncoats. If they could betray Anwar and Mahathir, they could just as easily betray the betrayer, Muhyiddin.

If Muhyiddin were to appoint any of these slimy characters to his Administration, then Parliament should act right away. At its scheduled meeting of March 9, MPs should pass a vote of no-confidence on him following which the Agung should appoint Anwar Ibrahim as the people's mandate of the last election still holds. At this perilous time Malaysia does not need an expensive, divisive, and rancorous election.

Readers' Rating: * *
Sampling of Readers' Responses:
"Parliament's sitting has been moved to May. They need time to shop."
"Wouldn't appointing Anwar be the same act of recycling has-beens?"

Spare Malaysians The Apology – Just Get Out!

February 27, 2020

[News item: On Wednesday, February 26, 2020, Prime Minister Mahathir appeared in a nationally televised address apologizing to Malaysians for having triggered an unneeded and very divisive political crisis by resigning unexpectedly just days before. He had earlier remained uncharacteristically silent. Then after his sudden unexpected resignation, he quickly reaccepted the position as "Interim Prime Minister" that the Agung had offered Mahathir.]

That television address was vintage Mahathir. There he was blaming everyone but himself for the political crisis. However, he was no hero; he was hiding in his house, skipping his office in the few days following his resignation even though he had re-accepted the post back after the Agung had offered him the post back.

Spare Malaysians the apology. Quit the half-assed resignation charade. Just get out! If Mahathir could lecture the leader of the Free World (President Trump) to resign, so too could I to this divisive and polarizing Third World autocrat who has long overstayed his welcome.

The chaos Mahathir had inflicted upon and the distrust he had sowed among Malaysians through his latest conniving move will remain long after he is gone, forever blighting the nation. By contrast, the burden imposed by his predecessor Najib Razak, though humongous monetary-wise, was at least quantifiable. Najib paid the price by going to jail. There is no price tag to this latest Mahathir's folly. Nor would any punishment be adequate. Besides, the man knows no shame.

This is the ugly reality of Mahathir and his now conveniently forgotten Vision 2020. Instead of a leap into the First World, he has plunged Malaysia into the typical Third World political chaos and the usual third-rate power brawl. Imagine seeing lawmakers trotting to the palace for their two-minute "interview" with the Agung! If not for their misplaced joyful expressions, they resembled faithful Catholics lining up for their Sunday confessionals, what with their fancy formal attire. It also reminded me of my school days when our entire class was summoned one by one to the principal's office because no one had owned up to writing on the blackboard the insulting message to our teacher. At least we had the excuse that we were kids then; these MPs are adults and getting paid well by taxpayers.

While Mahathir indulges in his many fanciful savior delusions, billions have evaporated from Kuala Lumpur Stock Exchange (KLSE) and the coronavirus remains a looming lethal threat. Local schools continue to deteriorate, and Malaysian academics their blissful indifference if not ignorance. As the new Minister of Education, the post he had appointed himself to, Mahathir is too busy trying to "save" the nation, after he had wrecked it.

Mahathir's latest antic recalls the dark ugly days following the 1969 General Election that saw the UMNO-led coalition losing its supra majority. Mahathir himself was booted out of his own parliamentary seat in that election. The ensuing brutal race riot forever scarred Malaysians. It has barely sealed over. This latest Mahathir's monkeying threatens to remove that scab and reopen the old ugly wound, and with all the ensuing putrid pus and stench. The ugly viciousness of the rioters and senseless sufferings of the innocents caught in the crossfire of that riot are wrenchingly recounted in Hanna Alkaf's prize-winning autobiographical novel, *The Weight Of Our Sky*.

Mahathir claims to be a voracious reader. Give him a copy of that book. That might just refrain him from continuing to play with his highly incendiary race card. Extend the gift to the racists in DAP and UMNO, that is, if they could read English and appreciate elegant writing. As for those chauvinists wrapped in their religious robes in PAS, well, their reading repertoire does not extend beyond ancient musty Arabic *kitabs*.

The divide in 1969 was between Malays and Chinese. That was horrific enough. Today Mahathir has bested that. He drives not only Malays against non-Malays, but also Malays against Malays. Now that takes some doing! Without any trace of embarrassment, he called for a "unity" government. This from a leader who could not even unite his own party, the smallest in the ruling coalition. As usual, the irony escapes the man. He is in his own delusional world. For a man who is always confident if not cocky with the media, the image Mahathir projected in his televised address was of a leader overwhelmed by events. The format he chose was also one to spare him the inevitable tough, awkward questions.

Nonetheless the old ugly Mahathir's conniving streak was still evident. He blamed politicians for the current chaos. As an unnecessary reminder, Mahathir had blamed Abdullah and Najib for the failure of Vision 2020, forgetting that he chose those two duds. Likewise, Mahathir's New Economic Policy failed because of those "lazy Malays" who "easily forget."

Mahathir is a bitter man, intent on settling old grudges, a schemer too smart by half, the no-longer-agile old flying squirrel who had missed the last branch. A more reflective metaphor would be the pyromaniac caught with a matchstick during an inferno claiming to start a "controlled burning." His supporters see Mahathir differently, heaping accolades like "sly fox of Malaysian politics," "masterstroke genius," and "master strategist." A few described him as "Machiavellian." This classic quote from *The Prince*, "It is better to be feared than loved, if you cannot be both," is inappropriate for Mahathir. He is neither feared nor loved.

The future of Malaysia must be without Mahathir. As what exactly that would be, it is up to citizens, not the palace or Mahathir. The mandate that Malaysians gave Pakatan Harapan last May 2018 still holds. As such after accepting Mahathir's resignation, the Agung should have asked the present head of Pakatan, Anwar Ibrahim, to assume office. He should remain so until Parliament in an open, transparent, and formal session, with robust debates that could be witnessed by all, asserts otherwise. At which point Anwar should resign and either have another Pakatan leader take over or advise the King to dissolve Parliament.

Mahathir, the interim Prime Minister, advising the Agung to dissolve Parliament was the Mahathir in his trademark spiteful mode.

Decisions arrived in private can be very different from that made in the open or following robust discussions. This is quite apart from Timur Kuran's "preference falsification," where one's public utterances and professions are often at variance with one's private convictions. A backroom deal, whether in a luxurious palace or a smoky bar, is unacceptable.

The Agung's current remedy, presumably modelled after the Perak one following a similar debacle there after the 2008 state election, would not satisfy voters. Who could forget the spectacle of the Speaker of the Assembly being dragged out or the Raja Muda humiliated with having to wait for hours to deliver his royal address! Spare Malaysia those odious scenes again.

There was a silver lining to this recent dark cloud in that Malaysians had prevented Mahathir from anointing yet another dud (his third) of a successor in Azmin Ali. Yet there he is again today, Mahathir pushing for yet another in the person of Muhyiddin Yassin.

Readers' Rating: * *
Sampling of Readers' Responses:
"Never has the country encountered and experienced a more selfish, shameless, and egotistical politician."

"Wolf in sheep's clothing. We all thought he would be the statesman riding into the sunset. Now it's clear the wolf intends to stay and pillage the country for his own ends."

"I was one of the many working to convince the fence sitters to bring change through the ballot paper. When Dr. M came along, I was delighted that finally this man wants to wash away his past sins and redeem himself and the nation from the plunderers. Never can I imagine one so close to the deathbed could still harbor evil plans. Does his soul merit redemption and forgiveness?"

"You have summed up Mahathir the man and how he has gone about getting what he wants very well indeed! Vision 2020? Like me, this vision thing is inflicted with cataract of the political variety!"

"Couldn't agree more. This man makes Machiavelli look like an angel!"

The Flying Squirrel That Missed Its Last Branch

February 24, 2020

[News item: There had been endless distracting speculations since the General Election of May 2018 when Mahathir became Prime Minister for the second time whether he would later make way for Anwar Ibrahim. That was apparently settled at a meeting on Thursday, February 20 when leaders of the ruling coalition agreed to give Mahathir the freedom to choose his timing. Alas all that ended when on the very next day Anwar's putative deputy in his Keadilan Party, Azmin Ali, schemed to derail the plan and have Mahathir join the opposition coalition thus sidelining Anwar and his Pakatan Party. That resulted in Mahathir's unexpected resignation as Prime Minister as well as leader of his party. Azmin was kicked out of his party when his nefarious scheme was exposed.]

Had Mahathir been satisfied with only in getting rid of Najib Razak as Prime Minister in the May 2018 election and not "volunteered" himself to be Malaysia's seventh Prime Minister, his stocks would have soared and remained in the stratosphere. He would have been rightly anointed a national hero for having saved Malaysia from that international crook and thief Najib.

Malaysians would also have overlooked if not forgiven him for his role in Najib's rapid ascent and rapacious greed. Najib was but Mahathir's political child, his ugly legacy. Najib's 1MDB mess, together with his unprecedented greed and obscene ostentation, is but a variation on the theme of Mahathir's many earlier sordid scandals. Remember the Bank Bumiputra debacle, London Tin fiasco, and Pernas' expensive bailout during the Asian contagion of his son's teetering shipping company? Those and many others as yet unrevealed are all Mahathir's unmitigated blunders, so well captured by *reformasi*'s vote-getting rallying cry of a few decades ago – *korupsi, kolusi dan nepotisme* (KKN, or corruption, cronyism, and nepotism).

Malaysia is still reeling from that. Look at Malaysia Airlines today, yet another sorry example of Mahathir's crony capitalism. The difference between Najib's greed and Mahathir's cronyism is only quantitative, not qualitative, matter of degree, not kind. Even that could be debated as no one has as yet tallied up ringgit-wise the cumulative costs of Mahathir's blunder. Today, at a time when Malaysia should be celebrating Mahathir's much-ballyhooed Vision 2020 that would see entering the elite club of developed nations, he has instead thrown the country into an unwanted, unneeded, and very destabilizing political crisis. It was your typical Third World variety leadership tussle. As for Mahathir, he has not said a word on his "vision." It is now more truthfully a delusion. Worse, a nightmare.

Where was Mahathir during this moment of crisis? Holed up in his The Mines luxury estate. His Deputy Azizah, together with leaders of the Pakatan coalition, had to chase him down, first at his office (he had *ponteng* [absconded] that Monday morning), then his official residence, before finding him holed up in his private home. He was a skunk, slinking away but not before leaving his stink all over the place.

A man who always had been at ease with the media suddenly found himself desperate to escape from it. None of the usual smooth press conferences with his trademark silly snide grins and snickering belittling sarcasms on those who disagree with him. The man who only a week earlier had the gumption to tell President Trump to resign, suddenly found himself tongue-tied and camera-shy.

Two iconic pictures capture best the silly and futile drama of this past few days. One was of Deputy Prime Minister Azizah sitting on the bench outside Mahathir's private residence, with Anwar standing, arms folded, exuding confidence. The other coalition leaders with him, Lim Eng Guan, was casually standing at the side, while Mat Sabu was busy texting on his cellphone. The implied message from their body language: You old rat; we have you cornered. We can wait all day here for you.

That snapshot eerily reminded me of the pathetic scene when American troops finally trapped Saddam Hussein in his desert rat-hole hiding place. They had cornered their slimy target. They could wait all day; Saddam could come out and surrender with the television cameras recording it live, or rot in there.

The other searing sight was of Mahathir in the back seat of his limousine, alone, sans his wife who usually accompanies him on such important missions, his face glum, with defeat smeared all over it. He was on his way to the palace to hand in his resignation. That was far from the portrait of a victor. What a way to cap your career, the hitherto ageing but still (he thought) agile flying squirrel who had missed his last tree branch.

In personally confronting Mahathir at his home that Monday morning, Anwar had shown that he was not in the least cowered by the old man's usual antics and silly scheming. Anwar however described the meeting as "very satisfying." That's confidence verbalized succinctly!

Make no mistake. This past weekend's *sandiwara* or contrived drama could have ended badly for Malaysia. The endless frightening chatters on WhatsApp and other social media brought back ugly reminders of the horrors of May 1969. In my reckoning, Anwar had saved Malaysia from that. He also saved Mahathir from committing his third and possibly irremediable blunder or strike-out.

Mahathir's first was his having the incompetent and soporific Abdullah Badawi succeed him back in 2003. Abdullah dozed away while his "Fourth Floor boys" were busy self-aggrandizing themselves and destroying Malaysia in the process. Credit Mahathir for owing up to that error and successfully undoing it.

Mahathir's second strike-out was his aggressively promoting Najib Razak to overthrow Abdullah. Najib did nothing to advance himself. He was just happy to be the instrument and beneficiary of Mahathir's effort. Credit Mahathir for once again recognizing his error and going about to remedy his second mistake, but not before Malaysia was saddled with 1MDB and other crushing loads.

Whether Mahathir was responsible for Najib's Barisan defeat at GE 14, or whether Mahathir was merely the flying squirrel who flickers his tongue claiming credit when the coconut fronds above swayed in the breeze, does not interest me. I am just relieved that Najib and his ilk are defeated with a few of them now facing serious criminal charges.

Ponder this. Had Anwar not confronted Mahathir this past Monday morning and exposed his scheming to his face, Mahathir was set to commit his third strike-out. Drive around KL today and plastered all over town are tall billboards with faces of Mahathir and Azmin Ali, with privilege and a smug sense of entitlement pouring out of the latter's pores. No mistaking the implied message there and elsewhere – Azmin would be Mahathir's next (his third) dud successor.

This Azmin character, with his degree from an *ulu* (boondock) American state university, fancies himself an expert in economics, but he could not manage his family's microeconomics. He skipped on paying his family's luxurious travel bills. Even his mother has disowned him. His relations with his own siblings are dysfunctional. That is understating it. Nonetheless Azmin deludes himself into thinking that Malaysians would trust him to bring harmony to Malaysia's diverse society.

The only saving grace to this weekend's third-rate political drama is that Malaysia is spared Mahathir's third strike-out. This deadbeat *pengkhianat* (traitorous) Azmin is now out. That is reason enough to celebrate. If Mahathir is anywhere as smart as he thinks he is, he should thank Anwar and the other Pakatan leaders for saving the nation from yet another Mahathir's blunder.

Readers' Rating: * * * * *
Sampling of Readers' Responses:

"We are all being duped by this wily old fox. He is the maestro who endorsed the script from A to Z."

"His resignation from the party was actually part of the script to make him look good and that it was not he who abandoned the Pakatan Harapan-led coalition."

"Now that he is the interim PM and soon will be appointed the PM for good with unilateral power to make decisions without Pakatan Harapan Presidential Council interference. Ain't he the grand master of deception."

"The sly old fox is still in control."

"Malaysia is still reeling. Look at Malaysia Airlines. The difference between Najib's greed and Mahathir's cronyism is only quantitative, not qualitative; matter of degree, not kind."

"Most of the comments agreeing with you seem to be from non-Malays and maybe some urban Malays. You try to put Malaysia into a Western democratic mold. You forget Malays form the majority in Malaysia. They come from rural backgrounds and their thinking and life are still somewhat conservative. Religion and Malay culture are still influential on their lives and choices."

"Najib learned every tactic from him [Mahathir]; he was the PM who ruined Malaysia, a country blessed with rich natural resources, fertile land, and plenty of water."

"I think he checkmated himself this time."

Malaysia's (And Malays') Darkest Moment

January 12, 2020

[News Item: On January 8, 2020, Latheefa Koya, Chief of the Malaysian Anti-Corruption Commission (MACC), released wiretaps on then-Prime Minister Najib Razak's phone. The world heard, among other things, a late midnight call by Dzulkifli Ahmad, then a public prosecutor, tipping off Najib on impending criminal charges against Najib, as well as his (Najib) groveling up to the Crown Prince of United Arab Emirates pleading to him to backdate a loan agreement to protect Reza Aziz, Najib's stepson and one of the principals named in the United States Department of Justice's Asset Forfeiture Lawsuit of July 2016. Hearing His Highness repeatedly giving Najib a not-so-subtle royal shove-off and Najib not getting the message was painful.]

I had to take breaks more than a few times while watching MACC Chief Latheefa Koya's press conference of January 8, 2020. I had to, as I could not restrain my revulsion otherwise. Persevere I did however, only to be cursed with the darkest of moods at the end.

This is what Malaysia has turned into, her leader Najib Razak with utter impunity, unbridled arrogance, and egregious greed betraying the sacred trust citizens have placed upon him. Not just him but also his coterie of top officials. I was gripped with an even deeper melancholy, accompanied by utter shame and barely controlled rage, on realizing that those officials involved were all Malays. Many were later honored as Datuks, Datuk Seris, and Tan Sris. Is this what Malay leaders meant when a few months ago they held a much-ballyhooed gathering addressed by no less than current Prime Minister Mahathir under the banner of *Maruah Melayu* (Malay Dignity)? Is this what Malay culture has degenerated into?

Then amidst my gloom, a spark of hope, as in Dostoevsky's *The House of the Dead* where in the depth and sea of unimaginable inhumanity of a Soviet Siberian prison, a glint of humanity – a young man crying over the death of a stranger-to-him inmate. As for his reason, he replied to the narrator, "He, also, had a mother."

After hearing those MACC tapes, I too was desperate to find any sliver of honesty, integrity, and dignity amidst Najib's crowd of Malay officers and retinue. Then, there he (or she) was! We Malays (I assumed that the he or she who installed the wiretap was a Malay) also had one within our midst with honesty, integrity, and dignity. I would add, great courage! Imagine if he or she were to be caught! Yet there he (or she) was all along, hovering over but unnoticed, doing that daring deed of wiretapping the Prime Minister's personal phone! This hero or heroine loomed large though unseen and unheard. I hope that would remain so for I fear the consequences otherwise.

This brave soul saw evil being perpetrated. He (or she) was guided by our ahadith that says (approximately rendered) when you see evil being perpetrated, use your hand to stop it. Failing that or if it would be too risky, then use your tongue, meaning, voice your disapproval. And if even that is too dangerous, then at least disapprove of it in your heart, though that is the path least favored by Allah.

This brave soul used his (or her) hand to install the tapping device, and in so doing trapped the tongue of those evil doers, Najib and the equally traitorous prosecutor. I desperately want that brave upright individual to be a Malay because, God help Malaysia and that soul, if he or she were to be a non-Malay. Yet another sneaky *pendatang* (immigrant) trying to shame and "do in" an honest, upright Malay leader, they would howl. Malays, in particular Najib, already have difficulty digesting the role of that other chubby Chinaman, Jho Low.

Malays like me are in desperate need of that righteous figure now, even an anonymous one, upon whom we could share some sense of reflected cultural pride in this much too rare display of bravery, dignity, and integrity.

Confirming the authenticity of those MACC tapes would be an elementary forensic exercise. Meaning, those tapes are genuine. Further, no one has denied them or claimed that they were concocted by slick actors and actresses, or rather actress. There was not even a sly "Sounds like me but not me" or "taken out of context" denial. Nor did we hear any "Correct! Correct! Correct!" affirmation as with the other earlier infamous videotape involving a senior lawyer and an equally senior judge who would later become the nation's Chief Justice.

What surprised me was not the tapes' content. That ugly reality that present Malay leaders are corrupt to the core and top civil servants (again mostly Malays and UMNO partisans) lack an iota of integrity is not news. You do not need those tapes to validate that. That is the saddest and most painful part for me as a *merantau* (expatriate) Malay to acknowledge.

More revealing were the responses of the participants, or lack thereof to the tapes' release. Most remained silent. Rosmah, whose voice was also recorded in that taped phone call, managed only, "I have nothing to say!"

Then there was the rubbish from Najib claiming that those tapes vindicated him! Note, and of great significance, he did not deny the taping or its contents. There is a term to describe those who have difficulty discerning fantasy from reality. The good news there is that the malady is treatable.

I always knew that Najib was not terribly bright. However, I did not realize he was that stupid as to use an unsecured land line to speak to a foreign head of state on a very sensitive matter. The man also lacks dignity; his shameless groveling to the Arab Crown Prince was despicable. I wonder how many other heads of state who had communicated with Najib over the phone and discussed 1MDB or other serious matters of state would feel now? Rest assured that those tapes were only the tip of the proverbial iceberg.

To those who claim the tapes' release was *sub judice*, violated due process, or an invasion of privacy, it is significant that so far no one has filed a court motion or police report. The reason is obvious – the behaviors of those whose voices were recorded were so egregious and beyond the pale. I am surprised and saddened that those who complained about the propriety of the tapes' release have not seen fit to condemn the participants in the tapes. Focus on what those tapes reveal. Does anyone approve of what they did?

Meanwhile Inspector-General of the Police (IGP) Hamid Bador was waiting passively to receive those tapes. He should have responded thus: "This is serious! I am on my way to see Latheefa right away to secure those tapes."

Those who argue that the tapes should have been handed to the police first and dispense with the public release, consider the police "investigation" of the other infamous tapes like the so-called *semburit* (anal) videotape of two consenting men frolicking in a Sandakan hotel. That dragged on (I mean the investigation) and at the end, "NFA!" (No Further Action)"

The actions of those individuals caught on the MACC tapes thought they were doing the patriotic thing to protect their leader, the classic Hang Tuah excuse. It is this perversion of our noble values that is so destructive. That prosecutor who tipped Najib of the criminal investigation was later promoted to be MACC Chief and given a Tan Sri. There's more. He was later videotaped holidaying abroad (probably celebrating his reward, I mean promotion) cavorting with a female other than his wife. Worse is yet to come! This slimy character had the audacity to give a Friday sermon on – yes, you guessed it! – the evils of corruption! Next JAKIM (Islamic Agency) would invite him to give a Friday sermon on marital fidelity. That's the degradation of our culture and of Islam in Malaysia today, but that is another and a very long chapter.

Save unconditional denials, the Keeper of the Rulers' Seal Syed Danial should ask the Agung and his brother rulers to rescind the titles awarded to those knaves. The Syed should not be like IGP Hamid, *menunggu arahan* (awaiting directive). I am proud that the Ruler of my state of Negri Sembilan had already rescinded 15 months ago Najib's and Rosmah's royal honorifics.

There was another shocker on the Council of Rulers' non-action. Latheefa's predecessor Shukri at MACC had apprised the rulers twice on 1MDB and the need for immediate action. The Rulers refused. Shukri called Duzlkifli a *pengkhianat* (traitor). From what we know today that term could apply to many more.

In the pantheon of infamy, those MACC tapes would be in the same league with Nixon's equally infamous Watergate tapes. With Nixon, it was the missing part that undid him; with Najib and his ilk, the contents.

To MACC Chief Latheefa Koya, continue your excellent work. Give 'em hell! You already struck fear among the corrupt. Let them have more sleepless nights believing that their past conversations could also have been tapped. As to that brave righteous soul who tapped Najib's phone line, my heartfelt gratitude. You are my North Star; you personify "Duty, honor, country!"

Readers' Rating: ✶ ✶ ✶ ✶ ✶
Sampling of Readers' Responses:

"Surely ex-MACC Chief Abu Kassim had done well for Malay dignity. So despair not Bakri Musa!"

"You, sir, give us a glimmer of hope during our nation's dark, embarrassing, and shameful moment in history."

"They were all executed in the name of '*agama, bangsa dan negara*' [religion, race, and nation] ... old lyrics written by the oldies Third World leaders of Bolehland."

"There are, and always will be righteous and good Malays, our people are not devoid of them. We just have to find them and put them in the right place at the right time."

"The revelation [release of the tapes] is both unwarranted and is nothing more than for political pretenses. Firstly, the comparison with the Watergate Tape is flawed as that was done at a time when Nixon was in power .... Secondly, the timing of the revelation also invites public suspicion of its ulterior motive to divert public attention from another video scandal that the Attorney-General had decided not to press charges. This [latter decision] attracts more condemnation but escapes your attention."

"Let's move on to a better Malaysia ... [with] a leader who has integrity, charisma, and wisdom ... instead of looking at "kulitfication" [skin color]."

V: PRISTINE ISLAM

Chee Hoi Lan's Maulidur Rasul Award And Islamic Adoption

October 12, 2022

[On the occasion of observing the birthday of Prophet Muhammad, s.a.w., the Trustees honored Chee Hoi Lan with the Maulidur Rasul's Ibu Sejati (Exemplary Mother) Award. She is one of the few non-Muslim honorees.]

What an uplifting news item, the Agung honoring retired 83-year-old kindergarten teacher Chee Hoi Lan with the 2022 National Maulidur Rasul Award Malaysia – Ibu Sejati-Keluarga (True Family Mother)! Kudos to the selection committee and those who nominated her.

Chee is the mother of Rohana Abdullah whom she had adopted when Rohana was two months old. No, there is no error with that sentence. Chee is Rohana's mother. Rohana was given up by her birth mother, an Indonesian maid who had worked for Chee and was later forced to return to Indonesia as per Malaysia's strict immigration laws.

That was in 1980 when Indonesia was a chaotic repressive country under that goon Suharto. Rohana's birth mother decided that her daughter would be better off remaining in Malaysia. It revealed volumes of her relationship with her employer that she had entrusted her daughter to Chee even though she was not a Muslim. Recognizing the baby's mother's Muslim heritage, Chee took extra effort to ensure that the baby was brought up in the Islamic tradition.

Chee's award, apart from recognizing her extraordinary generosity and unconditional love for Rohana, highlights current understanding on the concept and dynamics of motherhood (and also parenthood). It is as much biological as sociological. Depending on circumstances, one may take precedence over the other.

Muslim thinking and practices on adoption have remained rigid and not kept up with modern understanding as well as realities and complexities. The primacy of biological parenthood remains in Islam, as well as in many other traditions. This needs to be reexamined, what with adoptions, orphanages, and foster parenthoods becoming widespread. Then we have surrogate motherhood and in-vitro fertilization with other than the husband's sperm. If Muslim thinking were to remain unchanged, that would be as if despite satellites and people flying around the world, we still think the earth is flat.

Islam recognizes only biological parenthood. Nonetheless the Qur'an as well as prophetic traditions exhort us to be kind to orphans, with the concomitant severe punishments otherwise. This Islamic "kindness" however, is limited only to things material, such as properties and living provisions. It does not extend to that most elemental need of any child, the emotional sense of belonging to and of being an integral part of a loving family. Even the material things are circumscribed. An adopted child is denied lawful inheritance (*faraid*); adopted parents could only bequeath gifts (*hibah*), and then to no more than a third of their assets. There are other subtle as well as not-so-subtle, overt as well as covert, and consequential as well as trivial matters to remind the adopted child that he or she remains different and separate from "real" or biological children.

At marriage, the *kadhi* still insists that an adopted daughter get her biological father's consent even though he may never have appeared in her life or memory while growing up. As for the trivial, an adopted daughter still has to don a hijab in front of her non-biological brothers and male relatives. These and other rituals, as with the practice of naming "illegitimate" children as "bin" or "binti Abdullah," are there to remind them that they are "different," meaning, not a "real" child of the family. That bin and binte Abdullah appellation effectively brands the kid for life and beyond. Such are the "awesome (curious) powers of the Registrar-General of Births and Deaths," in the words of Alima Joned, former Dean of Law at the University of Malaya and now an attorney in Washington, DC., in a Law Journal article.

Western societies place a premium on the traditional family. That takes precedence over the child's presumed faith at birth. This can be heartbreaking for mothers who by court order have to give their child to a family who does not share their faith.

Malay society is blighted by easy divorces and the taking of multiple wives. I have not come across any local sociological studies but anecdotally the dynamics of those children (more so the sons) are similar to Black children in America with absent father figures. I wonder whether such dysfunctional phenomena as Mat Rempits and school dropouts are but manifestations of this "absent father" syndrome.

I was touched by a recent documentary of a Chinese girl who went (accompanied by her adopted American parents) on a visit to her old village in China in search of her biological parents, a common yearning among adoptees. She found them and was taken aback at the highly emotional demonstrations of guilt trip that they had laid upon her to regain her affection as well as to excuse their giving her up at birth. That confused the teenager, but her secure adopted parents reassured her.

"Yes, you came from her tummy," referring to the biological mother, "but you came from our heart!" The daughter returned home to America with her parents.

"Open adoption," where birth parents are allowed varying degrees of access to the child, is now common in the West. Muslim adoption practices have elements of that. However, it too is not without its own complications as recounted by one mother of an adopted child (Vanessa McGrady) in her riveting memoir, *Rock Needs River.* One positive with open adoption is that the child has access to her family's medical history. With today's genetic testing, that is becoming less of an issue.

We still read with horrifying frequency of abandoned babies in Malaysia. California has Safe Haven Law where parents and others may safely surrender infants within 72 hours of birth with no charges filed and no questions asked. Outside Emergency Rooms, fire stations, and churches is a warm attractive cot placed just for that purpose. I have yet to see one at Malaysian mosques.

I hope our ulama are not satisfied with just awarding Chee with this singular honor. It should inspire them and us to work with social workers, child psychologists, and lawmakers to make all babies wanted and loved. Issues such as faith and bureaucratic identity (as with race) are trivial if not irrelevant.

Readers' Rating: * * * *
Sampling of Readers' Responses:

"We can't claim to love God but despise one another, regardless of race, religion, or royalty. God is love and love is God!"

"Currently all registered Children Welfare Homes run by non-Bumis can take only non-Bumis"

"Pregnant Muslim teens are scorned by society."

"Once in a while one is moved and challenged by such real-life stories."

"For a more compassionate and merciful society."

"Yes, she truly deserves … [it]. May her spirit lift her up to Heaven!"

Let Us Undertake Our Own Hijrah

August 14, 2022

[The hijra (migration) of Prophet Muhammad (May Allah's blessing be upon him!) from his hometown of Mecca to Medinah in 632 AD to escape the persecution from his own tribesmen was such a pivotal event in Islamic history that Caliph Omar later decided to mark the Muslim era from that date.]

I was touched by my Imam Ilyas Anwar's Friday, August 5th, 2022, Awal Muharram 1444 *khutba* (sermon). Awal means first in Arabic, and Muharram, the first of the twelve months of the Muslim year.

Prophet Muhammad's hijrah (migration) to Medinah from Mecca in 632 AD was such a pivotal event that the second Caliph (Omar) retrospectively made it (17 years later) the beginning of the Muslim calendar. To be precise, that hijrah did not take place 1444 years ago rather 1400 as the lunar-based Muslim year is shorter than the Gregorian one by 11 days. Further, hijrah was completed on the tenth day of the third Muslim month (Rabi al Awal), and not during Muharram.

Hijrah, my Imam Ilyas reminded us, means to migrate, to leave something and start anew. The Prophet, *s.a.w*, undertook it because he was being hounded by his fellow Meccan tribesmen intent on killing him and with that, his divine mission. Islam's message of justice posed an existential threat to them and their existing order.

Imam Ilyas reminded us that hijrah could be physical or spiritual. As for the physical, Muslims have no equivalent Abrahamic burden of being in a permanent state of exile (diaspora), dispersed in alien territories and to return to the promised land upon some messianic intervention. To Muslims, every new country is a promised land, an opportunity for a fresh beginning.

When the Prophet, *s.a.w.*, undertook his hijrah, it was more to preserve and transmit the divine revelations he had received, less for his personal safety. Although the hijrah was the command of Allah, nonetheless the Prophet, *s.a.w.*, took all necessary worldly precautions. It was far from a spur-of-the moment decision typically associated with "escaping." Nor did he depend only on Allah's protection. For example, the Prophet, *s.a.w.*, had arranged for a guide, mapped out his route carefully, and prepaid for the animals that would transport him and his companions. He also enlisted the help from non-Muslim shepherds to cover his tracks in the sand. This last point should disabuse UMNO [Malay-based political party] and PAS (Islamic Party] chauvinists' unfounded distaste of working with non-Muslims for the country's good.

To the Prophet, s.a.w., careful planning did not conflict with and was indeed part of *tawakkul* (what Allah has bestowed or planned upon us). This point, Imam Ilyas reminded us, is often missed by Muslims, now and then. To be pedestrian, predestination notwithstanding, one should always look both ways before crossing a street. That is a necessary and much needed reminder as well as antidote to the entrenched fatalism ("Leave it to Allah!") of Muslims prevailing not just among uneducated simple villagers.

In leaving Mecca the Prophet, *s.a.w.*, went from a homogenous society of his Bedouin tribesmen to a then plural and diverse one in Medinah, with its established Christian, Jewish, pagan, and polytheistic communities. There he used Islam's touchstone of justice to govern, not whims, revenge, hatred, or desire to dominate. He demonstrated as much as he preached this new faith, following the Qur'anic injunction (Surah Al-Kafirun 109:6): "Unto you your religion, unto me, mine."

That simple, pragmatic, and peaceful creed is today missed by many, and not just the zealots.

In Medinah the Prophet, *s.a.w.*, emphasized civic engagement and good communal relations. Among the first things he did was set up marketplaces. He did that even before building a mosque. Being a merchant, he knew that trading was the best way to create and increase social bonds and interactions among people. It still is. As such I find the current Malay obsession with "Buy Muslim First" an aberration and counterproductive, from the business sense as well as faith-wise. As a vendor you would want the widest possible customer base; as a consumer, the best product and price. With the greater profit from the former, and the money saved with the latter, you would have that much more to donate for *zakat* (tithe).

The Prophet, *s.a.w*, lived the message of Surah Al-Ma'idah (5:8), approximately translated, "Bear witness to justice and not let hatred for a people lead you to be unjust. Be just, for that is nearer to reverence and to God."

That inspiration from the Prophet's hijrah was demonstrated to me by a student refugee from Ethiopia. She related her perilous journey escaping the land of her birth. What kept her going through her harsh ordeals trekking across the parched desert and sailing across the treacherous Mediterranean in winter was remembering the Prophet's own hijrah. While she was being hounded by those who were other than her own kind, and thus more understandable though no less painful, the Prophet, *s.a.w.*, was being chased out by his own tribesmen. As such the pain must have been that much more wrenching.

In Surah Al Nisaa (4:97) the Angels reprimanded those who had wronged themselves using the convenient excuse that they could not escape their plight. "Was not God's earth vast enough that you might have migrated?" That should be the sharp rebuke to those who would use the ready rationale of "They always do it this way here!" to justify their evil conduct. That was what that Ethiopian student did by migrating. As for those jingoistic Malay nationalists with their endless exhortations *of hujan emas di negri orang, hujan batu di negri sendiri* ... (There may be showers of gold abroad but hailstorms in your native land but ...) in discouraging us from our own *hijrah*, heed Rumi's wisdom:

"Muhammad says, 'Love of one's country is part of faith.' But don't take that literally! Your real 'country' is where you're heading, not where you are. Don't misread that hadith."

Rumi too had done more than his share of hijrah. As for not going to where there are showers of gold, you are depriving yourself of Allah's bounty. Worse, you are belittling it. In this regard, my Minangkabau tradition of *merantau* (wandering) is one to be celebrated and emulated.

Imam Ilyas's Awal Muharram khutba was refreshing for yet another reason. As I view on social media of similar sermons elsewhere, I was struck by two sad observations. While my Imam exhorted us to be inspired by hijrah, most Sunni Imams emphasized the ritual aspects of Muharram as with fasting on the tenth day. Meanwhile the Shi'ites are consumed with re-living the senseless tragedy of Karbala when the Prophet's grandson was butchered, and his body desecrated. Those ulama missed or skipped the essence and key lessons of hijrah.

As we enter the Muslim New Year of 1444 let us again as per my Imam Ilyas, internalize the noble values and aspirations of that initial hijrah. Heed our beloved Prophet Muhammad (May Allah be pleased with him!):

المهاجر من هجر الخطايا و الذنوب المهاجر من هجر ما نهى الله عنه

(*ālmhāǧr mn hǧr ālḫṭāyā w āldnwb ālmhāǧr mn hǧr mā nh□ āllh 'nh*)

[We do not have to physically migrate, rather abandon all that Allah has forbidden.]

Readers' Rating: *
Sampling of Readers' Responses:

"The ummah (community) and *Bangsa* (race) ... need a new enlightened Ataturk ... not new (old) Mahathir to demolish and rebuild."

Ramadan – A Month Of Generosity And Forbearance

March 31, 2022

[During Ramadan AH 1443 (April 2022), in a departure from the traditional Muslim practice of reciting the entire Qur'an (*qatam*), I focus instead on exploring the meaning and significance of Surah Al Fatihah, the short opening surah that is recited in all prayers.]

First of Eight Parts: Personal And Societal Impact of Ramadan

This Sunday April 2, 2022, Muslims will begin our month-long fasting from sunrise to sunset. I remember my first summer Ramadan in Canada in the late 1960s. I wrote my parents back in tropical Malaysia seeking advice on how to fast when the sun would not set for nearly 20 hours.

They replied that they did not have the answer. However, after consulting with our family Imam there, my father reminded me that Ramadan was not meant to be Allah's torture test upon us Muslims. As such I could fast according to Malaysian time if that would make it easier. Ramadan, he went further, goes beyond fasting. It is a season to acknowledge our Creator by being generous to and forbearing of others, including all His creations.

Consider generosity. It is said that the Gate to Heaven would remain open during Ramadan. Also reflecting His Generosity, Allah first revealed the Qur'an to Prophet (May Allah be pleased with him) over 14 centuries ago during this month. Muslims give *zakat* (tithe) during Ramadan. To emphasize this point, charitable deeds done during this holy month is said to be amplified "a thousand times." No surprise that Muslim organizations plan their fund-raising during this period. Likewise the traditional communal "breaking of the fast" (*iftar*) is a treasured ritual with Muslims.

Those emphasis on generosity and forgiveness notwithstanding, I have yet to see Muslim nations grant clemency to their citizens during

Ramadan. In fact the reverse! Two weeks before Ramadan, Saudi Arabia, Islam's birthplace and center of the faith, executed 81 prisoners. Some mercy! Such generosity!

In our preoccupation with rituals Muslims forget that fasting and *zakat* are two of the four mandatory foundational practices of our faith. Implicit with *zakat* is wealth creation. You have to have wealth before you could give *zakat*. In this respect Islam is spared the theology of the ennoblement of poverty implicit in the biblical "The meek shall inherit the earth," or the eastern practice of sending monks to beg in the streets.

Muslims should strive to be wealthy so we could give *zakat*. That the opposite is the reality among Muslims reflects the extent to which our faith has been debased. Our ulama belittle worldly wealth acquisition, emphasizing instead only the variety presumed to be valued (as they see it) in the Hereafter.

Beyond material wealth, and far more important but less acknowledged, is that we should also (if not more so) be generous of our time and talent. I was reminded of this early in my career. I was called to the Emergency Room (ER) deep in the night during one Ramadan. Having your sleep interrupted, especially after a day of fasting, has a way of putting you in a foul mood, more so if you expect the case to be what we private physicians euphemistically refer to as "uncompensated care." I must have made quite a ruckus in preparing to leave for the hospital, enough to wake up my wife. Upon finding out the cause of my frustration, she got up to hug me.

"Bakri, this is Ramadan!" she soothed me. "A blessed month," she continued, "a time to be generous!"

Those words calmed me. From then on, I learned to take my ER calls in stride, treating them as my commitment and contribution to my community that had been so generous to me and my family.

We may not always be able to be generous with our time, talent, or wealth, we can be in being more accepting and tolerant of the faults and failings of others, as well as of our own. Often that is the most meaningful. I remember how tolerant my parents were during Ramadan. While red marks on my school assignments would ordinarily trigger blistering lectures on the importance of being diligent, during Ramadan I would instead get a comforting "try harder and do my best next time!" Likewise with our evening dinners during Ramadan; those would be extra special with added treats. As for communal iftars, in premodern Malaysia the local lords would, in a reversal of roles, host the local commoners. It still is the tradition in many places today.

Fasting in its infinite variations is practiced by many faiths, east and west. Together with caloric reduction in general and ketogenic diets in particular, fasting today draws much medical attention for its many proven health benefits. Thus "We are what we eat!" could be augmented with "When we eat." Fasting in itself is not a novelty for our body; we do it when we sleep. The added element to Ramadan is the associated disruption of our diurnal rhythm. However, research on shift workers showed that similar altered diurnal rhythm carries significant adverse health consequences.

What gives?

Modern research shows that ketone bodies play a much greater role in the brain (and elsewhere) beyond being an alternate source of metabolic fuel. Ketogenic diet was once the mainstay to reduce children's epileptic seizures. Ketones affect the excitability of neurons as well as the levels of certain neurotransmitters. Hence the calmness of marathon runners and the heightened spirituality among Muslims during the holy fasting month. Ramadan, and daytime fasting generally, induces this state of nutritional ketosis that in turn influences our mental state.

The Qur'an looks with great disfavor (*makruf*) upon those who would "sleep off their fast." Then we would be no different, metabolic-wise, than shift workers. Instead, we are to maintain our regular activities and enhance our charitable deeds during Ramadan. Thus I find the common practice in Muslim countries of curtailed official and business hours a perversity and against the spirit of Ramadan. They should be expanding their hours to accommodate the public and customers. That is, be generous with their time and services.

Though a physician, as a Muslim I emphasize more this spirit of generosity and forgiveness implicit with Ramadan over the many health benefits associated with reduced caloric intake and consequent metabolic ketosis of fasting. The latter benefits only oneself while the former, society. May this Ramadan heighten our spirit of generosity and may we be generous not only to others but more so to ourselves.

Readers' Rating: * *

Sampling of Readers' Responses:

"Insightful sharing, Dr. Bakri Musa, but I must make one correction. Blessed are the poor in spirit, for theirs is the kingdom of heaven .... Blessed are the meek, for they will inherit the earth …(Matthew:5). Poverty is not ennobled in the Bible nor does "meek" mean weak but rather it encompasses traits like humility, patience, and compassion."

"Ramadan goes beyond fasting. It is a season to be generous and forbearing of others. Agree 100 percent! But why not practice this all year round? Why have a specific month to be and do good?"

Second of Eight Parts: Living Surah Al Fatihah
April 3, 2022

The tradition for Muslims in Ramadan is to partake in a communal recitation of the Holy Qur'an, completing it (*qatam*) at *lailatul qadar*, the "Night of Power." That was when, as per Muslims' narration, Angel Gabriel first revealed Allah's message to Prophet Mohammad, *s.a.w.*, some 1440 years ago. *Lailatul qadar* is believed to be one of the odd nights of the last ten days, the 27th being most favored.

This Ramadan I have a more modest, and to be hoped for, achievable goal. I strive to search for and live the full meaning of just one surah, and a very short one, Al-Fatihah, the opening surah with only seven easily memorized ayats (verses).

My choice of just one short surah versus attempting the entire Qur'an was a tacit acknowledgment of my own limitations, as well as in deference to the wisdom of quality over quantity. I was also inspired by Bruce Lawrence, the non-Muslim retired Professor of Islamic Studies at Duke. In initiating a series on understanding the Qur'an, he and his colleagues chose one surah and "owned" it. That exercise was uniquely insightful.

A study by a group of scholars at the Universiti Pendidikan Sultan Idris showed that over 90 percent of Malay students do not understand Surah Al Fatihah despite the heavy emphasis on Islam in their curriculum. That reflected the general pathetic state of Islamic education. God's first revelation to Prophet Muhammad, *s.a.w.*, was *"Iqra"* (read). Through reading we learn to acquire new knowledge and from there, to practice (*amal*) it, and in the process improve ourselves.

To Muslims, Surah Al Fatihah is divine revelation. That is a matter of faith. Little merit to or benefit gained from debating that. One does not have to be fluent in Arabic to sense the inner rhythm and exquisite beauty of the surah. Nor does one have to be a Muslim to appreciate its aural splendor and absorb its transcendent wisdom.

Just as a born English speaker needs help to appreciate Shakespeare, so too Muslims, Arabic as well as non-Arabic speakers, with our Qur'an. We should leverage all our modern insights to better comprehend it. Understanding a text blends with its capacity to stimulate ideas as well as what the reader brings to it, as per Elizabeth Rosenblatt's "Reader Response" theory of literature. It should thus not surprise anyone that the Qur'an would be read and understood differently by a Bedouin desert dweller of the 7th Century versus a Muslim diaspora in 21st Century urban West. The Qur'an is a living document, "for all mankind and at all times." As such, it cannot be detached from current knowledge or accepted wisdom.

The late Tunisian philosopher Mohammad Talbi brought his insights on French Literature to reading the Qur'an, giving us yet another dimension as well as a much richer meaning and deeper appreciation. The *pesantran*-tutored and Harvard-educated Indonesian Ulil Abdalla noted that traditional Eastern reading of the Qur'an is ritualistic and formulaic; modern Western, analytical and practical. Both approaches are useful and complement each other.

Religious learning in the Islamic world today is consumed with recitations but little actions, Talbi's "illness of speech." He would rather have us "not parroting what had been discovered ... rather searching for what constitutes the essence ... " of Islam. Malaysians have a laconic acronym echoing Talbi's lament: NATO (No action; talk only!).

Early jaundiced orientalists dismissed the seeming literary jumble of the Qur'an as incoherence, akin to the astronomically challenged looking into the star-lit night sky and seeing only scattered blobs of lights. To me Al Fatihah is less recitation, more comprehension; less gourmet recipe, more profound aphorisms; less night stars, more my northern star. Like the rest of the Qur'an, Al Fatihah guides me more for this world. As for the Hereafter, *Allah hu alam*! (Only He knows!)

I lament the current sorry state of Islamic discourses in Malaysia — long and loud on sound but alas dim and short on enlightenment. The obsession is on the Hereafter, and the intellectual traffic all unidirectional. Hours would be spent glorifying the various names of the surah, as if putting different labels explains things. Al Fatihah is already beautiful and exquisite; heaping more superlatives adds little. As per the character in the celebrated novel *Saman* by the Indonesian writer Ayu Utami, "*Apakah keindahan itu perlu dinamai?*" (Must a thing of beauty always have a name?)

The emphasis on such religious occasions is on dazzling the audience. For example, one mufti could not complete a simple sentence in Malay, promiscuously inserting long incomprehensible Arabic at the slightest provocation. Never mind that his listeners do not understand a word of Arabic. Yet another triviality would be to engage in endless controversies, as whether the surah has six or seven ayats, revealed in Mecca or Medinah, or should it be recited audibly or in silence during congregational prayers.

Such needless disputes are not without their consequences. The earliest and most traumatic was on the question of whether the Qur'an was created or eternal. That tore early Muslims apart, and for little purpose. Heed the Qur'an's message, or at least try to; that should be the principal pursuit.

An American alim on a visit to Malaysia spent hours expounding on this surah, mesmerizing his audience with his exquisite *tajweed* (recitations). He waxed lyrical on Al Fatihah's beauty, dazzling his listeners with his erudite renditions of ancient tomes. At the end of his long marathon session, he claimed that he could go on for another couple more hours!

He must have thought himself very effective for his listeners posed no questions at the end of his lengthy monologue. Preachers like this character have minimal respect for their audience's precious time and insult their intelligence with irritating repetitive, infantile, rhetorical questions. They have minimal insight on how adults learn, as for example our short attention span.

As for ancient scholars, they have made their prodigious contributions and we owe them a huge debt of gratitude. However, their world was very different from ours, and so were their problems. Today, as asserted by the Sudan-born American scholar Abdullahi Ahmed an-Naim, the challenge is to make the Qur'an relevant to and align with contemporary universally accepted norms of constitutionalism, human rights, and gender equity, among others. Dismissing Western interpretations as but another manifestation of orientalism insults readers' intelligence, quite apart from being patronizing to your listeners.

I find much of current Islamic discourses irrelevant, akin to listening to lectures on mental health where the speaker would expound long and loud on Freud and Jung but silent on anti-depressants, neurotransmitters, and modern neuroscience insights.

Ulama, like all leaders, have an awesome responsibility. In embellishing the supposed miracles of Al Fatihah they could be imparting a misguided message. When you are sick, you must seek expert medical care, or in a pandemic as with the current Covid-19, get vaccinated, wear a mask, and avoid crowds. Only then recite Surah Ash Shifa (The Curer, Al Fatihah's other name) for Allah's added protection. Malaysians do not need to be reminded that the first and largest outbreak of Covid-19 followed a Tabligh gathering in February 2020 where they undoubtedly recited Al Fatihah umpteen times.

Al Fatihah is also Umm Al Qur'an (Mother of the Qur'an). In contemporary parlance and practice, that would be the equivalent of a book blurb, the back cover or inside flaps of the dustcover. Apart from telling potential readers something about the book, it also serves as a "hook" to grab them.

There has been a gratifying increase in the number of English translations of the Qur'an in recent decades. Unlike earlier ones, these later translators, Muslims as well as non-Muslims, remain faithful to the challenging task of both elucidating the divine message and replicating its exquisite beauty. That notwithstanding, I have yet to see a translation that captures Al Fatihah's poetic beauty. It is after all more poetry, less prose.

My purpose here is to explore Al Fatihah's meaning so it can continue to guide me. Mine is not a *tafseer* (commentary and/or translation), far from it! Nor am I preaching. My pursuit is towards greater understanding of this most-recited surah. To paraphrase Robert Frost, I begin my journey with much delight and hope to end with some wisdom.

Readers' Rating: *
Sampling of Readers' Responses: None

Third of Eight Parts: Invoking Allah And On Being Grateful
April 7, 2022

The first ayat of Al-Fatihah is approximately translated as, "In the Name of Allah, the Most Gracious (Ar Rahman) and Most Beneficent (Ar Raheem)." "Approximately translated" is a necessary caveat. Certitude is not my forte or practice.

Invoke means to cite or appeal to a higher authority. It could also mean to petition or seek help. With Muslims, the highest authority is Allah. That is a matter of faith. Secularists invoke the constitution; royalists, the King. With the former you would need expert lawyers to argue your case through the courts; with Kings, their royal courtiers. Islam, unlike other faiths, puts no intermediaries between you and Allah – no priests, bishops, or popes. Sheikhs, ayatollahs, and the plethora of JAKIM (Malay acronym for the religious authority) bureaucrats are but *bida'ah*, a perversion of the faith. With judges and kings, you could see the tangible consequences of their interventions. Not so with Allah. To repeat, believe in Him and His power is but a matter of faith.

Ar rahman and *ar raheem* have the same root as *rahim* (womb), a powerful feminine imagery. That notwithstanding, Allah is always referred to in the masculine, an anomaly and tradition that defy explanation. Raheem thus carries a womb/fetus relationship between God and mortals, one of nourisher, sustainer, and protector. It also implies essentiality–an embryo requires a womb to develop.

That imagery also hints at limits or boundaries. Experimental artificial wombs notwithstanding, a fetus needs a womb. Likewise with us mortals and Allah. Once we transgress His boundaries, our relationship to Him and He us, changes as an aborted fetus to its mother. That is the central message of all scriptures.

The second ayat begins with *Al hamdu* and ends with *raab bil alameen* before going to the third which repeats the two frequently recited attributes of Allah, *ar rahman and ar raheem. Al hamdu* is often translated as praise. That is inadequate to express its full meaning and sentiment; it implies more – thankfulness, satisfaction, and most of all gratitude. Thus that phrase is uttered after a hearty meal, a lucky break, or on receiving good news. *Syukur* (gratitude) expresses a similar meaning. Idiomatically as well as expressive-wise, it is comparable to the Christian's Hallelujah!

Just to be able to wake up in the morning and say *Al hamdu* in our *fajar* prayers is gratitude enough. Think of those who could not. Life is precious! No surprise there coming from me, a physician. Al Fatihah reminds us of our good fortune and not take it for granted.

The traditional translation of *raab bil aalameen* is "Lord of the Universe." Some pedants make a fine differentiation beyond the grammatical between *raab bil* versus *raab bul*. Considering that the Al Fatihah as well as the entire Qur'an began as an oral tradition, it would take a very fine ear to distinguish between *bil* versus *bul*. Only when written could the difference be apparent. That is my way of saying that it is trivial.

The Malay word for God is *Tuhan*, only one letter longer than Tuan (master). Ever wonder why Malay leaders are Tuans – aloof and imperial if not God-like towards their subordinates? It is a deferential and almost slave-master, non-questioning relationship. There are other words to describe God and His attributes that have similar meaning as *rabb*, as with *maliki* of the beginning in the third ayat.

Tarbiyah (to nurture or develop one's full potential) has the same root as *rabb*; hence Tarbiyah Schools. Taken in this context, *rabb* has less the meaning of a lord as in a lord-servant relationship, more a nurturer, as with the earlier womb imagery of *rahman* and *raheem*, or a teacher and her pupils. I prefer this to the controlling and submissiveness implied by the appellation "Lord."

More relevant is the phrase *aalameen*. The Malay word *alam* or universe derives from this; hence the accepted translation of Lord of the Universe. *Alam* also has the same root as *ilm*, knowledge; hence the Malay word *ilmu*. Thus that phrase could be more appropriately translated as "God who has equipped us with the tools to gain knowledge." This ayat (sentence) implores us to use all our God-given senses and faculties including *akal* (intellect) to gain knowledge, and then use it to benefit us and our fellow humans. Scientists peering into outer space or biologists exploring the inner secrets of viruses are exercising the full meaning of *aalameen*.

Ancient Muslims interpreted that ayat thus; hence the flowering of knowledge during the first few centuries of Islam. They were not at all perturbed or shied away from learning from the atheistic Greeks or hedonistic Romans. To those ancient Muslims, knowledge is knowledge; it ultimately results from Allah regardless whom He chooses as His intermediary on earth.

Back to *alam* and its root *ilm* (knowledge), when Muslims expound on a religious or any topic, they would always end with the humble expression *Allah hu alam*, only Allah knows best (or have full knowledge or true interpretation of that). Implied is that their interpretations or conclusions are but tentative, until someone else could give a more meaningful one. That makes the certitudes of Malaysian ulama that much more jarring if not "un-Islamic!"

Muslims today are obsessed with the "Islamization of Knowledge" fad to the extent that we refuse to learn from or even acknowledge the contributions of the West because of its presumed secularism and thus Godlessness. We delude ourselves with our arrogant assumption that there is a uniquely Islamic version of knowledge, wisdom, and reality.

Knowledge ultimately emanates from Him. That He chose to dispense the insight on the concept zero to a Hindu, the secret of gravity to an Englishman, or the structure of the polio virus to a Jew is not for us to question but to learn, use, and add to that wisdom.

Of the 99 attributes of Allah, the two, *ar rahman* and *ar raheem* are often paired, as with the opening of all surahs, except for Surah 9. As Muhammad Shahrour wrote in his *The Qur'an, Morality and Critical Reason*, Allah does not need to display His literary prowess or rich vocabulary. As such there must be significant differences between *rahman* and *raheem* for Him to pair them. Some interpret *rahman* as a noun, an attribute, while *raheem*, actions. Others would have the former apply to all His creations while *raheem* only to believers. That interpretation however would not square with His attribute of justness.

Ar-rahman also always precedes *ar raheem* and never *ar-raheem ar-rahman*. The beginning and end of a sentence are the two pivotal positions; the middle, less so. The first is for emphasis; the end is what we remember last or most. Does that imply *ar raheem* merit a higher status than *ar rahman*? That cannot be. *Ar rahman* seems more important as reflected by the fact that an entire surah (55) is known by that name. *Ar raheem* does not merit that singular honor.

One explanation would have *ar rahman* connoting immediacy and spontaneity while *ar raheem*, deliberate and permanent. However, that still does not explain why *ar rahman* always precedes *ar raheem*, implying the precedence or relative emphasis one has over the other. Why not other pairings of Allah's attributes, as with Al Adil (The Just One) and Al Ahad (The One), or Al Badi (The Incomparable) and Al Baaqi? (The Everlasting)? Both pairs have comparable arresting alliterations; the second pair in addition also rhymes.

It is tempting to conclude that the *ar rahman* and *ar raheem* sequence is only for poetic reasons, to rhyme with the rest of Surah Al Fatihah. Against that argument would be the fact that the Prophet, *s.a.w.*, was very much aware of his early detractors who dismissed him as a "mere" poet, and the Qur'an simply poetry, profound and elegant but nonetheless still poetry. To claim rhyme for that sequence of *ar rahman ar raheem* would only add to that cynicism. I have also yet to find an explanation as to why that particular pair of Allah's attributes have to be repeated so soon as in the third ayat. It cannot be for emphasis as that would imply His other attributes less important.

As is evident, despite my having uttered Bismillah ... a zillion times, I am still seeking answers as to why it is *ar rahman ar raheem*, and not the other way around, or any other pairings of Allah's 99 attributes.

Readers' Rating: *
Sampling of Readers' Responses:

"Alhamdulillah, you are one non-religionist who responds to the repeated question in the Qur'an to its readers/listeners: *A fala ta' qilun* [So will you not reason?]

"You are better in explaining all about the Divine in Al Fatihah than all the ulamaks I heard since I started schooling!"

"Thanks for the insight. Never thought of connecting Al Hamd with *Rabbanalakal-Hamdu* until you *kupas* [analyze] it this way."

Fourth of Eight Parts: Lord of The Day of Judgement
April 10, 2022

Approximately translated, the fourth ayat of Al Fatihah, *Maaliki yaumid deen*, means "Master of the Day of Judgment."

Two problems crop up with the interpretation of *maaliki* as master or king. First as alluded earlier, that imagery does not match or reinforce the gentleness and femininity of *ar rahman* and *ar raheem* implied by their root word meaning womb. King or master is always male, and brutal. Second, servants, the flipside of "Master," have no choice — obey or else. Not so with Islam. As per Surah Baqarah (2:256), again approximately translated, "There is no compulsion in our faith. The right direction is clearly distinguished from the wrong." There is freedom in Islam, both to believe as well as not to believe. As per the American scholar Abdullah An Naim, a faith coerced is no faith.

There is yet another interpretation, that is *maliki*, with the shortened ma instead of maa to mean owner, a difference without any meaning as kings were "owners" of their subjects in those days. As for *yaumid deen* (Day of Judgement), *ad deen* means faith, religion, or Islam, together with the associated rituals, prayers, and observances. Extracting from the use of the word elsewhere in the Qur'an, a much broader meaning to *ad deen* could thus be deduced, as with norms, established order, or staying within the boundaries laid by Allah in the Qur'an and all earlier scriptures.

The Day of Judgement would come to you when you breach Allah's boundaries. You do not have to wait for some faraway universal moment when we and all other mortals before and after us would be awakened up from our graves to face a mass assembly in front of Him to answer for our worldly deeds and misdeeds, *a la* the school assemblies of our youth, with God as the powerful headmaster ready to cane in public our errand fellow humans. More useful to view the Day of Judgement as a concept. We will be held accountable for and enjoy or suffer the consequences of our actions at some point in time in the future.

That interpretation resonates with me. As a student, if you are diligent your day of judgement could come as soon as at the end of the year, as reflected in your excellent test scores and with that, a coveted scholarship.

Now that would be heavenly to any student. Not to trivialize Paradise, it was for me decades ago.

Conversely, if you are promiscuous or engage in risky behaviors as with abusing drugs, then your day of judgement too could come much sooner, as with your being afflicted with debilitating if not fatal HIV and hepatitis. Likewise if you were to be corrupt, as Najib and his fellow crooks of 1MDB notoriety are now enduring.

As for one's fate on the Day of Judgement, scriptural-wise, Allah in His Beneficence would tip His hand and give some worldly hints or preview. As per the 14th Century Sufi scholar Ibn Ata Allah al-Iskandari in his *Hikam al-Attaiya* (The Book of Wisdom), "If you want to know your standing with Him, look at the state He has put you in now." (Aphorism No: 73.)

Two centuries later John Calvin echoed Ata Allah, and with that he reformed Christianity and gave rise to the famed Protestant work ethics. Western Europe was transformed into a modern capitalistic society that elevated by a quantum leap its citizens' wellbeing. Like Muslims, Calvin also believed in predestination – one's fate is "written in the book" – but he developed that concept further. That is, God in His wisdom would give signs upon those whom He would favor in the Hereafter, echoing Ata Allah. With that everyone worked very hard so as to be seen as His "elect," the chosen ones.

Same scripture, read differently. I wish Muslims today would heed Ata Allah's wisdom: Your conditions today would be a hint of your fate in the Hereafter. It is a perversity defying rational explanation that Muslims would dismiss worldly successes; "real" success to these misguided souls would be in the Hereafter. Meanwhile they endure their own hell right here on earth.

The Indian Saadhguru said it best. If you think that the other place would be so much more sublime, why not leave for it now? Allah's most precious gift to us is our life. Belittling that would not be showing *syukur* (the *al hamdu* – gratitude) to Him. The best expression of our gratitude to Allah would be to lead a life that would please Him, meaning, be of service to our community and fellow mankind, in short, be Allah's *insan soleh* (exemplary mortal).

Former Prime Minister Najib does not need to wait for his *qiamat* (Day of Judgement) as he is enduring his own hell right now with the public shame and humiliation, as well as knowing that he could spent the rest of his life in the slammer. His public bravado cannot conceal his shame and inner turmoil. His days of hell are far from over. Najib had breached Allah's womb and now suffers the fate of an aborted fetus.

The Day of Reckoning is real and could be sooner than expected, as Najib is finding out much to his (and his family's) sorrow and anguish. That should be incentive enough for us to keep on the straight path.

Readers' Rating: *
Sampling of Readers' Responses:

"Scholarship of the Al Qur'an and Surahs [is] intriguingly more palatably served by you than experienced from my first introduction/attempt at understanding/reading it."

"An altogether delightful culmination of prosaic-poetical yet elegant verbosity, though invoking the ire of the 'hierarchically conscious' … Have you considered changing your 'calling' or at least moonlighting?"

Fifth of Eight Parts: We Worship Thee Only And Thine Aid We Seek

April 14, 2022

This fourth *ayat* is commonly interpreted as: Only Thee (meaning Allah) do we worship and (only) Thine aid we seek." The first part, Muslims worship only Allah and no one else or objects, is central to our faith. There is universal agreement on that. Many however would also extend that exclusivity to the seeking of help from Allah and no one else; hence the adding of "only" before the "Thine aid we seek."

Exclusivity of worshipping Allah means that Muslims do not deify Prophet Mohammad, *s.a.w.* Nor do we worship rocks and shrines. Many look askance at the venerated ritual of *tawaf*, the circumambulating of the *kaabah* during Hajj, and the visiting of graves of prophets or shrines of venerated scholars to seek help. Islam has no tradition of saints so as to avoid this particular trap.

Does this exclusivity of worship also extend to our seeking succor and help only from Him? The Qur'an repeatedly exhorts us to be kind to and help others. That builds and enhances social bonds. If we were to interject "only" to the second part of the fourth ayat as with "only Thine aid we seek," that would negate the Qur'an's other messages.

If you are sick, you seek help from a physician. Yes, you should also pray. That however would be in addition to and not a substitute for seeking medical help. I once had a challenging case and went through with the family all the possible complications of surgery as well as the risks of not doing it, part of the informed consent protocol. Anticipating the difficulty of the surgery, I had also gone over in my mind a thousand times of all possible surprises that could confront me.

Then as we were about to wheel the patient to the Operating Room, the wife held my hand together with her husband's and said, "I know you are not a Christian Dr. Musa, but would you mind joining us in the Lord's Prayer for Jim?" I readily obliged.

"Oh God in Heaven," she prayed. "Please guide Dr. Musa and his team through the operation. Help him make the right decision and guide his healing hands as he removes the tumor from my husband. I ask this in Your name, Ameen."

I was moved by her brief, plaintive, and meditative words, as did the rest of my team. I thanked her, adding that I would have said a similar prayer. We all pray to the same God.

The surgery was successful, and my patient had a smooth recovery. What I remembered most during the procedure was how calm I was, my initial jitteriness had vanished, and everything went as planned. To me that is the real power of prayers.

When I was a surgeon at General Hospital Kuala Lumpur in the mid-1970s, I was told that the legendary Dr. Syed Alhady who had just retired a few years earlier had made it his practice to recite Al Fatihah quietly before he scrubbed. Today in America we have "surgical pause" or "time out" where every member of the surgical team would remain quiet as someone goes over the "check list," a practice adopted from the airlines' cockpit crew protocol. Today when I am in a plane during turbulence, I pray to Allah to guide the pilot so his decisions would lead to safe maneuvers. I also pray that the Good Lord would shift the storm away from our path or deflate its energy.

I once saw a picture of a pilot at a Malaysian airport praying on the tarmac in full view of his embarking passengers. I would be more assured (and so too the passengers I presume) had he been thorough with his preflight routine. I am also certain that Allah would entertain that pilot's prayer if he were to do it in the privacy of his cockpit seat. A busy, noisy and dirty tarmac is not the most conducive place for praying, or the gathering of one's thoughts.

That aside, the safety of a flight requires the diligence and competence of many, the mechanics, ground crew, and air traffic controllers, among others. A pilot needs all their help, plus God's guidance. A Turkish airline crashed in Paris because the ground crew did not secure the cargo door. A Singapore Airline jet rammed into heavy construction equipment at Taipei Airport because the ground construction crew did not post adequate signs. Malaysia Airline Flight 370 disappeared into thin air because military air traffic controllers in Northern Malaysia preferred their sleep and ignored the strange blips that intruded on their radar screens deep in that fateful night of March 8, 2014.

While we worship only Allah, we need and must seek help from others. The Qur'an reminds us that we need our families, friends, and neighbors. As a professional, I need and seek help from my support staff.

Za'aba, the "Father of Malay Grammar" and an acknowledged religious scholar in his own right, ridiculed the hallowed Malay ritual of *zikir* (collective recitations of the Qur'an at funerals and special prayers) as begging. We beg for handouts from the government while we are alive, and we beg for prayers from others when we are dead, he wrote in his widely quoted *Perangai Bergantung Pada Diri Sendiri* (The Habit of Depending on Oneself).

There is a fine but discernible difference between praying versus begging. To Za'aba, much of Muslim praying is but begging. As Muslims we pray only to Allah as this ayat of Al Fatihah asserts, but we must also seek help from others. Most of all we must put in our best effort.

Readers' Rating: *
Sampling of Readers' Responses: None

Sixth of Eight Parts: Guide Us Along The Straight Path
April 14, 2022

"Guide us along the straight path," exhorts Al Fatihah's fifth ayat. In geometry, a straight line is the shortest distance between two points. As life's many lessons have taught and continue to teach us, the shortest path is often not the best or even quickest. Thus we cannot take that literal meaning of the Qur'anic straight path.

This ayat is the core of Al Fatihah. One interpretation would have the "straight path" be one of moderation, of not swaying to or be distracted by either side. The imagery often used is a path lined on either side with hidden alleyways, with *syaitan* (Satan) enticing you to enter one of them and be distracted. That at least implies some effort or willful decision on one's part to stray. As per our physics lessons, momentum alone would have us maintain our straight path. Keeping on a straight line is our natural tendency, our *fitra*. As in physics, it takes force to alter our velocity (direction and or speed).

Life is far from a smooth passive and steady flow downstream that would carry us at our leisure to our destination. Instead it requires constant conscious effort on our part to go upstream where the water is pure and cool. Anything less and we would end up stuck in the muddy delta and be flooded by the effluents of those upstream. That imagery reflects reality better.

Another would have the straight path be not breaching the boundaries on either side, as per our prophet's counsel: In everything, moderation; the striving for balance, echoing Aristotle's "golden mean." Consider courage, one of Aristotle's twelve virtues. Too much of it and you become reckless, endangering yourself and others; too little and you would subject yourself to be preyed upon. The straight path would be Goldilocks's baby bear's porridge of being just right, not too hot or cold.

Counterbalance that to Barry Goldwater's (the 1964 US Presidential candidate thrashed by Lyndon Johnson) infamous "Extremism in the defense of liberty is no vice; moderation in the pursuit of justice, no virtue." A direct assault on Aristotle's golden mean. Intellectual comparisons of the two aside, there are other issues with Goldwater's brash assertion. Little purpose in pursuing that.

The two Qur'anic extremes could refer to pursuits in this temporal world versus the Hereafter. Allah would not like us to be praying all the time or endlessly praising Him. He does not need our praises. Instead as per the Qur'an, He wants us to go out into the world and do good. Maintain the straight path and the destination will take care of itself.

I find Muslims' obsession, heightened during Ramadan, with the garnering of religious "brownie points" to be cashed in at the Pearly Gates distracting if not counterproductive. Do "good" on a certain night and that would be as if you had done it for a thousand nights. That sounds so, well, accountant-like. It trivializes the scripture. Besides, why only during Ramadan? Ill fortune could strike your fellow beings at any time, requiring you to dispense help to them.

As for limits, the word Qur'an shares the same root as *qariah*, boundary, as with the *qariah* of a masjid, the district served by it. Limits and boundaries bring forth the imagery of *raheem* (womb) mentioned earlier. While the Qur'an glorifies freedom, it does impose limits. Your freedom stops when it intrudes on mine, a harsh reality demonstrated during this Covid-19 pandemic. Your personal choice not to wear a mask stops when you threaten my health. To quote the American jurist Oliver Wendell Holmes, freedom of speech does not extend to shouting "Fire!" in a crowded theater, unless of course there is a fire. Freedom without boundaries is anarchy.

Muhammad Shahrour in his *The Qur'an, Morality and Critical Reason* introduces the concepts of limits. To his interpretation, Allah through the Qur'an sets only the extreme limits, and it is for the community collectively to decide where within that broad range to draw the line. To Shahrour, the Qur'anic cutting of the hand as punishment for thievery is the extreme limit; it does not mean that it should be the punishment for thievery. To Shahrour it would be more important and beneficial to society if we were to "cut off" or remove thieves from society, as with incarcerating them.

Yet another interpretation would have that fourth ayat mean not a straight path but an uphill one. That implies some effort, akin to going upstream in a river. Unless you maintain your effort, gravity would pull you down, gravity being the metaphor for life's constant, universal temptations and distractions.

Yet another interpretation emphasizes the *suratul*, taking its root word in *sirat* and *sarata*, meaning to swallow and be part of something bigger, as the tiny rain drop falling to the ocean and being made part of or swallowed by it. The ocean is a common metaphor to describe Allah's powers. Imam Ghazzali used it frequently in his encyclopedic contributions. Just as the power, secrets, and benevolence of the ocean are infinitely manifested at its shores, waves, and deep under, so too Allah's. "Guide us along the straight path" is rightly considered the pearl of the Qur'an, with us pleading to Allah to make us, a tiny drop of humanity, be part of His vast rich ocean.

Mustaqeen is translated as to arise, to actualize one's potential, as a seed would with soil, water, sunlight, and other nurturing elements grow into a vigorous plant, blossoming with beautiful flowers and producing bountiful fruits to benefit the community. Meaning, strive for constant improvement and self-corrections to reach our goal as a productive human being capable of contributing to society, as Allah wants us to be. That is the straight path. As for pleasing God, He is in no need of our praises. Instead, follow His dictates to make us better human beings. Now that is a worthy pursuit.

Some differentiate between those who have the knowledge and despite that still pursue other than the straight path, versus those who choose it because "they know not what they are doing." A heavier burden falls on the former. Operationally however, the consequences would be the same. Likewise the differences on quantity (magnitude) versus quality (nature). As per Surah Al Ma'ida (5:32), whoever kills a person ... it shall be as if he has killed all mankind. Surah An Najm's (53:32) differentiation between major and minor sins notwithstanding, the consequences are far more important than the act itself. Running a red light or being drunk may be a minor sin (a misdemeanor if you like) but not if through it you cause an accidental death of an innocent bystander.

As per the wisdom of Ata Allah al-Iskandari in his *Hikam al-Attaiya*, "Your obedience does not benefit Him and your disobedience does not harm Him. He has only ordered you to do this and prohibited you from doing that for your own gain." (Aphorism No: 211)

Readers Rating: *
Sampling of Readers' Responses: None

Seventh of Eight Parts: Those Whom Allah Favors
April 17, 2022

Guide us along the path of those whom You have favored, we pray to Allah as we recite the sixth *ayat* of Al Fatihah. As Allah does not let us know whom He favors, this and the last *ayat* ("Not those who have incurred Your wrath") serve more as a Rorschach test of sorts. That notwithstanding, the Qur'an does hint of certain individuals whom He would favor.

For Muslims, topping that list would be Prophet Muhammad, *s.a.w.*, together with all earlier prophets. Sunni Muslims would also include the four Rightly Guided Caliphs: Abu Bakar, Omar, Uthman, and Ali, the last being the Prophet's cousin and son-in-law. Shiite Muslims have a more exclusive list; they have much less favorable views (putting it mildly) of Abu Bakar, Omar, and Uthman.

Next those Heaven-bound as per the Qur'an would be the *shayids* (martyrs), those who died in Allah's cause. That word today has a radically different meaning, thanks to 9-11, the Talibans, and other Islamic extremists. As is evident, whom society deems worthy of being *syahid* reflects more on it than on the individual.

Beyond that, characterizations of those whom Allah favors come from hadith, sayings attributed to Prophet Muhammad, *s.a.w.* One has it that a prostitute was admitted to Paradise because she once brought water to a dog dying of thirst; likewise a man for picking up a thorn on a path thus preventing others from injuring themselves. In terms of professions held in high esteem by Allah, we can assume that the lady's would not even be on His list. As for dogs, they are not the favorite animals of Muslims. Yet Allah in His wisdom deemed her worthy of that exalted place for her single good deed to a dog.

Imagine then the rewards awaiting veterinarians! Yet Malays were in an uproar over pictures of veterinary students petting their dog-patients.

As for the man who removed the thorn, if that were to be the reward for such a simple good deed, how much greater would it be for the engineer who built the road or bridge so villagers could bring their produce to market or their sick ones to the hospital in town?

That of course assumes the bridge to be safe. If through corruption or negligence the bridge were to collapse in the first rainstorm, then it would be but a dangerous trap, an attractive nuisance, in the language of American tort lawyers. Its builders would then be criminally liable.

Another group of *syahids*, relevant today, would be victims of pandemics. Funeral rites could be dispensed for them as those would be redundant; they already have reserved slots in Heaven. That makes good public health sense for among the major factors spreading a pandemic would be contagion through funeral rites. China controlled its devastating Manchurian plague of 1910-11 when the emperor decreed that all bodies be burned in mass graves. Traditional Chinese funeral rites are even more elaborate than Muslim ones, perfect portal for spreading lethal communicable diseases. Heed the prophet's message. When there is a plague, do not go there; if you are already there, do not leave – the essence of quarantine.

As for prophets and their reserved slots in Heaven, was that because of their prophethood or great deeds? Prophet Muhammad, *s.a.w.*, emancipated the ancient Bedouins, making them give up their tribalism, spousal abuses, eye-for-an-eye sense of justice, and their odious practice of female infanticide. Would leaders who perform comparable good deeds deserve similar rewards even if they had not been specially dispensed with Allah's prophethood? Or the reverse, someone selected as a prophet but failed to live up to God's high expectations. Prophet Muhammad, *s.a.w.*, expressed his own lack of confidence in executing Allah's command when given his first revelation in the cave near Mecca.

China's Deng Xiaoping, a communist and thus an atheist, uplifted hundreds of millions of Chinese out of poverty within a generation or two, a feat unmatched in history. The closest would be medieval Western Europe with the introduction of capitalism. That took centuries and impacted a much smaller fraction of the then global population. With his monumental accomplishment, would Deng merit a slot in Heaven? If he did not because of his presumed Godlessness, at least hundreds of millions of Chinese today enjoy their heaven on earth, compared to the hell their parents and grandparents endured during Mao's disastrous Cultural Revolution, or under earlier Emperors with their "Mandate from Heaven."

Along the same line, would the developers of polio vaccines deserve to be in Heaven, or is it only for Muslims?

I once posed this question in a religious class. I went further and asked the students to name individuals whom they know personally who should be in Heaven. I was touched by their responses. One offered his favorite teacher, another our Imam Ilyas Anwar, and a third, her mother. When her classmates dismissed her choice, belittling her mother's efforts as being obligatory maternal duty, she defended it by saying that her mother did it well and with love, in contrast (presumably) to the burgher flippers who do it as a job.

To me it would not be Heaven without the likes of such luminaries as Sudirman, P. Ramlee, and Saloma there. They had brought joy to and uplifted the hearts of millions with their melodious voices. As for the promised 72 virgins that would await me should I end up there, what would be the comparable rewards awaiting my loving wife? After all it would not be Heaven for me if I were to be deprived of her company. Such are the difficulties when we confuse imageries and metaphors with concepts and ideas.

Readers' Rating: *
Sampling of Readers' Responses:
"Indeed, Heaven would not be complete without the likes of P. Ramlee, Saloma, and Sudirman!"

Last of Eight Parts: Those Who Have Incurred His Wrath
April 21, 2022

Al Fatihah's last ayat exhorts us to avoid the path of those who have earned His wrath. That may be obvious but remember even demons like Pol Pot had their admirers and wannabes. Prime Minister Najib Razak stole billions from the rakyat. Despite that, he still has many loyal, exuberant *"Malu Apa Boss Ku"* (What's there to be ashamed of my boss?) followers and supporters.

I make no apologies for mentioning Najib in the same paragraph with Pol Pot. The difference between him and that Cambodian cretin is one of magnitude, not kind. The gruesome killing of the innocent Bahraini banker and Mongolian model may not be on the same scale as Pol Pot's genocide, but then think of the thousands of Malaysians who succumbed to Covid-19. Had the billions not been siphoned from 1MDB, and Malaysia not been burdened by its subsequent humongous debt, the nation would have had more than ample funds to secure an adequate supply of Covid-19 vaccines early on. As for the banker and model victims, the Qur'an reminds us (5:32) that if you kill one person, it is as if you have killed all mankind.

Leaders have an extra special and heavy burden. They must go beyond doing good; they must also prevent evil. Najib failed at both. Worse, he perverted the pristine values of our faith, as with his financing Hajj pilgrimages from his pilfered funds. He mocked the sanctity of our hallowed rituals with his cynical attempt at "sanitizing" his loot, thus degrading our faith.

Najib hoodwinked Malaysians by claiming that the billions secretly deposited into his account were but gifts from a Saudi prince. Najib exploited the religious sentiments of Malays and Muslims. To us, anything from the land of the Arabs is halal, *rezki* (bounty) from Heaven. Even Meccan flies are halal!

It may be harsh to condemn Najib during Ramadan, a season to be forgiving. However, he has yet to admit his wrongdoings. On the contrary, to Najib he did something exemplary, worthy of praise, not censure. Najib should be condemned lest he be emulated by others. When society honors its corrupt, then it has a very serious problem. The most obscene picture this Ramadan was of Najib Razak, a convicted criminal, being invited to the palace for *iftar*. That speaks volumes not of Najib but the man who invited him, the Agung.

More offensive, however difficult that would be to imagine, Najib posted that picture, as well as one of him with the Agung, both gleefully grinning, on social media. The only thing more jarring at that royal *iftar* would be if the Chief Justice were also to be there, what with Najib's final appeal coming up.

Back to Al Fatihah, if that surah is the essence of the Qur'an, could there be a comparable *ayat* that is the Qur'an's kernel? That question was posed to Malaysian undergraduates at a meeting organized by the UMNO Club of New York and New Jersey in 2011 where I was part of the invited panelists. The students' responses touched and taught me much about our Glorious Qur'an.

One student recalled his *fajar* (dawn) prayer at the Grand Canyon National Park late one summer. Engulfed in the cool, high desert morning air, he could just glimpse the northern rim through the soft ray of the emerging sunshine. Deep below was the shimmering ribbon of water flowing at its leisure, guarded by sheer magnificent cliffs on both sides. Those contain many secrets of the past, while the river supports the multitude of life forms all the way to the Gulf of California. Above, the vast expanse of the cloudless sky with no pillars supporting it. It was as if Allah had revealed to this student "All His Splendor," as per Surah Al Qaf (50:6 – Letter Qaf)).

Visitors to the Grand Canyon cannot but be struck by the spirituality of the place. Even if one were not religious, one would be constrained from blemishing it. To scratch graffiti or litter with your plastic bottles would be blasphemous. Indeed to Native Americans, the Grand Canyon is sacred; it also should be to every visitor.

Another student recalled her experience at a New York City event. She was struck by the diversity of the attendees, their stark differences in skin color, facial features, languages spoken, and of course their food and attire. It brought to life for her Surah Al Hujurat (49:13) where Allah said that He could have made us all of one tribe but chose not to so we could learn from each other.

Yet another recalled her classmate's ordeal fleeing her native land. What made that classmate endure it all was recalling the Prophet's own migration to Medinah. While she was hounded by other than her own kind, and thus understandable though still not excusable, the Prophet, *s.a.w.*, fled from his kin and fellow tribesmen. The pain must have been exponentially more unbearable. She found comfort in Surah An Nisa (4:97) that admonished those who partake in sin in their homeland using the excuse of local conditions. Is Allah's earth not vast enough for one to escape (migrate), that ayat rhetorically asked.

That exercise prompted me to ponder the Qur'anic ayat most meaningful to me. Earlier I discussed Surah Al Fatihah's fifth ayat, "Keep us along the straight path." Parallel to and carrying the same pristine principle would be:

$$\text{الأمر بالمَعْرُوف والنَهي عن المُنْكَر}$$

(al-amr bi-l-ma'rūf; wa-n-nahy 'ani-l-munkar)

Command good; forbid evil. Stunning in its brevity, clarity, and verity. That phrase is repeated in a few other places. To me that is the Qur'an's essence, its golden rule; the rest are but commentaries. The Qur'an gives many ready examples of "doing good" (be kind to orphans and wayfarers) as well of the meaning of evil (killing, adultery, etc.). If you rob, kill, or destroy then it matters not how many times you pray or go for Hajj. If you build your community, keep your rivers clean, and nurture the environment, then whether you don a hijab or how exhilarating your zikir is trivial by comparison.

As for contemporary discussions on Surah Al Fatihah, I find the arrogant certitude of some preachers intolerable. They remind me of the all-knowing imperious physicians of yore, their utterances and prescriptions unchallenged. They were, well, God-like. As a physician I am glad not to be of that generation or persuasion.

We also trivialize this great surah if we were to reduce it to a Genie-in-a-bottle. Rub or recite it, and miracles would magically happen. Likewise, we would not be expressing our *syukor*, the *al hamdu* of the beginning of Al Fatihah, if we dismiss Allah's most precious gift to us — our life and this wonderful world — as being but a mere mirage and that our "real" existence and universe await us in the Hereafter.

The American Islamic scholar Ebraheem Moosa, then at Stanford, summed it best for me during a talk he gave to our small Muslim community here in Morgan Hill one Ramadan many years ago. The day you think you have fully understood the Qur'an is the day you die. Ameen to that!

Readers' Rating: *

Sampling of Readers' Responses:

"There are no innocent bystanders. When you don't fight the wrongs because you're afraid your *rezeki* (bounty) may be affected, then you're not innocent."

"Indeed a refreshing tafsir of *ummul kitab* (mother of all books) thanks!"

"Wow! 'Qur'an's kernel.' Thanks for this!"

An Eid ul Fitri To Remember!

May 9, 2021

[Eid ul Fitri is the Muslim celebration to mark the end of the fasting month of Ramadan. It is a joyous time for family and friends. Each has special and treasured memories to savor. Last year because of the Covid-19 pandemic we had to dispense with our usual communal gathering.]

This Thursday, May 13, 2021, *Insha' Allah* (God willing!) our small Muslim community at the southern tip of Silicon Valley, California, will celebrate our Eid ul Fitri. It will be extra special for many reasons!

This year we will once again be able to celebrate as a congregation, a precious joy denied us last year because of the Covid-19 pandemic. Now thanks to the enlightened leadership of our Governor Newsome, together with the collective prudence of our greater community to follow sensible public health guidelines, plus the brilliance of our scientists and their vaccines, we have "flattened the curve." With the predictable warm California spring sunshine, we will pray on the lawn of our beautiful community center. We will of course still maintain social distancing and don our face masks. That will complement our festive attire.

Unlike many Muslim communities elsewhere today and in the past, we announced our Eid day based on calculations, dispensing with the traditional proviso, "conditioned on sighting the new moon." Besides, by

May 13 we would have fasted for 30 days. By our lunar calendar, no month exceeds 30 days.

We opted for the scientific route less on reviewing the treatises of yore, more for practicality. In the beginning we too had, as per tradition elsewhere, to rent a facility for two consecutive days, just in case the new moon would not be sighted at the predicted time. We decided very early on that the extra rental costs could be better spent on the needy. Allah would not look kindly upon us wasting precious funds on empty halls. Hence the rationale for going by the reliably predictable "secular" calendar.

Hari Raya, as we Malays call Eid ul Fitra, brings forth many memories. Most are, as expected, warm and pleasant, a joy to recall and share. Few less so and would bring only tears and regrets.

Growing up in a kampung in Kuala Pilah, Negri Sembilan, I remember well my parents and grandparents recalling their past Hari Raya "celebrations" during the desperate era of the Great Depression and the horrific years of the Japanese Occupation. In their retelling there was never a hint of anger or regret, only gratitude to have been able to celebrate however modest with friends, family, and community despite the austere times and trying circumstances.

Now it is my turn to tell my children and grandchildren of my past Hari Rayas. Three come to mind right away. First was last year when, unprecedented, we had to dispense with our traditional communal gathering. Our Imam Ilyas Anwar could hardly hold back his tears when he delivered his Eid 'sermon' virtually. Bless him, he paid tributes to the engineers, scientists, and entrepreneurs who made possible the Zooms and Facebooks so we could remain connected albeit only virtually during this pandemic.

I saw similar touching scenes in our Intensive Care Units where nurses would hold their cellphones to desperately ill Covid-19 patients so they could in their final moments 'see' and bid their loved ones goodbye. Those wonderful media platforms also let me have my own Raya "gathering" with my extended family.

Second was Hari Raya of 1997 when my family and I were visiting Malaysia. Like Muslims, the Chinese and Jews follow the lunar movements for their calendar. That year Hari Raya and Chinese New Year occurred on the same day. The government rightly seized on that fortuitous once in a thirty-three-year occasion to remind citizens of the virtues of embracing tolerance and cultivating harmony. Businesses too joined in with their uplifting commercials celebrating the two joyous occasions. Petronas in particular carried memorable catchy jingles and endearing images of inclusiveness in their advertising.

Those wholesome messages notwithstanding, there was nothing warm or uplifting in the Hari Raya sermon I heard that morning at the International Islamic University Mosque in Petaling Jaya. The Imam venomously lashed out at those who dared elevate non-Islamic festivities to the exalted status of Hari Raya, a direct assault on the government's noble intentions.

I have low tolerance for long soporific sermons, but the ferocity of the Imam's fulminations kept me awake. "During our *Raya* we go to mosques," he bellowed, "while they go to casinos!" Words like heathens and blasphemy as well as "Hell!" and fiery fires spouted forth freely from his frothing mouth like an angry rabid dog, irreverently incongruous in a place of worship and during a traditionally forgiving season.

Later that afternoon at my brother-in-law Ariffin's "Open House," before we enjoyed the cornucopia of delicious offerings, this young imam gave an invocation, first in Arabic and then English. Afterwards a non-Muslim guest whispered to me how touched he was with the *du'a*. That was a much-needed antidote for me, what with the earlier outpouring of poison I had to endure at the mosque.

My third Raya that I remember for all the wrong reasons, was in 1976. I had just started my job in Kuala Lumpur (KL). After being away for almost a decade and a half I was anticipating very much the Hari Raya that year. My father had also reminded me that all my siblings and their spouses as well as their children would be present. There may not be another similar opportunity, my mother chimed in.

After arranging for appropriate coverage, I left for my parents' house in Seremban. The next day after returning from Raya prayers at the nearby mosque, I received a desperate long-distance call. My medical officer could not get hold of my covering consultant, and one of my patients had gone sour.

"You can't leave," my mother pleaded, "your brothers and sisters are not here yet!"

I had to. Thanks to the deserted highway and streets I made it in time. Later that day and the next, what with my having to stay near the hospital, and with every Malay "*balik kampung*," (returning to the village) I managed a leisurely delightful tour of the city.

My mother was right. There would never be another Hari Raya when we all could be together again. My precious lesson? Enjoy the moment while you can!

On this extra special Hari Raya, I send the traditional Malay greetings, "*Ma'af, Zahir, dan Batin*!" (I seek forgiveness and express my gratitude in all sincerity.)

Readers' Rating: * * *
Readers' Comments:

"As usual, imparting the simple and true divine message for all."

"Unfortunately, our idiotic government that did not know what to do in fighting Covid-19 and makes us revisit 2020 Eid ul Fitri."

The Special Blessings of *Lailatul Qadar*

May 2, 2021

[The month of Ramadan, with its obligatory daytime fasting, brings forth heightened spirituality among Muslims. Tradition has it that the Qur'an was first revealed to Prophet Muhammad, *s.a.w.*, on one of those odd nights during the last ten, the 27th being most favored.]

On Sunday evening May 2nd, 2021, Muslims entered our last ten days of fasting for the month of Ramadan. It is said that the first ten are for seeking Allah's Mercy; the second, His Forgiveness; and the third, refuge from Hellfire.

Muslims also believe that one of those odd nights of the last ten days to be especially blessed. Dubbed *lailatul qadar* (the Night of Power), one's worship on that blessed night would be amplified by an All-Generous Allah as if we had been performing it "for a thousand months!" Hence the frenzied spiritual activities during those last ten days.

Legend has it that a particular clan was successful because its patriarch once saw a patch of ice upon returning from his *taraweeh* (special Ramadan prayer) at the mosque. That ice patch symbolized Allah's *borkat* (bounty) as well as miracles. Imagine ice in the desert, or tropical Malaysia! Truly a miracle!

It was during one of those nights over 14 centuries ago that Prophet Muhammad (May Peace Be Upon Him!) received his divine revelation high in the cave of Mount Hira. From that came the Qur'an, a "guide for all mankind at all times and till the end of time."

In his sermon last Friday, April 30, 2021, our Imam Ilyas Anwar asked us to reflect on the state of the Bedouins at the time of the prophet. Blighted by a multitude of ills, the list was long, from gruesome female infanticide to rampant vicious tribalism, and from indentured servitude to outright slavery. The obscene inequities between the poor and the privileged would offend anyone's sensibilities, except that they did not. The Prophet's solitude in that cave was to seek answers for this social aberration – his people's unconcerned acceptance if not willing embrace of this state of *jahiliyyah* (ignorance).

The result? The Holy Qur'an, the revelations from Allah to Prophet Muhammad (May Allah bless his soul). That transformed the Arabs. Today it guides a quarter of the global population.

Prophet Muhammad was Allah's Last Messenger, the last mortal God talked to. In our post-prophetic era, we can thus no longer climb the mountain tops or go into prolonged seclusions to seek guidance from God. We seek it in the Qur'an, using the unique faculty Allah has endowed upon each of us – our *akal* (intellect).

Ancient Muslims used their *akal* to unravel many of nature's mysteries, from the movements of celestial bodies to the inner workings of ours. They were pious ulama as well as observant scientists. They did not have the arrogance to classify knowledge into secular versus religious, or Islamic versus non-Islamic. That particular *bida'ah* (adulteration of our faith) would come much later. Those ulama of yore accepted that all knowledge is from God. We are to seek that knowledge, share it, and use it to benefit humanity.

Contrary to the fulminations of many, I see no contradiction between faith and reason. Each complements the other. An unexamined belief is not worth having, and blind faith is no faith. When scientists explore the world within and beyond, it is their belief that there is something worthy to be discovered, whether that search is for life in outer space or the inner secrets of the Covid-19 virus.

Malaysia today differs only in degree from the Prophet's Age of Jahiliyyah. Corruption is endemic, its loots viewed as *rezki* (blessings), and the corrupt honored. Gross inequities are deemed to be the natural order. Meanwhile Covid-19 ravages on.

During this *lailatul qadar* I implore Malay leaders to reflect on the sorry state of the nation and be inspired by our Holy Prophet to do the right thing. Go beyond the rituals of Ramadan. That would indeed be a blessing for all Malaysians.

Some view Allah's special bounty during *lailatul qadar* as the supremacy of predestination over freewill. Indeed *qadar* means just that — fate. As with *akal* (reason) and *iman* (faith), fate and freewill complement, not contradict each other. We live in a world of probabilities. Even electrons circling the nucleus of our atoms are expressed in probabilities. One's freewill or conscious decision not to text or drink while driving would ensure a high probability but not a guarantee of a safe journey. If a drunk driver were to come into one's lane or a boulder crashed down the hillslope, that's fate!

Reinhold Niebuhr's serenity prayer best reconciles fate and freewill. "God, give us the grace to accept with serenity the things that cannot be changed, courage to change the things that should be changed, and the wisdom to distinguish the one from the other."

During this *lailatul qadar* let us reflect, as our Prophet did on the state of his community over 1400 years ago, on the challenges facing ours. If that is too daunting, then limit it to the social unit we lead, as with our family. If that is still overwhelming, then focus on our individual challenges so we could become a better person. Make "The Night of

Power" be the stimulus for serious introspection, one worthy of the effort of "a thousand months."

Early in my career I was called to the Emergency Room (ER) deep in the night during one Ramadan. Having your sleep interrupted, especially after a day of fasting, has a way of putting you in a foul mood, more so if you expect the case to be what we politely refer to as "uncompensated care." I must have made quite a ruckus in preparing to leave for the hospital, enough to wake up my wife. Upon finding out the cause of my frustration, she got up to hug me.

"Bakri, this is Ramadan!" she soothed me. "A blessed month," she continued to plead with me, "a time to be generous, of ourselves and of our time as well as talent."

Those words calmed me. From then on I learned to take my ER calls in stride, treating them as my commitment and contribution to my community that had been so generous to me and my family. Yes, I missed more than a few significant events in my family's life, as with being late or absent at my children's birthdays and school plays. Nonetheless that revelation from my dear wife many Ramadans ago helped me achieve my personal *ikigai*, the Japanese philosophy on the meaning of life. I love what I do and I am competent at it, while society needs my service and I am well compensated for doing it. *Alham dulillah*! (Praise be to Allah!)

Readers' Rating: * * *
Sampling of Readers' Responses:

"The last ten days of Ramadan are our last chance to reflect and seek forgiveness from Allah. Sadly, our politicians are not at all concerned. Corruption and politicking remain the core activity amongst some of them."

"If only our leaders are as wise as your wife .., we could do better with her wisdom. Bless her, you, and your family!"

"One of the best reflections on life, faith, and knowledge!"

"Even your duty as a doctor is *ibadah* [worship or service to God] too!"

"A refreshing read! A bit different from the usual 'waiting for the moment when the angel would appear to grant all of one's wishes' on that night."

"*Takde sebut pun dalam Qur'an. Lailatul Qadar ini cerita Arab kuno!*" [Not even mentioned in the Qur'an. *Lailatul Qadar* is but an ancient Arab lore!"

Reflections On *Awal Muharram*

Review of Muhammad Shahrour's *The Qur'an, Morality and Critical Reason. The Essential Muhammad Shahrour.* Translated and Edited by Andreas Christmann. K Brill, Leidin, 637 pp, 2009. ISBN 9004171039

August 23, 2020

Last Thursday August 20, 2020, after sunset, Muslims ushered in our New Year. Awal Muharram (the first of Muharram) symbolizes peace and reflection. Reflection because 1441 years ago our Prophet Muhammad, *s.a.w.*, undertook his *hijrah* (migration) to Medinah to escape his persecutors in Mecca. So momentous was the event that the Companion of the Prophet, Omar, later decided to begin the Muslim calendar from that date.

As for peace, there was nothing peaceful about that epochal journey. The prophet escaped an assassination attempt by having his nephew Ali sleep in his bed that night. Legend has it that Allah made the prophet invisible to his pursuers. Invisible perhaps, but not weightless for the prophet had prudently scattered dirt to cover his tracks!

Like then, peace still eludes much of the ummah today. The majority are trapped in dehumanizing poverty, appalling injustices, and brutal autocracies. In the latest "Islamicity Index," not one Muslim country made it in the top thirty.

Volumes have been written to explain this sorry state. Some pine for Islam's own Martin Luther. Conveniently forgotten is that during its few centuries the Islamic civilization was the beacon for the world. What went wrong?

This was the question that intrigued one Arab engineer, Muhammad Shahrour. His epiphany came early. He remembered as a youngster hearing a sermon in his local mosque right after Syria was humiliated in the Six-Day War with Israel. "We have strayed far from the ways of Allah," his Imam bellowed. "We do not fast, and our women have discarded their hijabs," he excoriated his flock.

Israeli women wore bikinis, yet their armies prevailed, Shahrour reflected. That prompted his lifelong self-study of the Qur'an. No easy task for a man who was a professional engineer (Dublin PhD) with a thriving consultancy, quite apart from his academic duties.

Shahrour dispensed with those voluminous ancient treatises. Those are what produced today's ulama and scholars like his Imam, he reasoned. To his scientific mind that would be akin to reading Freud and Jung when the world is into neurotransmitters and dynamic brain imaging.

Shahrour began his commentaries on matters religious in the 1990s, and until his death last year he had published over a dozen books and countless essays. He had also been interviewed numerous times. Though ignored by the establishment (lucky; he could have been branded an apostate and dealt with accordingly), he was (and still is) a phenomenon among literate Arabs. *The Qur'an, Morality and Critical Reason: The Essential Muhammad Shahrour*, a translation, is his only book in English.

To Shahrour – and all Muslims – the Qur'an is Allah's words, "for all mankind at all times and till the end of time." It explains itself, *a la* Christianity's *sola scriptura*. Shahrour was advantaged and emboldened to re-read the Qur'an as Arabic was his mother tongue.

He began with the concept of non-synonymity. Allah is precise in his choice of words. Thus Al Kitab (The Book) and Al Qur'an must not mean the same thing. When Allah used both in the same *ayat* (sentence), it is not for reasons of style. They have separate distinct meanings; it is for us to discern them. To Shahrour, the Qur'an as we know it consists of two parts. One, the early Meccan verses expressing universal values and aspirations. He called that the Al Kitab (The Book). That contains the same revelations dispensed to earlier prophets like Jesus and Moses. They are but variations on the theme of the Ten Commandments.

Two is the Al Qur'an, which adds to the confusion. It comprises the Medinan *ayats* revealed as the Prophet was establishing the first Muslim community. Those dealt with the practical realities of governance more so in a plural society of 7th Century Arabia. By necessity those revelations have to be in forms and language comprehensible to and executable by his constituents. Our error, now and in the past, is in reducing the Prophet of Allah to a divine fax machine, mechanically and mindlessly spouting out His message.

To make the Qur'an relevant to contemporary society, Shahrour would have us read and interpret it as if it were revealed yesterday. Only then could it be as transformative to us as it was for those ancient Bedouins. I use this example. Consider that had Allah chosen His Last Messenger to be an Eskimo, would the Qur'an's imagery of Hell be one of blazing eternal fire or a dark frozen dungeon?

The late Fazlur Rahman had a comparable approach to the Qur'an. That is, deduce from its particularities the underlying governing principles (connect the dots as it were), and then apply or extrapolate them to current challenges. Both demand considerable intellectual exertions. Endlessly quoting the Qur'an, no matter how exquisite the *tajweed*, would not do it.

There are many apparent contradictions in the Qur'an. The Meccan verses assert there be no compulsion in religion; the Medinah, kill the apostates. Ancient scholars applied the concept of abrogation to reconcile those differences, whereby later verses "abrogate" earlier ones.

Shahrour rejected that. Allah is Perfect and All-Knowing. He does not need revisions, editing, or abrogating of His words. Instead, the Medinah verses reflected the specific challenges facing the early Muslims as they struggled to deal with their enemies who were intent on destroying this new movement that was challenging the existing order. Those Medinah verses are thus the exceptions to the central message of Al Kitab; the exceptions proving the general rule.

To Shahrour, the Qur'an cannot contradict what we know from our senses and rational thinking. If our observations show that the earth rotates around the sun, then that must be so. If the Holy Book were to say otherwise, then we have misread it. Thus Islam was spared Christianity's Copernicus conundrum.

Shahrour's take on the infamous Surah An Nisaa (Women) 4:34) was most enlightening and refreshing. He read it as per ancient word usage, not formal Arabic grammar. That was not developed till long after the Qur'an was revealed. He made the point that the masculine and feminine forms in those ayats refer not to men or women, rather leaders (the dominant partner, who may be men or women) and followers (who may be likewise), and the dynamic relationship between the two. Thus those ayats have wide applicability beyond the family, as with organizations.

That is a more sophisticated reading than the contorted interpretations of Muslim feminists. Husbands disciplining their wives should thus be read more generically, as with leaders their wayward followers. Malay leaders would do well to reread Surah An Nisaa as per Shahrour's insight.

His other significant contribution is the concept of limits, derived from his understanding of calculus and engineering. To Shahrour, Allah defines only the extremes or limits of punishments, as with cutting of hands on one end to forgiveness and restitution on the other. Within those parameters it is for society through communal consensus to determine the appropriate level.

Shahrour's enlightened views resonate far beyond the Arab world. However in Indonesia, a doctoral candidate had to withdraw his dissertation on Shahrour as it triggered the wrath of the local ulama and widespread howling controversy. They took umbrage at Shahrour's interpretation on consensual sex outside of marriage. To him, the Qur'an condemns only where force or coercion is involved, inside or outside of marriage. This criminalization of consensual sex is a later *bida'ah* (adulteration of the faith).

Malaysian ulama would have rape victims marry their tormentors, and abused wives continue 'pleasing' their husbands. Meanwhile Muslims are comfortable with *muta'ah* (temporary marriages). It is said that brothels in Tehran have ulama ready to solemnize such ultra-brief 'marriages,' for a fee of course! Elsewhere in the secular world that is called pimping.

Back to Malaysia, the religious police should quit snooping around parks and hotels looking for *khalwat* (close proximity). They should instead focus on rapes, spousal abuses, and forced as well as child marriages.

My prayer on this Awal Muharram and the new year of AH 1442 is for Allah to shower His blessings on the soul of Muhammad Shahrour, and for his books getting wider reading. Muslims are in desperate need of this gush of fresh air to blow away the thick cobwebs encasing those ancient texts as well as contemporary minds.

Readers' Rating: *
Sampling of Readers' Responses:

"The late Imam Khattab of Toledo Islamic Center ... gave a similar interpretation of those issues.... As an engineer I find the Qur'an cannot be understood adequately without the knowledge of science, art, humanity, and mathematics. The Qur'an calls itself the Book for those who think. Thanks for sharing!"

VI: THE PERNICIOUS RISE OF MALAY ISLAMISM

Malaysia Needs Less, Not More Religion To Combat Corruption

Book Review of M. Kamal Hassan's *Corruption And Hypocrisy In Malay Muslim Politics. The Urgency of Moral Ethical Transformation*. EMIR Research, Kuala Lumpur, January 2021. Paperback, 277 pp; RM69.90

July 31, 2022

[After remaining silent for decades, Malay ulama and scholars are finally waking up and voicing their concerns on the corruption that is fast becoming the norm in Malay society. This is one such albeit belated voice.]

The book's title, and with that the content, is spot on and timely. The author's central point is that Malaysia's current problem is one of Malay Muslim politics and leadership, not of Malaysians generally. His second, the disunity and polarization of Malays. He has much less to say on this, or whether it is related to the first or a separate issue.

Kamal Hassan is no ordinary Malay. A scholar with an Ivy League doctorate (Columbia), he was the first Holder of the Malaysian Chair for Islam in Southeast Asia at Georgetown University. At home he had a long sterling academic career at the International Islamic University, ending as its third Rector in 2017. He had been honored with a Tan Sri and Datukship, as well as the national title of Professor Ulong (Distinguished Professor) and the prestigious Tokoh Anugerah Akademik Malaysia (National Academic Figure).

On Kamal's first point, I remind Malaysians that the state of non-Malay politics or the standing of non-Malay politicians is also far from being pristine. Recall the 1985 criminal conviction in Singapore of the Malaysian Chinese Association (MCA) leader, one Tan Koon Swan. That took down the hitherto massive MCA's Deposit Taking Cooperatives.

Not to be left out, the Malaysian Indian Congress too had its own unsavory and equally expensive MAIKA Holdings mess.

All that is little consolation for Malays. While Malaysian Chinese could look to exemplary leadership of their kin south of the causeway and on Mainland China, Malays are bereft of such inspiring examples. As for Malaysian Indians, the current mess in India and Sri Lanka would make Malaysia shine by comparison. Nonetheless both Malaysian Chinese and Indians could look with pride and satisfaction on their achievements in education, commerce, and other endeavors. There is no comparable compensatory glory for Malays. Malays used to bask (unjustifiably in my view) on the successes of such government-linked companies (GLCs) like Petronas, but Bank Bumiputra and now 1MDB squashed that. Besides, GLCs are public, not Malay enterprises.

Kamal Hassan is compelled to write because he is "disillusioned, dismayed, and ashamed" of the deteriorating state of Malay leadership, made worse since the General Election of 2018. "To make matters worse," he continues, "the involvement of the factor of political narcissism appearing to the public as a well-meaning 'savior' [Kamal's quote] in spite of advanced age, turned the political turmoil of the last few years into a complex phenomenon of political maneuverings, machinations and hypocrisy which are unprecedented."

No marks for guessing who that political narcissist of advanced age might be! Nonetheless Kamal should be more explicit as future readers could have difficulty identifying this geriatric culprit. For another, the man might just heed Kamal's counsel and reconsider not contesting the next election, as he (the culprit) now threatens to do. Of greater significance, Malays may remember Kamal's wise words come the next election. The ageing political narcissist Kamal referred to, and the man responsible for Malaysia's current curse of corruption, is of course Mahathir. It began with his "direct negotiations" of public contracts, massive expansion of GLCs, and the infamous money-printing "Approved Permits" back in the 1980s when he was Prime Minister.

While the costs of those shenanigans as well as the latest 1MDB debacle were humongous, they were at least quantifiable. Not so the damages Mahathir inflicted upon Malaysia and Malays by entrenching the current culture of corruption and rent-seeking activities as well as his endowing first, the inept Abdullah Badawi, then the egregiously corrupt Najib, followed by the scheming, incompetent Muhyiddin, and now the unbelievably clueless Ismail Sabri as leaders. These duds were all mentored by Mahathir. To be fair, how such untalented characters could rise so high reflects as much on our culture.

Kamal Hassan's remedy? A "Theocentric Leadership Paradigm." In short more religion, Islam to be specific.

However, all these Malay leaders have undertaken multiple Hajjs and Umrahs. Many have private suraus at their palatial residences and host regular *zikir* (remembrance of Allah) sessions during Ramadan. No, more Islam would not help. Jailing these corrupt leaders would. China, a communist and atheistic country, goes further. There they shoot them, and in public too!

Islam in Malaysia today is less a guide to the "straight path," more a set of mindless rituals. It is this perversion of the faith that makes Malays view the loot of corruption as *borkat* and *rezki*, Allah's bounty. As for "theocratic leadership," Malaysia already suffers from what Georgetown University legal scholar and Malaysian-born Yvonne Tew refers to as "stealth theocracy," where ambitious politicians and others eager to ride the Islamic tiger have corrupted the courts and other institutions. These *penunggang agama* (religious opportunists) pose the greatest threat to Malays and Malaysia, not the *pendatang* (immigrants). More pertinent, I cannot find any Muslim country, with or without theocratic leadership, that ranks high on the clean governance index.

Look at Iran. Imam Khomeini drove more Muslims out of the faith than Stalin could ever hope to achieve. Kelantan, the poorest state in Malaysia and with the highest rate of domestic abuse, child marriages, and yes, Internet pornography viewership, has long been ruled by an avowedly Islamic party.

A more practical, effective, and readily achievable solution to Malaysia's entrenched corruption is to fire the current Attorney-General, Chief of Police, and Head of the Malaysian Anti-Corruption Commission. Then conduct a global search, seeking help from the FBI, Scotland Yard, and others. While there is no shortage of honest, competent local talents including among Malays, but because of the community's current polarization (Kamal's second observation), finding one viewed as nonpartisan would be tough. As for local non-Malay candidates, those too are plentiful. The challenge there is to find one not politically tone deaf, as with not being able to speak the national language and then be proud of that fact, as with Tommy Tomas. Malaysians tolerate that in a foreigner but not one locally born and bred.

On to mundane matters, books are expensive in Malaysia. As such local writers and publishers must do their part to reduce that. A paperback format as this one is a solution. Another would be reducing the number of pages. Adopting standard publishing guidelines would achieve this by dispensing with the unnecessarily wide side margins and the line spacing between paragraphs, references, glossary as well as with the index. Copyright infringements aside, there is little need for extensive quotes. Putting them in smaller fonts would also help with page economizing. Chapter II of this book is but a reprint of the Sultan of Perak's long speech and extensive quotes from others. Likewise with hadith and Qur'anic verses, their page-consuming Arabic scripts are unnecessary; brief approximate translations should suffice. Adopting accepted referencing practices, as with 2:126 for Surah Al Baqarah, Ayat 126, would also save ink and paper.

This book is the lament of a respected scholar. It deserves wide readership for the observations and more importantly, robust discussions of the offered solutions. The publisher is confident of the first; it put "First Edition" to the copy I have! There is a Malay version, *"Korupsi Dan Kemunafikan Dalam Politik Melayu: Perlunya Disegerakan Transformasi Moral-Etika,"* at RM49.90 compared to the English at RM69.90. Whether that reflects lower cost of production or assessment of market value, *Allah hu alam* (Only Allah knows!).

Readers' Ratings: * *
Sampling of Readers' Responses:
"The writer is right about less not more religion to fight corruption. I go a step further ... Islam is the root cause of the troubles we have among Malays."

".... The problem with Malaysia is [that] ... we failed to produce morally and ethically upright Muslims because Islam is largely ... ritualistic, not spiritualistic. The same person who prays next to you is the same person who takes *rasuah* [bribes]. That boils down to our ... understanding or rather lack of understanding of Islam."

"Malays have Islam as their group religion but individually Malays have no real morals nor basic ethics."

"... [I]slam's greatest enemy is certain type of Muslims."

"The type who is greedy, corrupted .... This greed is in all religions but in Malaysia [it] is on a different level. That's all because they use *ketuanan* [presumed racial superiority] as an excuse!"

"Great review but I wouldn't agree with yours and the author's conclusions. This is perhaps due to non-definition of the words "religion" and "theocentricity". You probably concluded "we need less religion" because you have in mind the meaning of "religion" and "theocracy" to be mindless, ritualistic and legalistic practices of Islam."

"Religions are just man-made sets of laws and regulations but with God (also man-made) attached."

Malay Ummah's Many Phantom Enemies

June 11, 2022

[The religious establishment was upset that many young Malays were interested in the festivals of other faiths and communities. In this case, it was the Japanese Bon Odori Festival to honor the spirit of ancestors. Earlier the ulama were apoplectic over the Oktoberfest, and before that, Yoga in the Park program.]

Viewing the plethora of Malay religious sermons on social media, as well as from reading current mainstream headlines, I am reminded of the observation of a character in Naguib Mahfouz's *The Cairo Trilogy*. "At times a person may create an imaginary problem to escape an actual problem he finds difficult to resolve." At least that Mahfouz's character is aware of her limitations. Malay leaders on the other hand are consumed with fighting one phantom enemy after another and declaring repeated victories!

There is no shortage of critical challenges facing the ummah, from child brides and atrocious divorce rates to rampant drug abuse and entrenched corruption. Yet Malay leaders and ulama are fixated on manufactured enemies like the Japanese Bon Odori Festival. Earlier they hyperventilated on the presumed threat from Oktoberfest.

Yet they and their followers remain silent when that *"pengkhianat negara"* (national traitor) *aka* Former Prime Minister Najib Razak convicted of massive corruption was invited to an official palace dinner. Malay rulers with vulgar tastes are the norm; we have long lived with that. The current Agung's immediate predecessor had to resign after his cavorting with a Russian beauty queen was exposed. The current Agung's late father was no figure of moral rectitude either. He left a trail of wives from East to West. His son, the present Agung, his Sandhurst education notwithstanding, is no different.

It is not surprising that this degenerate trait would spread beyond the political and royal classes. Consider that Sidek Hassan, former Chief Secretary to the Government, the Establishment's highest officer, admitted in court during the Najib trial that he was being paid RM30K per month, a figure that exceeded his official salary, to be on the board of the infamous 1MDB for "doing nothing." There is more. He was honored with a Tan Sri and made Chairman of the Enforcement Agency for the Integrity Commission. Truly Orwellian!

Sidek's successor as the top civil servant, Ali Hamsa, was no sparkle either. He died recently so I am restrained in my comments except to say that he, after 'meticulous' examination, declared that 1MDB's affairs were "clear and above board." Yes, Ali Hamsa was also a Tan Sri. As a side note, both attended some *ulu* (boondock) American universities.

Royal rulers are by statute exclusively Malays, while the political and administrative classes are increasingly becoming so through practice. The other exclusively Malay leaders are the ulama and religious scholars.

Throughout history, as Noah Feldman noted in his *The Fall And Rise Of The Islamic State* ulama and scholars were the ummah's formidable bulwark against tyrannous rulers. Read the biographies of these ancient luminaries; many had suffered the wrath of their evil rulers. For most however, then and now, the ahadith "Heaven is full of rulers who befriended scholars while Hell, of scholars close to rulers" describes better the reality.

Malaysia has gone far beyond; the state now fully coopts the ulama. This blight began with Mahathir Mohamad. Early in his tenure as Prime Minister he tried to ingratiate himself to them so as to be seen as the "champion" of the faith. He succeeded only in emboldening them. They ridiculed him for his illiteracy in Arabic (the language of Islam) and lack of formal religious credentials. Imagine if you will an English-illiterate expounding on Shakespeare's subtleties, they sniffed! Mahathir tried to ride the Islamic tiger to fame and glory only to end up with the beast nearly devouring him. Crudely put, they crapped on him.

Today's Malay ulama, far from being a bulwark against tyranny, are very much part of the problem. Listening to their sermons and observing their actions I am struck by two disturbing thoughts. One, the total irrelevance to and ignorance of contemporary challenges facing the ummah when delivering their sermons. 'Delivering' is the appropriate word, or 'reading' as their sermons are all canned, produced by a central government bureaucracy.

Two, the obsession is with death and the associated destructive theology of belittling Allah's greatest gift – our precious life. This more than anything else prevents Malays from making our rightful contributions to society, hence our current sorry state. This preoccupation with chasing Paradise causes the ummah to suffer hell in this world. Malays should instead heed the wisdom of the 13th Century Sufi scholar Ata Allah Al Iskandariah: If you want to know your standing with Him in the Hereafter, look at the state He has put you in now (*Hikma Ata'iyya Al-Hikam's* Aphorism No: 73).

Malay ulama have failed to give full meaning to the Qur'anic injunction: Command good and prohibit evil. True piety, the Qur'an goes on, does not consist of turning your face towards east or west ... rather your spending on the needy and freeing humans from bondage (2:177). The greatest bondage trapping individual Malays today is our poverty of skills and intellect, thus our lack of competitiveness. Endless *zikir* (pleadings to The Almighty) would not solve that, improving our schools and universities would.

Our collective cultural bondage makes us accept the loot of corruption as *borkat* (bounty from Allah). We were easily bought when 1MDB crumbs were used to finance Hajj and suraus. As for Sidek Hassan's monthly RM30K *borkat*, that was but spilled gravy compared to what *kafirs* Tim Leissner, Jho Low, Roger Ng, and others had gained.

A cautionary note. For my fellow Muslims despairing of the current state of the ummah, it is worth reminding that "assassin" is an Arabic word and "amok" a uniquely Malay cultural trait. The recent interest in Mat Kilau, the lone warrior who rebelled against the British, and one Private Adam who went amok against a sultan, are early warning signs. The other necessary reminder is that even the most compliant society has its limits.

Readers' Ratings: * * * * *
Sampling of Readers' Responses:

"Agree with you ... religion should not be part of governance. It should be separated and not interfere with how the country is administered .... It should not interfere with the civil and criminal laws of the nation."

"Some ulama are co-opted by the state but that does not mean independent ulama who criticized the government, or the current religious direction of the country don't exist."

"Spread the word around about our leaders' hypocrisy, incompetence, and corruption."

"Your disgust and fury resonate [with me]."

"Well said! Hoping that we will reach the tipping point sooner than later—before there's no turning back!"

The Continued Unbridled Corruption of Malay Ulama

September 19, 2021

[Islam in Malaysia is less a religion, more a bureaucracy. The ulama class has been totally co-opted by the state, with Imams now becoming the handmaiden of the politically powerful. If that is not bad enough, the religious leaders are now becoming as corrupt as secular Malay leaders. The good news is that the ummah (community) is finally awakening to this fact and beginning to assert itself, much to the discomfit of the government and the ulama class.]

Malaysia's premier public intellectual and academic architect Tajuddin Rasdi lamented in a recent column that in his 40 years of listening to local sermons, not once did he hear the khatib address much less condemn the egregious corruption among Malay leaders. That is what happens when the state has co-opted the ulama class. Religion then becomes yet another sinister state apparatus and the ulama now the handmaidens of the politically powerful.

This ulama-ruler complex has not always been the case, in Malaysia or the greater Islamic world. In the preface to the recent re-release of Elijah Gordon's *The Real Cry of Syed Shayk al-Hadi*, Ahmad Farouk Musa, another public intellectual and academic cardiac surgeon, writes, "To Al-Hadi, the lifestyle of the ruling elite was morally corrupt, decadent, and unjust. They, aided by the teachings of conservative ulama, have led the ummah to our current abysmal state."

I would delete the restrictive adjective "morally" as Malay leaders are corrupt and decadent in every way beyond just 'moral.'

Shayk al-Hadi was of the reformist Kaum Muda of the early 20th Century. "Do not be deceived by the titles and accolades of your dignitaries for they are the source of all the miseries that have befallen upon you. They ... oppressed and ... continue oppressing you," Ahmad Farouk quotes Al-Hadi.

Harvard's Noah Feldman in his *The Fall and Rise of the Islamic State* noted that throughout history, the ulama class remained the only effective bulwark against the excesses of rulers. When rulers stray from God's laws, as with being corrupt, then the ummah would no longer be bound by those rulers' edicts, those ancient ulama asserted. Nay, the ummah must go beyond; they are duty-bound to get rid of those errant rulers.

The delusional detachment from reality noted by Tajuddin Rasdi is today the hallmark of local sermons and religious discourses. Listen to the *ceramahs* of the various "celebrity" ulama on Youtube. The prime exhibit is the ever-pompous Dr. MAZA (he does not need his full name; his acronym is enough, like the famous grammarian Za'aba) would at the slightest provocation overwhelm his listeners with his long Arabic quotes. No one had ever "fact checked" his claims as his listeners could not understand Arabic. His is not to enlighten but to dazzle his listeners. Once in a panel discussion in front of an urbane audience, Dr. MAZA left in a huff, demonstrating yet another ugly trait of Malay ulama – their inability to handle criticisms, challenges, or to be questioned in any way.

Another social media preacher is Azhar Idrus. This odd character has not quite figured out his real calling, whether to be an Imam or a stand-up comedian. His folksy delivery in his distinct Terengganu accent, plus some trite jokes, enthralls his listeners. He forgets that his dialect alone elicits prolonged laughter in sophisticated company.

That these ulama have large loyal followings reveals much of themselves as well as the Malay ummah.

Contrast these ulama with my Imam Ilyas here in California. In a recent Friday sermon before Labor Day holiday for example, he reminded us to honor and respect workers. He quoted Prophet Muhammad (May Allah bless his soul) that employers should pay their workers before their (workers') "sweat dries up." They, whether cleaning the parks or taking care of the elderly are providing much-needed community services. They are doing God's work as much as if not more so than those cloistered in houses of worship endlessly doing *zikir* or reciting their holy texts.

Those who abuse and cheat their workers deserve the wrath of Almighty, Imam Ilyas added. Today, thousands of Malaysian workers have had their paychecks delayed or withheld. Few treat their workers with respect. When I was in Malaysia in the mid-1970s, I was stunned to see a prominent Islamic scholar treating his maid as a slave. It is a common sight in many Malay homes today to have their "servants" eat separately from the main family. As for my pay when I was in Malaysia, I did not get my first check till three months later, and then not in full. And my employer was a self-proclaimed Islamic government!

When Pope John Paul II died, Imam Ilyas paid tribute to this great religious leader, recalling his early condemnation of apartheid and the Gulf War, as well as his historic visit to the Ummayad Mosque in Damascus, a former Byzantine-era church, where he respectfully removed his shoes and kissed the Qur'an.

In that sermon Imam Ilyas Anwar reminded us that Allah has the final prerogative on who would enter Heaven, an indirect dig at those who proclaim that their faith is exclusively privileged, an arrogant claim made not just by Muslims.

Malaysian ulama schooled at prestigious foreign institutions are no different. Afifi Al-Akiti, the current darling of Malays being that he is the first Malay to be appointed Fellow at one of Oxford's colleges, is an example. When asked during a seminar in Kelantan (attended by no less than the sultan) on the current state of corruption and breaches of faith by Malay leaders, he demurred, using the excuse that he had been away from the country for so long. A cop out!

One could excuse local ulama as they are on state payroll. Al-Akiti however is paid by British taxpayers. As such he is free from the constraints of his Malaysian counterparts. The man is capable of eloquent protest as when he condemned Islamic terrorists in his "Defending The Transgressed By Censuring the Reckless Against The Killing of Civilians." That received widespread praise. I wish he had been as brave and unequivocal in condemning corruption among Malay and other Muslim leaders.

Alas when it comes to corruption in Malaysia, mousy Al-Akiti is no Tariq Ramadan, his fellow Oxford don. During a visit to Malaysia, Tariq Ramadan condemned in no uncertain terms the rampant corruption among Muslim leaders, Malaysians included. In the finest display of prophetic tradition, while Ramadan could not stop corruption in Malaysia with his hands, he used the next best thing, his tongue, by lashing out.

Alas Al-Akiti dared not even do that. Only Allah knows whether he condemned Malay corruption in his heart.

Therein lies the problem, and tragedy. Until Malay ulama assume the mantle of their ancient brothers by being the bulwark against errant corrupt leaders, the ummah will continue to suffer.

Readers' Ratings: * * *
Sampling of Readers' Responses:

"Nabi, *s.a.w.*, *bersabda barang siapa korup bukan dari golongan aku.*" (Our prophet, *s.a.w.*, asserted that whoever is corrupt is no longer part of my community.)

"It takes courage to speak against corruption ... [as that] would affect their rice bowls or ... be ostracized by those in power. They do not have the strength or resilience to face those challenges as mentioned above."

"Structural barriers with deep historical roots are impeding progress in Muslim countries. They score below the global average on key criteria used to evaluate democracy and socioeconomic development, such as literacy rates and life expectancy. Islam and Western colonialism are commonly cited as the sources of these issues, but such explanations are problematic and serve to propagate Islamophobia, anti-Westernism, and the misdirection of blame. Instead, and as this report will argue, the main cause of authoritarianism and underdevelopment in many Muslim-majority countries is the alliance between Islamic scholars (the ulema) and state authorities."

"Their alignment is not due to stupidity. They are in fact quite intelligent. The question is where do their interest lie? If it is in their interest to dumb down the population to maintain their hold on power ... they would continue doing that."]

VII: APPALLING MALAYSIAN EDUCATION

Reserve Residential Schools For The Poor

April 18, 2021

[The decline of Malaysian national education at all levels is obvious and profound. Witness the mushrooming of international schools and private institutions of higher learning in the country despite their high costs. Malay parents of lesser means are now opting for National-Type Chinese Schools in droves, much to the chagrin of Malay nationalists. These trends will only accelerate.]

I was visiting my old village a few years ago and was discussing with the local teachers the sorry state of Malaysian education, in particular rural schools. One of them took that as my blaming the teachers.

"How can we be inspired?" she protested. She went on to relate that while in the past there were more than a few bright kids in her class to create some sparks, today those few would have gone into the many residential schools.

Now that Malaysian schools have reopened, that teacher's lament and perceptive observation came to me as I read the many congratulatory remarks in social media made by and for proud Malay parents whose children had been selected into these residential schools. There is merit in having these magnet schools. Farmers give special care and attention to their promising saplings, ranchers their prized heifers and young bulls. They are the future; they will increase the quality of the output of a farm or ranch. Likewise with a nation.

Old established Singapore's Raffles Junior College and the much newer South Korea's Daewon and Minjok are now de facto "feeder schools" for the Ivy League. When those students graduate and return, they would uplift the nation. To prepare for those elite universities, these students sit for recognized international matriculating examinations like the British GCE "A" Level, American Scholastic Aptitude Test (SAT), and the International Baccalaureate (IB). They do not bother with local third-rate counterparts like the Sijil Tinggi Persekutuan (Higher School

Certificate) or *Matrikulasi* (Matriculation). Those schools prepare for their students early, upon entering high school and thus have at least four years of preparation. Some Malaysian residential schools also prepare their students for IB and GCE A level, but only after they have sat for their local Sijil Persekutuan Malaysia at their eleventh school year. Thus, they have a truncated preparation of at most only two years.

By contrast India opted for a different strategy for her brightest. She targeted not the schools but at the undergraduate level, as with her elite 23-campus Indian Institutes of Technology (IIT). Those students then would strive to enter leading graduate programs in the West for their MBAs and PhDs. Many current leading American scholars, professionals, and executives of Indian origin trace their academic roots to IIT.

Malaysia also has comparable targeting with her five "research" universities. Unlike India, Malaysia does not have much to show for her effort. It would have been far more effective and cheaper if those "top" five universities were to improve their undergraduate programs *a la* IIT. Instead, they are on a futile chase for "global ranking" and produce gluts of PhDs with their half-baked "research" published in predatory journals.

It takes considerable time, money, and effort just to take part in those ranking surveys. Accept the fact Malaysian universities will never make to the top 200 within the next few decades. So why not focus on more achievable goals, as with increasing the employability of your graduates by making them bilingual.

The criteria for success as with the IIT-like approach could also be readily measured, as with how many of your graduates get accepted to elite universities. Another would be whether their programs are recognized internationally. University of Malaya's medical degree was once accepted by the British Medical Council, thus paving the way for its graduates to take further training in Britain. Today Malaysian medical degrees are not recognized outside of Malaysia for purposes of further studies or employment.

Malaysia sends her educators to and hires consultants from such countries as Finland but fails to learn the most elementary lesson. That is, successful schools, whether in Malaysia, Finland, or America, are more likely when there is commonality of purpose and efforts among teachers, parents, and the local community. As for the curriculum, Finnish and

German high school graduates are all fluently bilingual, the second language being English. That is worthy of Malaysia to emulate.

If rich successful Malays were not to send their children to these residential schools, they would by default support the local schools. Their children's success would depend on that. Further, as their children would be among the bright ones, they would add much-needed sparks to the class and inspire their fellow classmates as well as the teachers. Beyond that, these residential schools could then provide more opportunities for others less fortunate to have the same superior opportunities that you once had. Besides, your children would have far better living conditions at home than they could ever hope to have even at Malay College. Imagine, their own room, broadband access, and definitely much better food! As for intellectual stimulation, you could provide that far better than those teachers. Last and most important, your children would absorb your family's values.

Imagine the multiplier effect on the Malay community if all residential schools were to be restricted to the children of the poor or those who would be the first in their family to go to university. There must be some pride among successful Malays not to let their children be the ward of the state. In essence that is what their children would be if they were to attend these residential schools.

I am appalled that Malay leaders like Mahathir would on one hand chastise Malays for being too dependent on the state while at the same time send their children to these residential schools. They have no shame. Worse, their children too are now sending their children to these schools. When will they learn the lesson that they are preaching?

Readers' Rating: * * *
Sampling of Readers' Responses:

"I am reminded that during those crucial early years, two Education Ministers, namely Mahathir and Anwar, were responsible for many 'reforms' in our school system."

"If after 60 plus years of Merdeka, positive development in education is hardly in sight, it's a definite show of failure .... We aren't short of brainy people and resources, so what's the problem with uplifting our standards to be on par if not above the countries mentioned?"

"Big towns need not have residential schools. Education Ministry should select a number of schools in major towns to be elite schools so students do not have to leave their homes ...."

"Affirmative action is to assist the poor. Every CEO kid [at these residential schools] is denying a deserving case."

"Education? I'd think twice before speaking of it at these premises ...."

"You speak what I would like to speak of my observation in residential schools."

Unsolicited Advice For The Next Minister of Education
Tackle The Basics First

January 5, 2020

[News Item: With the defeat of the Barisan Nasional in the 14th General Election of May 2018, Malaysia for the first time had a Minister of Education someone from other than UMNO. Then on January 2, 2020, less than two years at the job, following a private meeting with Prime Minister Mahathir, Education Minister Maszlee, a former academic, submitted his surprised resignation to be effective the very next day. He did so on the advice of "Ayahanda" (father-figure) Mahathir. In his nearly 20-minutes press conference, surrounded by his top officials, Maszlee blamed the media for focusing on controversial issues like pupils' shoe color and the introduction of *jawi* while ignoring what he thought were his spectacular successes, as repairing dilapidated schools and providing free breakfasts in rural schools. Foremost he highlighted his Ministry's Annual Report, the first Ministry to do so. His was released even before the year ended! It was clear, at least to him, that he had done a super job. Being magnanimous, he is returning the "gift" of being Minister of Education back to his father figure. Early in his tenure Maszlee took time off for Hajj, presumably to thank Allah for that gift.]

The challenges facing Malaysian schools and universities are as monumental as they are obvious. The newly appointed Minister of Education Maszlee Malik tried to be a hero in attempting to tackle all at once. He would have been much wiser as well as more prudent – and likely to succeed to boot – had he focused first on the more fundamental and pressing issues. Defer the peripheral and distracting ones like students' shoe color. Likewise, assessment of UEC (Chinese School Certificate), holistic or otherwise, should not be his top priority, nor the introduction of the *jawi* script.

The Ministry of Education (MOE) is the biggest personnel as well as budget-wise. Beyond that, its policies and pronouncements impact the nation far more than any other portfolio, and for generations to come. Malaysia today still reels from educational policies instituted way back in the 1970s.

MOE is also the most prestigious ministry, as reflected by the fact that all Malaysian Prime Ministers had once been Ministers of Education. [Note: the exception was Ismail Sabri, a few years later.] No wonder Maszlee thought of himself as a rising political star with the granting of the special "gift."

Maszlee's first challenge relates to the very management of the Ministry. The other pertains to its policies. Both are interrelated. Failure to address the first would doom the second, and both would consume and exhaust his time, talent, and energy. There would be little time to undertake a Hajj or umrah during his tenure, more so very early on as he did. Besides, Maszlee's top priority should have been the salvation of young Malaysians, not his.

If Maszlee lacks executive experience or management talent (clearly he does), then he should have enticed someone to assist him on that crucial front. Be humble. He should not have considered himself innately multi-talented or had a hitherto hidden executive gem. He was but an untenured professor.

Management problems are not unique to MOE. The entire civil service is blighted with this onerous burden of intractable bloat and incompetence. That is more than a burden. The massive bureaucracy impedes effective policy execution, and at times works against it – the entrenched self-interest of the so-called "deep state."

Delegate power and authority to the periphery. That would dispense with the need of a huge bureaucracy at head office. Grant universities their autonomy. Then all you would need would be a clerk to prepare the checks for you to sign every month or quarter for those campuses. That one initiative would rid MOE of its Director-General for Higher Education, his deputies, and their assorted highly paid support staff. Let the universities choose their own Vice-Chancellors, Deans, and Professors, or what color of drapes for their faculty lounge. The Minister's control and influence should only be through such macro levers as the funding mechanism and his appointees to the governing boards.

Peruse MOE's organizational chart, replete with such bureaus as the Islamic Education Unit, Institute of Translation, and Institute of Language and Culture. Get rid of them. Private publishers do a far superior job of publishing and translating, and at no cost to the government.

The new Minister's focused vision and MOE's sole aspiration should be to prepare young Malaysians to be competitive for the new global realities so they could contribute. And only that. Heed the wisdom schoolteachers Pak Harfan and Bu Mus drummed into the handful of precious young minds entrusted to their care, in Andrea Hirata's bestselling novel *Laskar Pelangi* (*The Rainbow Troops*): "... [B]*ahwa hiduplah mu untuk memberi sebanyak-banyaknya, bukan untuk menerima sebanyak-banyaknya.*" (Live so you could give as much, not to receive.)

To paraphrase, be a proud contributor to society, not its dependent. That is also the best and most succinct encapsulation of the purpose of education, to prepare the young for those objectives. Help young Malaysians achieve that goal by ensuring that they are fluent in Malay and English, as well as be science literate and competent in mathematics. Teach those four subjects daily, at all levels, and in all schools, including religious ones. Fictional Pak Harfan and Bu Mus taught their pupils English, STEM subjects, and music in their very modest Muhammadiyah Islamic *pondok* school.

Consider this glaring anomaly. Malaysia is in desperate need of competent teachers of English. Yet not a single public university has a dedicated Department of English, and there are no English-medium Teachers' Training Colleges. This jarring disconnect, obvious to all, is missed by those in MOE, as well as the personnel selected to run the universities.

Leverage the funding mechanism to make every public university have a dedicated Department of English. Make a pass in MUET (Malaysian University English Test) mandatory for university admissions. Quadruple the number of scholarships for those pursuing English and STEM. That would be a good start. Discontinue scholarships for Malay Studies as well as Islamic Studies as the country already has a glut of those graduates.

Make MUET mandatory for all teachers and MOE personnel. Their promotions and continued employment should depend on it. That one initiative would be far more effective and consequential than all the endless exhortations of leaders and educators on the importance of the English Language.

With mathematics, if Malaysians were to have some elementary competency in it, they would not dismiss Vietnam's impressive six percent economic growth rate versus Malaysia's meager four as "that country growing at only two percent faster." Vietnam is growing 50 percent faster! If Malaysia's rate were to drop to three, then Vietnam is growing at 100 percent more, or twice as fast.

Beyond that, make 13 years of schooling the new standard. Modify the last two years (Sixth Form) for those not academically inclined to focus on vocational subjects. By reinstituting Sixth Form, the Ministry could dispense with its massive and expensive *matrikulasi* division. You would also be spared its quota controversy. The universities too could then dispense with their resource-wasting "foundation" and *matrikulasi* courses. Universities should focus on doing what other institutions could not do, that is, education at the undergraduate, graduate, and professional levels, as well as undertaking research. Again, use the lever of funding as well as your appointees to the universities' governing boards to achieve those ends without having MOE micromanage those campuses.

Teach the young critical thinking. Dispense with regurgitation. Pak Harfan asked his students to pen essays describing Heaven as they envision it. That demands both critical as well as creative thinking. Again, another glaring absence, as with English, no public university in Malaysia has a dedicated Department of Philosophy.

In a plural society like Malaysia, education should go beyond. It must also be a major if not the instrument to integrate her young. When young Malaysians learn and play together at school, the nation would be that much better. Diversity in the classrooms also enhances learning.

Today, Malaysian schools are dangerously segregated along racial and religious lines. Cutting down the hours devoted to if not eliminating entirely religion from national schools would go a long way in making those schools attractive to non-Malays.

Most of all, the one attribute the new Education Minister must have and instill in his officers is the mindset that he and his Ministry does not have the exclusive wisdom and insight on what's best for Malaysian education and for Malaysian children. The Ministry should be a resource center and a facilitator, not a command and control one.

Readers' Rating: * * * * *
Sampling of Readers' Responses:
"I do not really think that Maszlee, Mahathir, or any senior Malay want or dare change anything that would impact the primacy of Bahasa."

"This is as good a blueprint for the Ministry to adopt."

"It is like a Professor of Business who can teach but cannot create business of his own."

"It is the quality of the teachers and their incompetence. Maszlee should talk to the teachers who are not proficient in English, Physics, Mathematics, and Chemistry but still teaching these subjects."

"Maszlee has zero capacity to be Minister."

VIII: MALAYSIA AND THE WORLD

Rich Malays, Poor Malays

December 23, 2022

[In his book *Rich Dad, Poor Dad*, Robert Kiyosaki relates how he had learned much from both his biological father as well as from his friend's (sociological father, as it were). The former taught him frugality and diligence even though those traits did not bring much security and stability while the latter, financial literacy and entrepreneurial skills that brought Kiyosaki both fame and wealth. Malays too could learn much from our two civilizational parents: Islam and the modern West.]

Two consequential external forces impacted the Malay world: the arrival of Islam and a few centuries later, European civilization. The effects of both are obvious, pervasive, and profound. We would do well to learn from and absorb the best of both.

In Anwar Ibrahim we have a leader who personifies this creative blending, extracting, and synthesizing the best as well as the commonalities of the two. He is at ease quoting Shakespeare as well as in correcting the Leader of the Opposition who had erroneously recited a Qur'anic verse, as Anwar did in Parliament recently.

That Leader of the Opposition typifies many current Malay leaders, with their "half-past-six" understanding of the West and of English specifically as well as their obsession with the superficialities of Islam and Arabism. They exploit our great faith with their politics.

Turkish commentator Soner Cagaptay put it best. "Islamism is not a form of the Muslim faith or an expression of Muslim piety. Rather it is a political ideology that strives to derive legitimacy from Islam."

In his bestseller "self-help" book *Rich Dad, Poor Dad*, Robert Kiyosaki relates how he had learned much from his biological father as well as his friend's (sociological father, as it were). The former taught him frugality and diligence even though those traits did not bring much security and stability while the latter, financial literacy and entrepreneurial skills that brought Kiyosaki both fame and wealth.

Kiyosaki's insight also applies at the societal level. For Malays, that would be Islam and British rule. Both are worthy inspirations and laudable examples but could also be a curse and burden. Choose one and ignore or negate the other, and we would be that much poorer. Instead, appreciate and absorb the positive values of both while dispensing the unsavory aspects.

Discerning the glint of the pebble from the sparkle of a diamond, or not missing the gem in our midst can be difficult. Nonetheless try we must, and be rigorous at it, with no presumptions or assumptions. A gardener must not mistake *lalang* weed for rice saplings. We pull the weeds out and early before they become rooted.

As a Minangkabau I am used to and comfortable with "synthesizing contradictions harmoniously," to quote Indonesian sociologist Taufik Abdullah in referring to our blending of Islam's patriarchy and our cultural matriarchy. As babies we are fed bland white rice and hot red chili early so we could learn to tolerate, nay, relish opposites!

Historical perspectives also help. European Renaissance owed much to the ancient Muslims. Granted, many of the early translations of Islamic works were by jaundiced authors out to prove that our Prophet, *s.a.w.*, was but a plagiarizer, nonetheless Europe's emerging from the Medieval Age owed much to those early Muslims.

Likewise, Islam brought the greatest temporal gift — the written word — to our hitherto oral Malay tradition, transforming it far beyond only the intellectual. Through *jawi* Malays could access the voluminous Arabic literature.

Our ancestors however did not learn much beyond *hikayats* and hadith. That was the greatest tragedy, a missed opportunity of unquantifiable proportions as those Arabs had also made huge contributions in the sciences, medicine, and mathematics (STEM). While Malay Islamic scholars today can recite voluminous treatises on *tahajut* (night) prayers, they are ignorant if not contemptuous of the scientific contributions or profound philosophical deliberations of ancient Muslims. Worse, today's Islamic scholars do not emulate the ancients' eagerness to learn; those early Muslims learned even from the kafir Greeks!

Those Muslims were also diligent students of what the Malay scholar Hamka referred to as the "second Qur'an," this wonderful universe that Allah had bequeathed upon us. They studied those celestial bodies and deduced from there their relationship to the seasons, as well as used them to plot navigational guides. They studied the human body, another great gift of Allah. The first effective handling of an epidemic – quarantining – was practiced by our Prophet, *s.a.w.* When you are in an area of a pandemic do not leave, and if you are outside, do not enter.

Our ancestors however did not learn much about commerce from those early Muslim traders. The consequence of our current obsession with the Hereafter reduces this great faith to the childish collection of religious brownie points to be cashed in at the Pearly Gates. As for the Hereafter, the 13th Century Sufi scholar Ibn Ata' Allah Al Iskandari said it best in his *Hikam*, "If you want to know your standing in the Hereafter, look at the state He has put you in now."

John Calvin later incorporated that in his reformist teachings, and from there emerged the Protestant work ethics. Capitalism and the emancipation of Europe followed. Same holy text but with a new twist in interpretation, it uplifted millions.

Malays proclaim loud and often that we are now free from colonialism. The vigor and vociferousness with which we do it (and the need to express that often) belie the truth. Malay elite still aspire to send their children to British universities. Malays cannot converse in our own language without the promiscuous insertions of English words or use bastardized Malay versions even when there are ready native expressions. The purpose there is obvious, not better and clearer communication but to display one's supposed prowess in English, a none-too-subtle sociolinguistic "one-upmanship." Likewise today, having a condo in London is still the ultimate bragging rights. By contrast few Malays have condos in Mecca.

Colonization is wrong regardless of whether that was part of a messianic "white man's burden." That notwithstanding, there was a thing or two we could have learned from the British. For one, they abolished slavery among Malays. For another, the British blunted the more egregious feudal elements in our society and introduced modern education. With English now the global language, that conferred significant advantages, at least for those Malays who took advantage of it. Most of all the British romanized our alphabet, a significant plus in this digital age.

Munshi Abdullah wrote that there must be something that we Malays could learn from the civilization that ushered in the Industrial and Scientific Revolutions. We would be condemned to perpetual poverty, spiritually and materially, if we fail to see the beauty and absorb the values of both Islam and the West. If ancient Muslims could learn from the kafir Greeks, we too could from our fellow Abrahamic believers, the British.

Readers' Rating: * *
Sampling of Readers' Responses:
"…[P]erhaps we now can understand why it is so difficult to get the "Malays" together and be generally united! Only the Islam factor is the common link that PAS is trying to use in their politics to gain power …. It is time we assert ourselves as Malaysians …. True nation building could only be achieved by this most accommodating and progressive mindset."

"… Malays [as a community] moved backwards when Malay kids stop learning English. Then you have crazy ustazes preventing you from seeking good living and playing active role in attaining economic progress."

"What irks me the most is the reference to Western values or *budaya barat* by some Malay ulamaks, without fail, with negative connotations, never mind those Western values also stress being on time in one's daily routine as opposed to being lackadaisical regarding time, as in Malay culture.

Ukraine Is Much Closer To Malaysia Than We Think
February 27, 2022

[There are many current eerie similarities between Malaysia and Ukraine. The obvious is the entrenched corruption of their leaders. The other is geography, *vis a vis* great powers in their respective region if not globally. For Malaysia, it is the long land border she shares with Indonesia *a la* Ukraine and Russia, and an even greater maritime one Malaysia shares with China in the South China Sea. Malaysia was involved once in a war with Indonesia, the *konfrontasi* of the early 1960s. Today Malaysia is in dispute with China in the South China Sea. Then there is the demographic dynamics; ethnic Chinese in Malaysia versus Russians in Ukraine.]

Regardless of the outcome of the current lethal conflict between Ukraine and Russia (still ongoing more than a year later), this much is indisputable. Ukrainians, both nationalists and pro-Russians, as well as the vast majority who just want to pursue a peaceful life, are already paying a severe and unrecoverable price. They will continue doing so for a considerable time beyond even if a peace treaty were to be signed today. As for the soldiers killed or maimed on both sides, well, not to be callous, theirs is an occupational hazard. To the millions of civilian victims, the consequent global gyrations as with Wall Street jitters and increases in gas and food prices on Main Street triggered by this conflict are trivial. Even to mention them seems insensitive if not obscene.

Ukraine may be thousands of miles away from Malaysia, but to Malaysians she is much closer emotionally. A routine Malaysian Airline Flight 17 from Amsterdam to Kuala Lumpur was shot down there on a clear day of July 17, 2017, killing all 298 on board. That scar is still raw. That innocent bystander victim incident was but an early manifestation and consequence of this later more tragic conflagration.

Beyond that raw emotion, Ukraine holds many other eerie similarities with Malaysia. Malaysians ignore those at their peril. For example, the world may refer to Ukrainians by that term but to them, the old, ugly and perennial ancient tribal dynamics of "them" versus "us" are very much operative; the "us" being ethnic Ukrainians; "them," those of Russian ancestry and speaking that language, as well as others of varied Eastern European ancestries. Some are pro Russians, others nationalistic (meaning, pro Ukraine), and many others if not the vast majority could not care less. They just want peace so they could go with their lives. The millions who have fled the country testify to that.

Malaysians may have difficulty differentiating those Eastern European sub-varieties of *orang puteh* (white man), as with Ukrainians versus Russians, together with other Slavic minorities, and may view the

Russian Cyrillic and its subvariant Ukrainian script as chicken scratch, but those differences are but surface ripples. They hide dangerous treacherous reefs just beneath.

What the world labels as Ukrainians apply to about seventy percent of the population. They are proud of their culture, heritage, and language. They also have their own heroes. A substantial minority however are ethnic Russians; they too are proud of their ethnicity, culture, and language as well as having their own separate heroes. Worse, their heroes are but villains to the majority of their countrymen.

Another disconcerting demographic reality that Malaysians should take note. Ethnic Russians are concentrated in the eastern part of the country, bordering Russia. In Malaysia, while Malays are the majority in the West or Peninsular, the picture in East Malaysia is far different. The mother tongue of the majority there is not Malay, the national language, but their own, be it Iban or Hokkien. Yet another volatile element, while Ukrainians and Russians share the same Orthodox Christianity, Malaysians do not even share the same faith. Even Muslim Malays are divided in our interpretations of Islam.

As for Malaysian "Russians," the Chinese, the paranoia of *Ketuanan Melayu* notwithstanding, they have seen the fate of their kin in Hong Kong and share the anxieties their brethren in Taiwan have for their "motherland."

Demographic demon aside, there are two other eerie similarities between Ukraine and Malaysia. One is geographic destiny. Former Foreign Minister Anifah Aman asserted that Malaysia has the same potential dynamics *vis a vis* China with respect to the brewing South China Sea conflict, as Ukraine to Russia today.

A simplistic assessment, at best. First, land borders are intrinsically more problematic than maritime ones. Besides, South China Sea is a wide stretch of water even without factoring in the unpredictable Monsoon. Second, Malaysia is not the only party to that dispute. There are other and far greater powers with direct interests. Japan for one; likewise Europe and America. Over thirty percent of global maritime trade flows through that stretch of water. As such those countries have even greater interest than Malaysia to maintain peace and stability, meaning the status quo, in the South China Sea.

Anifah's observation applies more to Laos and Myanmar. Vietnam also shares a long land border with China and is also a party to the South China Sea dispute. Vietnam had bloodied the Chinese nose more than once. If a crisis were to erupt in the South China Sea today, Malaysia would be but a minor player in all respects. We would of course be forced to take sides, but that would be a separate issue.

Malaysia's relationship with Indonesia, a country with a long land border with Malaysia, *a la* Ukraine to Russia, is more relevant. Recall *konfrontasi* of the early 1960s. That crisis was more the consequence of the conflicting personalities of the leaders of the two countries, Tunku Abdul Rahman and Sukarno. Notice how quickly that conflict was resolved once both protagonists were pushed aside. Likewise with Putin and Zelensky, even if they were not national leaders, it would not be difficult to imagine the two being drawn into a bar brawl with minimal provocation.

The last eerie commonality between the Zelensky Administration and the current one in Putrajaya is that both are corrupt and incompetent, a lethal combination. Ukraine was an economic basket case long before this crisis; it will be worse afterwards. As for endemic corruption among Malay leaders, just follow the current trial related to the 1MDB now being played out in the courtroom of Putrajaya and New York City. As for incompetence, well, ask the man in the street.

Far more consequential but less commented aspect to the current leadership in both countries is this. Kiev has its share albeit small but still influential cadre of ultra-rightwing, nationalist, white supremacists, enough for Putin to exploit it. The pro-Russian secessionist movement in East Ukraine did not develop *de novo*. Those "white supremacists" in Kiev have their local variant in Putrajaya, the *Ketuanan Melayu* types. Only sheer incompetence and lack of intelligence make them less destructive than they already are.

Unlike the earlier demographic demon and geographic destiny, this third blight is man-made and thus at least theoretically much more remediable. Perversely, the reality is far different.

As for the current tragedy, I am struck by this observation of one Kiev resident. On Tuesday evening in February 2022, he was having a nice leisurely dinner with friends in a restaurant. On Wednesday evening they were scrambling for their lives, hiding in an underground subway station.

That is the central lesson for Malaysians and citizens everywhere. If we do not pay attention to our leaders' greed, incompetence, and shenanigans, that is what we can expect. This was true in Kiev on Wednesday, February 23, 2022, as in Washington, DC, on January 6, 2021, with the storming of the US Capitol.

As for being Russia's neighbor, I am certain that the restaurants in Sweden (like Ukraine, a non-NATO member) are full this evening with patrons enjoying themselves. That is my way of saying to Malaysians to worry less on what is going on in Beijing or Washington, DC, and focus on the monkeys now at Putrajaya. It is one thing for them to plunder the nation for their greed, it is another for them to put Malaysians at loggerheads with one another or plunge the country into war with our neighbors.

Readers' Rating: * *
Sampling of Readers' Responses:

"I hope there is another similarity, albeit positively. Should these things happen here ... our leader(s) will stay put with the rakyat ... to defend the country and not accepting a safe ride to their villas elsewhere."

"Exactly! Ukraine has a former comedian, and we have plenty of comedians or *raja lawak* wannabes."

The Pandora Papers: The Lesson From America
October 17, 2021

[The Pandora Papers, the work of the International Consortium of Investigative Journalists (icij.org) and containing the secret overseas accounts of heads of states (current and former), celebrities, and business leaders, were released in October 2021 to international headlines. Malaysia had over 100 names on the list, which included a former Finance Minister and a Chief Minister of a state.

Of significance, no one from neighboring Singapore and only a few Americans appeared on the list.]

The Pandora Papers reveals a long list of the rich and powerful having substantial assets held in secret offshore accounts. Remarkable for their absence is that there are no American billionaires on the list. Also significant is that while Jordan's King Abdullah is on it, no Malay sultans are. However, do not cheer as yet!

Former Finance Minister Daim Zainuddin is on it. That speaks volumes of his faith in the local system that he had to invest abroad, and in secrecy. I would have expected that his job was or should have been to make Malaysia the choice destination for all investors, foreign and domestic; not fleeing from it.

Americans are not on that infamous list because they pay taxes on their global incomes, regardless of whether domestic or foreign. Having an account in tax-haven Panama would not affect your taxes. If you were to hide your income, then that would be a crime. For lawyers, they could be disbarred while doctors could lose their license. Further, Americans with assets or financial accounts abroad above a certain threshold must file annual reports to the Internal Revenue Service regardless of whether those assets earn any income. The report must include year-end value as well as the highest and lowest figures for the year, reflecting the associated transactions.

Malaysians are not taxed on their foreign incomes; likewise, income from certain entities owned by locals but incorporated or registered abroad. No surprise then that Malaysians have foreign accounts, quite apart from the secrecy and safety. Americans have little need for either as some states offer even more generous tax advantages, and one's financial and other data are private. Divulging or misusing that information could lead to criminal prosecutions or civil suits.

That also explains why Malay sultans are not on that leaked Pandora Papers list. They have little need for the Virgin Islands (unless they think those islands are full of virgins) as their assets are already secret in Malaysia, and nobody dares ask them to pay their share of the taxes. A few years ago the Sultan of Kelantan drove off with his imported luxury car from the port lot, skipping on the import and other taxes. The personnel did not even dare stop the man!

President Reagan was notorious for his antipathy towards taxes, yet he introduced the "alternative minimum tax" and other provisions that affected only rich Americans like him. Contrast Reagan to Finance Minister Daim. Unlike Reagan who closed those tax loopholes, Daim took advantage of them. That is a tragic commentary not only on him but also on contemporary Malay norms, culture, and values. It also explains why Malaysia, led by the likes of him, remain Third World in status and mentality.

I do not know and could not care less how Daims and the other Malaysians especially Malays on the list acquired their wealth. This much I am certain. Theirs, like the overwhelming number for Malays, were not inherited. Until they hit the bonanza of the New Economic Policy (NEP), Malays including the sultans did not have much. NEP through its corruption, nepotism, and rent-seeking activities changed all that. Nonetheless the assets of these *nouveau riche* Malays, despite their gaudy displays, are but pocket change to the Bezos, Gates, and Musks. The near banana-note value of the ringgit does not help.

With those super-wealthy Americans, unlike their NEP-bred Malay counterparts, one has minimal difficulty ascertaining where they get their fortunes. With Bezos, Amazon.com; the behemoth that simplifies my shopping as well as my viewing the latest movies, not to mention the cheap "cloud storage" for my books and precious family albums. Gates' software helps with my writing and publishing. Musks' electric cars and solar generators reduce global warming.

Name a product or service associated with these mega-rich Malays. Daim was once given (yes, given) state land for salt mining. Alas he is no salt mogul today. There were a few Malay names on the list who had sons at Malay College. Meaning, their children, like the other students there, were but wards of the state. Even their meals there were paid for by taxpayers. Really rich Malaysians would send their children to Alice Smith School or abroad, not Malay College. I do not know whether Daim's law education was also publicly funded. There are many Malays on that list whose education, from their local high school through graduate studies abroad, was paid for by the government.

Malaysia should emulate America and tax Malaysians on all their income, local and foreign. Then have them, including and especially the sultans, file annual reports if their foreign assets or accounts exceed a certain threshold.

Those secret foreign accounts are only part of the problem. Malaysia does not have gift, wealth, or inheritance taxes. There is no chorus to alter that either. Then there is the diversion of political donations, another conduit for corruption. Najib claimed that the Euros, dollars, and pound sterling hauled from his residence immediate post-14th General Election were gifts or political donations.

Piketty in his *Capital and Ideology* (2019) suggests global wealth and inheritance taxes to reduce inequality as well as to fund such cross-border challenges as global warming. Note, both are taxes on assets, not income, a concept that should be familiar to Muslims as that is also the basis for *zakat*.

Income tax discriminates against income and thus workers; asset tax, the wealthy. Asset tax would also bring Malaysia closer to an Islamic state, more so than introducing *hudud* (Islamic criminal law). Make the rates comparable to the low Qur'anic 2.5 percent and you would also discourage cheating.

Current Finance Minister Zafrul threatens to sue local journalists for exposing the Pandora Papers. I suggest that he focuses instead on amending current laws to discourage Malaysians from investing abroad. Then make Malaysia the safe haven for all investors, foreign and local. That would endear him to citizens and investors, quite apart from his saving hefty legal fees and wasting precious court time now overburdened with prosecuting the Najibs, Zahids, and other filthy, pretentious NEP-bred *nouveau riche* Malays.

Readers' Rating: * * *
Sampling of Readers' Responses:

"Bakri Musa has sensible and reasonable solutions to the present circumstances of Malaysians hiding their assets in tax haven countries."

"More important that we dig into the sources of those wealth."

"I blame myself for voting the corrupt, incompetent, God-fearless politicians. I hereby repent and do the right thing in the next general elections!"

" ... [A]nd the Speaker has decided that the Pandora Papers shall not be discussed in Parliament!"

"A rumor ... unconfirmed, widely spread story or statement. ... [M]ay or may not contain elements of truth [and] their veracity is anyone's guess .... The list definitely damaged the reputation of some ...."

Bureaucracy Turns A Kilometer Land Trip Into Hours

December 13, 2020

[The southern-most Malaysian city of Johor Baru may be visible from Singapore across the narrow Strait of Johore, but to cross over at either the old causeway or the new "Second Link" remains a challenge time and patience-wise.]

First Of Two Parts: The Northward Journey

Economist Milton Friedman once said that if the federal government were to be put in charge of the Sahara, in five years there would be a shortage of sand! That is what English instructors call hyperbole, an exaggeration to the point of being ridiculous. However, I do have a more proximate and real-world example of the capacity of governments to grind things down, if not muck things up.

The bureaucracies in Singapore and Malaysia combined have succeeded in making the just slightly over one-kilometer (1,056 meter to be exact) journey across the causeway linking both nations to last over an hour by rail. By road even longer, and unpredictable. You could walk or even crawl across faster. However, you cannot because the bureaucracies on both sides prohibit that. Besides, only the reckless few would attempt, what with the traffic. Some, as those with a death-wish and a back-up desire to be arrested, still try.

One could blame the bureaucrats but that would be true only for Malaysia. Consider that her former Prime Minister Najib Razak was convicted of massive corruption. With that, what do you expect of his civil servants? That excuse however would or could not apply to Singapore. Its government is clean and efficient. Its ubiquitous towering public housing projects which rival luxury condominiums of developed countries are testament to that. Its Changi Airport, among the best in the world, is an oasis for weary travelers.

What gives?

I made a recent overnight return journey from Woodlands, the northern-most part of Singapore, to Johor Baru, peninsular Malaysia's southern-most city, for a family wedding. From the glut of reviews in cyberspace as well as on the advice of locals, I chose the train, The Tebrau Shuttle, for its purported predictable timetable.

I had no difficulty booking online with KTM, the Malay initials for Malayan Railway that operates the train shuttle, except for two quirks. One, KTM charged my credit card right away but could not guarantee my tickets. Be patient, watch your e-mail, was KTM's website advice as I clicked "Proceed to buy." Two, the trip north was $5 Singapore dollars, and the return was also $5, but in Malaysian ringgit. At current exchange, that would be about $1.65 Singapore, or US $1.20.

The next day I received my confirmation, complete with seat assignment (for a five-minute ride!), but only for my return (or southward) trip. My credit card would be duly credited for the unsuccessful northward journey, but expect that to take up to two weeks, the e-mail continued, after its mushy "Thank you for choosing KTM" message.

I re-booked the northward part of my journey choosing a different time. Again, a day later, the same "Unsuccessful, your card would be credited" message.

When you have a corrupt Prime Minister, what do you expect of his government-owned railway? Then I switched to an on-line Singapore travel agency with its extra booking fee. The same "Unsuccessful ..." response a day later, as with my earlier KTM experience. Worried that my stateside credit card issuer would cancel my card for what looked like "suspicious activities," I gave up and explored the Singapore Bus Service (SBS) option, with its clean, punctual, and air-conditioned coaches.

I had no problem deciphering the bus routes and schedules, but not the fares. What a convoluted exposition and bewildering color-coding system! I could not comprehend much beyond the need for "exact change only." I have some familiarity with spoken Singapore English – Singlish – but I did not realize that there is also a written variety!

Singapore schools are all in English and their students score high on international tests. As such those promotional blurbs, on the various websites and bus stops as well as in their brochures, must have been outsourced elsewhere. China perhaps, explaining the gobbledygook English. As per the promotional blurbs, I as a tourist could get a day or week pass at attractive prices, but those could be bought at only a few locations, and none near to me.

So, with my pants' pocket sagging with coins, I was ready. The first No: 950 bus that stopped was full and only a few could board. No problem, the next bus would be only ten minutes later, so said the schedule. The next bus came, fifteen minutes late and full. It just whizzed by our stop!

My friend who had volunteered to guide me despite my earlier protestation that I did not need one as the signs and instructions were so clear, suggested going in the reverse direction to the Woodland Bus Interchange, only three stops away, so we could board the bus at its source. We did, and found a long queue already waiting but we managed to squeeze in. We congratulated ourselves for our foresight!

As we passed by our original bus top, our full bus too just zipped by without stopping. I felt sorry for those still waiting with their indoctrinated patience and obedience, but I could not conceal my smug smile for having outsmarted the system.

Singaporeans are very good at following instructions and not deviating from the rules. They have to; the city is after all a "Fine City," a fine for everything, including if you were caught with a half-empty gas tank crossing the causeway, lest you would be tempted to take advantage of the cheaper gas in Malaysia. There are huge billboards reminding you of the severe penalty for failing to "top off" at the border.

At immigration for exit out of Singapore, my Singaporean guide cleared with no difficulty in the "Singapore Passport" line with its automated machines. I, together with the hordes in the "Other Passports" queue, took much longer, with the lines fast lengthening. That finally cleared and we headed back to our Bus 950, this time a different coach, perhaps the fourth or fifth after ours, one that had just disgorged its passengers at immigration only minutes earlier.

The bus drive across the causeway took less than five minutes, what with the light traffic. We disembarked and proceeded down a long corridor (at least it was air-conditioned) to the cavernous Malaysian Immigration Hall. The multiple lanes under the "Other Passports" were all already long, and fast growing. There were the inevitable few who shifted from one line to another trying to anticipate the fastest moving, just like at Walmart checkouts back at stateside.

An hour later we cleared this bureaucratic hurdle. Then down to our buses to continue the journey to the terminal. There were dozens of buses waiting but no signs. That was not the only oddity. Despite the mob of passengers earlier, there were none looking for their buses except for a few bewildered folks like us. We found our 950 Bus empty with its doors closed and without a driver. A terminal worker suggested that we take any SBS bus as they all would end up at JB Sentral terminal, the final stop. We did, and we were the only passengers. Later I discovered that the other passengers had chosen to just walk to the terminal after clearing immigration. If I had known that it was a short distance, I too would have done so.

My bus trip cost under Singapore $4. That included the return journey which I would skip as I had purchased the train ticket on-line days before.

Readers' Rating: *
Sampling of Readers' Responses:
    "Yes, sir! Especially in Malusia!"

Second Of Two Parts: The Return Southward Journey

For the return southward journey, I chose the train using the ticket I had bought earlier online. I arrived at JB Sentral early as I wanted to explore the shopping center. I had worked as a surgeon at the nearby hospital back in 1978 and remembered well the old railway station with its cool, green spacious surroundings. All that had disappeared, incorporated into this massive edifice that included the transportation terminal, shopping arcade, and the immigration complex.

A brief walkabout was enough; the shopping complex was nothing special. As my ticket was for the 3 PM train, I inquired at KTM's counter whether I could exchange it for an earlier one. Not possible.

Then I saw a long line at another counter with the makeshift sign, "Tickets for 1, 2, 3, 4, 5 and 6 PM trains." For RM 5, I could get on an earlier train. With the sign in bold letters "Have passports ready when purchasing ticket" in full view in front of me, I forwarded my passport to the clerk after she issued my ticket. She gave me a puzzled look. Finally, "Go, go, go!" as she beckoned to the next in line. So much for the sign! It was just for show. No one obeyed it, least of all the workers. Little did I know then that was indeed a good and relevant metaphor for Malaysia. Nobody follows the signs, or rules.

At the departure lobby a huge sign declared, "Gate B – Train To Singapore." The lobby seats however were near empty. Strange, considering the long lines at the counter earlier. Soon I saw a line forming at the other end at Gate A, "Domestic Destinations," so the sign said. Except that everyone had their passports out, unusual for domestic destinations. The sign notwithstanding, it was the line for Singapore. I joined the crowd. A couple with a ticket printout (with its familiar scan code) similar to what I had for my later train was refused entry. The husband had to scuttle back to the KTM counter to exchange it for a "real" ticket. I checked my now unneeded return ticket printout. It said in bold, "Present at the Gate!" but I saw no scanner. That cleared, a long walk to immigration and another less-long queue. Then more waiting.

At last we were then let onto the platform. My ticket showed "Coach 2, Seat 14," but the coaches were not numbered, neither were the seats. I boarded the nearest one. Despite the earlier long lines, it was near empty!

On reaching Singapore and after surviving another long line under "Other Passports," I was out into the less long taxi queue. Finally, I thought.

Premature! The driver asked for my destination, and when I replied, he refused to take me. It was not worth his time for such a short trip. So back to the nearby bus stop, and a frantic search for exact change. Everyone else had passes.

My outward journey took over two hours, my return about an hour. Both were not at peak times, so said the apps on my smartphone. I reviewed the map; the total distance each way, including the one-kilometer causeway, was less than ten kilometers.

Imagine what a school kid, commuter, or frequent traveler between the two countries would have to endure every day. The power of and burden imposed by modern bureaucracies! It matters not whether the bureaucracy is competent and efficient as in Singapore, or corrupt and incompetent north of the causeway.

There must be a better way. Considering that there were few foreign faces amongst my fellow passengers, meaning, most were frequent border crossers, there could be special permits akin to America's Global Entry and Trusted Traveler Programs. That would eliminate the bulk of the lines. For another, sophisticated face-recognition technology could spare those bureaucrats from mindlessly and endlessly flipping through and stamping passports, at least for those regulars. The only technology I saw was the live web camera of the causeway giving you real-time view of the traffic and estimated driving time in both directions. As for electronic passport reader, that is available only in Singapore and for her citizens.

On reflection, there is a reason why there are no such innovations. At its core, immigration, border controls, or "Homeland Security" as we call it stateside, are but manifestations of a massive public works project. They serve no other useful purpose.

For Malaysia, the ugly reality is that the millions of immigrants now enter the country legally through work permits, the lucrative contracts for which are issued corruptly to families and cronies of ministers. Those workers then overstayed. Then there are the millions more who entered through the miles of unguarded coastlines and the equally porous land borders. If caught, well, that explains why even lowly immigration officials drive Lamborghinis!

There are plans to expand the immigration bays. The proposed Rapid Transit System between the two cities had been cancelled. The solution however is not in more or improved physical facilities but in eliminating the many soft barriers. Meanwhile Malaysia complains that her sand is being sold to Singapore, threatening the ecology. The solution there is simple. As per Friedman's wisdom, have the government take charge of the sand!

Readers' Ratings: *
Sampling of Readers' Responses:
"If it were efficient many would be out of a job, and most of them would be Malays."

"This bureaucracy thing has become a culture in this country. It seems like most government frontline workers are having a field day making life difficult for the ordinary person. I wonder why?"

"Most governments have such a problem, worse in 'democratic' countries."

"Bureaucracy means time consuming. Time is gold and saleable if the price is right. Long lines for waiting to be served means opportunity to sell time."

IX: CHALLENGES OF COVID-19 PANDEMIC

Goodbye 2020! You Taught Us Many Lessons

December 28 2020

[The Covid-19 pandemic began in China in November 2019. A month later it had spread beyond, wrecking disruptions, and taking countless lives along the way. One early public health measure to control the spread was the banning of public gatherings including congregational prayers.]

In his virtual "sermon" on a recent Friday, South Valley Islamic Center Imam Ilyas Anwar recalled with restrained wistfulness his first on-line Friday noon talk more than 40 weeks earlier. He was careful not to label that a sermon as there was no utterance of the traditional *"Iqama Salah!"* (the call to prayer) to signal the start of the Friday congregational prayer.

This disruption of our usual Friday worshipping routine was but a tiny blip compared to the overall global chaos triggered by the Covid-19 virus. This tiny elemental life-form continues to humble the modern world. Even America, the richest country and with a humongous defense budget, was no match for the virus.

At the end of 2020 as I stood in line with my co-workers to get the first of our two-dose BioNTech/Pfizer Covid-19 vaccine, I was struck by one thought. As a physician I am very much aware of the importance of vaccines more so for infectious diseases. However, what I saw in the facial reactions and body language of my coworkers that morning reflected something much more. It was as if we were being dispensed a much-needed ray of hope to what had been horrendous past many months.

It also brought back memories of my Malaysian childhood days back in the 1950s when I too was among the first to be given the polio vaccine at my school. There were no cards or digital records then to show that we had been vaccinated. Instead, we were slapped with a wide adhesive tape across our chest with the stern warning not to remove it, much like ranchers tag their cattle, minus the instruction. The relief on my parents' faces when I came home that day remains etched in my memory. My mother ran to hug me while uttering her not-so-silent prayers of gratitude. Being schoolteachers, they saw first-hand the devastations the polio virus had wrecked, more so on the young.

Unlike writers and artists who are effective and emotive in expressing their inner feelings, we physicians are drilled not to show ours. That morning the best that I could muster to express my gratitude after receiving my Covid-19 shot was to thank the nurse and uttered the usual complimentary remarks, "I didn't feel a thing!" That elicited a grateful sweet smile from her.

In truth I was the one most grateful. My gratitude also went far beyond, to the husband-and-wife team of Ugur Sahin and Ozlem Tureci way across the globe in Germany. They had worked diligently for years with their novel approach in developing this vaccine. As an aside, they were focused initially on treating cancer. My gratitude also went to their parents, Turkish immigrants to Germany. Unlike refugees who had no choice, legal emigration is a volitional act, with many conflicting motives and emotions brought into play. I do not know the circumstances that made the couple's parents to leave their native Turkey, but mankind is the beneficiary of their earlier decision.

The development of this BioNTech/Pfizer Covid-19 vaccine is instructive from so many angles. It displays the might and creativity of capitalism, and the private sector generally, in providing the needed massive infusion of funds, the allocation of skilled talents, and the subsequent efficient supply chain needed to distribute the product. Granted, much of the earlier basic research was funded publicly.

The other principal player was Albert Bourla, Greek-born and educated veterinarian head of Pfizer. The Greeks and Turks are societal equivalent of the Hatfields and McCoys. Yet they were able to overcome that heavy tribal baggage to work for the benefit of mankind.

Early in the pandemic, my Imam Ilyas called the members of the board of our local masjid to consider closing it temporarily. I recall his plea. He could not bear the burden should anyone in our congregation were to become ill because of our gathering. The next day we closed our masjid. Two days later, the state of California issued its edict banning mass gatherings, including at houses of worship.

Words cannot adequately express our congregation's gratitude to the foresight and wisdom of our Imam. We were spared the "fear God more than the virus" pontifications. In the end, that is the functional definition of an Imam or any religious leader: to lead the flock along the straight path and away from harm.

As we move forward in combating the coronavirus crisis in 2021, I pray that the ray of hope that shined on the day I received my Covid-19 vaccine shot blooms into its promised full brightness. At the same time let us not forget the humbling lesson of 2020 – that the tiniest life-form could halt human civilization and throw it in disarray.

Readers' Rating: * *
Sampling of Readers' Responses:
"Poetic justice to the arrogance of *Homo sapiens* and politicians in particular."

"2020 has done too much but it also teaches us many lessons!"

"Covid-19 ... is a definite message from God to mankind ... [that] has lost all sense of humanity and being humane. Greed and lust have engulfed man and become a religion where the end justifies the means. War, conflict, harm, sufferings, and unfair business remain the tool to be ahead of others. Gratitude to God ... is put aside. It is man's greed that incurs the wrath of God ...."

"Thank you for sharing your thoughts on the most difficult and disruptive 2020.... Indeed the world has never been tested this way and ... [we] have to embrace this unprecedented 'new normal.'"

A Very Different Ramadan, But The Essence Remains
April 23, 2020

[News item: With the Covid-19 pandemic still roaring and state-imposed lockdowns still a reality in much of the world, communal religious activities, like other mass gatherings, had to be curtailed to protect congregants' safety.]

It would be a severe understatement to say that this Ramadan is very different from all previous ones. What with the lockdown imposed in response to the Covid-19 pandemic, our central social and religious activities normally undertaken communally at mosques, suraus, and elsewhere are now suspended.

However, if we take our core religious values and commitments to heart, independent of rituals, circumstances, and places of worship, then we should be able to adapt to the current reality. This challenge is not unique unto our faith. We should be comforted by the fact that Islam had prevailed over many such tribulations in the past, from ravaging deadly plagues and barbaric Mongol invasions to the messianic secularism of Ataturk and the brutal despotism of Stalin.

We will get through this, *Insha' Allah* (God willing!).

For those fascinated with numbers and happenstance, there is much to celebrate this Ramadan. It is the rare one with five Fridays, and the symmetry of the Year 1441 of the Hijrah.

Our small (about regular 50-70 congregants on Friday prayers) Muslim community in Morgan Hill, California, continues to adapt to this new normal through the enlightened spiritual leadership of our Imam Ilyas. We acted preemptively by closing our masjid ahead of the state-wide ordered lockdown. Every Friday now at 1 PM, at about the time of Zuhur prayer, our Imam would go on live video to deliver his talk to the members of our congregation. We are careful not to label that a sermon as it is not associated with our regular congregational prayer, but the essence and intent remain the same – uplifting message for and active (albeit only virtual) engagement with our community members.

Likewise with this Ramadan. Every evening our Imam recites the Qur'an on live podcast and our congregation gets to follow with him. Again we are careful not to label that as *Taraweeh* but the essence and intent remain the same – to seek guidance and inspiration from our Holy Book. Indications are that our Imam will also have to deliver what otherwise would be his Eid sermon in a similar virtual manner.

It is not a surprise that our community, located as we are at the southern tip of Silicon Valley and with many of our members engaged in the information and hi-tech industries, has taken to this digital revolution with relative ease. After every one of these on-line sessions, I thank those pioneers and engineers who made possible this wonderful medium. It is the same technology that enables me to celebrate with my granddaughter her birthday, thousands of miles across the Pacific. More poignant, it is software like Facetime and hardware like smart phones that make possible for many to bid their last farewell to their loved ones dying of Covid-19, prevented as they are to be by their bedside.

I do not know whether those chip engineers and software designers are religious or not, but I am certain that Allah has a special place in Heaven for them. If, as an ahadith has it, that a man was admitted to Heaven for removing a thorn from a path thus saving others from possible injury, likewise those ingenious engineers who enable me to listen to my Imam and converse with my granddaughter miles away should also be deserving of such divine favors. I say this to counter the tendency among many Muslim intellectuals and other religious types to belittle or even ridicule these modern Western innovations. Yet they use them with enthusiasm, without ever giving thought much less express their gratitude to those who made that possible.

Knowledge is knowledge, with no artificial differentiation between religious and secular. This "Islamization of Knowledge" fad which asserts that there is a uniquely "Islamic" variant is the height of intellectual folly. It is but a massive intellectual fraud perpetrated upon the ummah.

Religious Minister Dzulkifli Al Bakri reminds us to be thankful and positive in spirit during this Ramadan. "Someone somewhere right now is fighting for his or her life. We still have ours, so be thankful and spend it in obedience of Allah." That was the theme of his Madrasah Ramadan message. He also has a special message for those selfless, tireless frontline workers. If they find it hard to fast, it is *harus* (leeway) for them to break it so their attention and ability to treat the sick would not be compromised. As a surgeon I know how exhausting it can be to attend to the sick. On more than one occasion I had to break my fast. I did so without regret or hesitation. My patients' needs always come ahead of my personal salvation.

That advice from former Mufti Al Bakri is wise, timely, and practical. As he reminded all, Ramadan is a month of charity. I cannot think of a more charitable deed than to be of service to your fellow human beings, more so when they need it most. In these trying times of Covid-19, there are many in such desperate state. Our *zakat* (tithe) is never more precious and needed than now. Please give generously and make this Ramadan special for them and us.

Ultimately that is the mark of devoted Muslims, how well we serve our fellow man, not how rhythmic our *ratib* (chanting). Likewise, a true Muslim leader is one who brings justice, peace, and prosperity to the people, not how overflowing his robe or eloquent his sermon.

May this blessed Ramadan bring peace, prosperity, and most of all good health to you and yours! Keep safe!

Readers' Rating: * * * *
Sampling of Readers' Responses:

"Great to hear local Ramadan stories from different parts of the world! May Allah bless us all! Ameen!"

"Dr. Musa, I am not a Muslim, you know that! But what you wrote was so nice. Have a blessed Ramadan!"

"Thanks for sharing .... I am a Buddhist, but it is good to understand how a progressive Muslim intellectual feel about Ramadan. Wish you a pious, restful, and meaningful Ramadan!"

Deny Satan An Easy Victory

April 12, 2020

[News item April 8, 2020: The faithful throughout the world are fuming that in their hour of need they are denied access to their places of worship to seek spiritual guidance and solace. For Christians with their Easter masses and Muslims the upcoming Ramadan and Eid, this unprecedented barrier put up by the secular authorities in response to the escalating Covid-19 pandemic is hard to accept or fathom, but a necessity in view of the serious public health threat this virus poses.]

Evangelical Christians in the American South, pious Muslims of Southeast Asia, and Hindu devotees in India continue to throng their places of worship during this Covid-19 pandemic despite the clear evidence of the dangers that they would pose to themselves and others. To them, Corvid-19 is but an instrument of Almighty God to punish mankind for its excesses. This conviction is expressed in such statements as "We fear God more than Covid-19," or "At times of difficulties we seek solace and guidance from Him and in His house of worship."

Myths, religious and otherwise, are difficult to challenge with facts or rationality. We are more likely to succeed if we were to replace one set of myths with another, one we hope that would be beneficial or at least less harmful. The myth of the superiority of the White Man gave way to that of Kipling's White Man's burden. That in turn yielded to the current conviction of the universality of Western values. That is much more benign and could even be beneficial. Viruses too are like myths. They can change (mutate) or made to, and in the process become harmless or even useful, as with the live polio virus vaccine.

As the scientific evidence has failed to convince those believers to alter their behaviors, I suggest mutating their myth while still retaining its religious framework of God, and of good versus evil. Convince them that Corvid-19 is not God's instrument but of His archenemy, Satan, intent on destroying mankind. It would be incumbent upon every believer to thwart the devil's machination. That also is the universal theme of sermons of all faiths throughout history.

Meaning, those who are Covid-19 positive must do their duty to isolate themselves or be forced to do so. The ancients caged their mentally deranged in the belief of containing the devil within them. It was for their own (and community's) good, they rationalized. We should do likewise with Covid-19 positive individuals (and those suspected of being so), except we don't cage but quarantine them. The purpose is the same, to protect them and the community. Likewise, those symptomatic Covid-19 patients must be 'exorcised.' The ancients had their candle-cupping, bloodletting, and skull trephining to let out the evil spirit. Modern medical interventions are but highly refined, considerably more hygienic, and therapeutically more effective albeit horribly very expensive versions of those ancient practices.

We could liken modern ventilators blowing positive pressure oxygen into the lungs as unseen forces of good driving out the evil spirit, akin to ancient shamans blowing into their victims' ears! Those healers of yore may not have been rigorously trained but they were well attired and equipped with their set of rituals and incantations. Likewise with modern medical personnel, with their personal protective equipment (PPE) and sterile technique rituals but *sans* those incarnations.

In ancient times those who succumbed to plagues deserved extra cautious treatment lest Satan would continue his evil intent through those contaminated remains. Thus their special dispensation from the customary funeral rites. In Islam, those victims are considered *syahid* (martyrs). As their place in Heaven is assured, there is little need for elaborate prayers and the other funeral rites.

That ahadith should not be regarded, as some misguided ulama have, as a license for believers to willfully expose themselves to achieve martyrdom. Religious devotion should not be wrapped in reckless courage and ignorant obedience. Instead, that ahadith is meant to serve as a balm to grieving families. They already bear the terrible emotional burden by not being by the side of their loved ones at the very end. They need that spiritual comforting. That prophetic wisdom is also congruent with safe public health practices. Imagine the contagion if family members were allowed their usual contacts with contaminated bodies.

Be wise and be pious. Do not let our bodies and those of our loved ones be the conduits for the devil's malicious intent. Wear masks and wash the devil off our hands frequently. Most of all observe social distancing even if that means staying away from our places of worship. Deny Satan an easy victory!

Readers' Rating: *
Sampling of Readers' Responses:

"Yes Doc! Well said! We will stay safe! Thank you for reminding!"

"The scientific method is essentially reductionist and hence is a blinded protocol. As such it is a great propaganda tool to manipulate the masses especially where there are enough people who put their faith exclusively in science…. When it comes to the bigger picture of life, the scientific method is woefully inadequate."

Religion Should Protect, Not Endanger Us

March 29, 2020

[News item: On March 17th, 2020, the Malaysian (Federal) Religious Department (JAKIM, its Malay acronyms) announced the closure of all mosques in response to the Covid-19 pandemic. Five days later it announced the creation of a special task force to handle the remains of Covid-19 victims. Both edicts affect only the Federal territories. There is still no effective federal/state coordination even on such important cross-state matters.]

It is humbling to note that an ultra-tiny packet of RNA genetic material could wreck such havoc on human civilization. Beyond the social upheavals and economic devastations, this Covid-19 virus also inflicts consequential but underappreciated impact on the individual psyche, both the healthy as well as the infected. Despite advances in neuro- and behavioral sciences, there is still a huge void in understanding this facet of the pandemic. This is where we need our spiritual and religious leaders. Just as there are no atheists in a foxhole, likewise there are no non-believers in a pandemic. We need and depend on a higher power to reassure us and to protect and sustain us.

In this regard I am heartened that my Imam Ilyas had recommended early the closing of our masjid even before the state mandate. We could do our prayers at home, he advised. Singapore's Mufti too did likewise. Religion is about priorities, he emphasized. The top priority now is not to endanger ourselves and others. He went further. His organization has put out an informative public service video demonstrating how the virus could spread through hugging, handshaking, and prostrating, all activities associated with congregational prayers. A church in America provides telehealth mental health services. It encourages its followers to maintain regular communications with their loved ones via phones, Facetime, and other virtual platforms. It offers tips on keeping the conversations hopeful so as not to burden others with your anxieties. Other suggestions include reading together passages from the Holy Book, reviewing family pictures, and the sharing of stories, more so of uplifting ones.

Many religious leaders neglect this crucial role of guidance. Malaysian ulama, all on state payroll, instead engage in sterile sermons. We should fear Allah more than Covid-19, they bellowed, and that the virus is Allah's punishment!

Words, more so religious ones or those emanating from faith leaders, have consequences. Those pronouncements had also resulted in Malaysia's second and much more devastating surge in new cases.

Imagine the lives saved, costs not incurred, and families spared needless grief had that Sri Petaling Tabligh religious gathering been cancelled. Nor has that crucial lesson been learned. There was a much bigger festival later in Indonesia, a nation ill equipped to handle the inevitable spike in new infections. Those ulama have yet to own up to their accountability for those preventable tragedies.

Religious leaders have minimal knowledge on medical and public health issues; they should not pretend otherwise. Instead they should endorse those public health measures, using their religious knowledge to buttress their arguments. Likewise, Malaysian professionals should not abrogate their responsibilities by giving those bureaucrat-ulama veto powers in important matters of public safety. Be guided by our prophetic traditions on how to act in a pandemic. If you hear of an outbreak in an area, do not go there. If you are already there, then do not leave. Cleanliness is part of faith, goes another. Our five daily prayers are preceded by wudhu, a general cleansing of the hands, face, and feet.

Yet Malaysians instigated by their ulama are obsessed with public ostentatious displays of their faith, with endless emotional *du'as* and mass *sembayang tahajut* (dedicated prayers). They should be reminded of another prophetic wisdom. First tie your camel securely, only then pray that it does not escape! In the current context, first observe social distancing and hand washing, only then pray and make *du'a* that He would spare you the dreaded virus.

On another front, imagine the anguish of bereaved families when they could not administer the traditional funeral rites, as with washing the bodies. Or worse, when they breach hygienic principles in doing so, thus endangering themselves and others.

Indonesia's Imam Das'ad Latif advice is instructive. He likened the pandemic to war, with the victims *syahid* (martyrs), destined for Heaven. As such funeral rites could be dispensed with, as with those killed in battles. Such soothing words from an alim are a balm to grieving families.

Stress, more so chronic ones, is deleterious to our immune system, and thus our resistance to viruses and diseases. This is aggravated by the associated loneliness, psychiatric symptoms, and life events. Prayers, meditation, and mindfulness alleviate stress. Modern neuroscience's greatest achievement is to integrate these observations at the molecular level, of how stress hormones affect neurotransmitters or alter the conformations of our genes and thus their expressions. Of greater significance is that those consequences are transmitted to the next generation and beyond, as indicated by studies on victims of mass starvation in China during Mao, and in the Netherlands during the WWII Nazi blockade.

In short, what my Imam Ilyas, Singapore's Mufti Nazirudin Nasir, and Indonesia's Imam Das'ad Latif are doing is harness their spiritual leadership to calm and guide their followers. By contrast, those fiery, science-challenged preachers put the fear of Allah in their listeners, aggravating their stress, the very antithesis of the purpose of faith.

Former Mufti and now Religious Minister Duzlkifli Al Bakri should be less an Imam, more an executive. With Ramadan around the corner, he should consult all the muftis to come up with a national consensus. Covid-19 does not recognize political boundaries, religious persuasions, or the calendar. Prepare people for the possible closing of mosques right up to Ramadan and Eid. We cannot risk turning Houses of Allah into Houses of Pestilence.

Religion is to guide and protect, not lead us into danger. Islam is a set of universal principles to guide us to and keep us on the straight path. It is not a compilation of rigid rituals to be mindlessly performed regardless of the consequences.

Readers' Rating: *
Sampling of Readers' Responses:
"Thank you, Doctor, for the insight on Ramadan and Eid. Christians will have to forego Easter too!"

It's Not God Versus Covid-19

March 22, 2020

[News item: On March 19, 2020, California's Governor Newson announced a state-wide lockdown affecting all 40 million people. The state, America's most populous, had until recently the highest number of confirmed Covid-19 cases, with my County of Santa Clara where Silicon Valley is located, leading the pack with over 302 cases, 108 hospitalized, and 10 deaths as of 4 PM March 22, 2020.]

Last Friday, March 20, 2020, the first day of spring and in the void of our mosque being closed ten days earlier, I spent the afternoon listening to on-line sermons and lectures from around the Muslim world pertaining to the current Covid-19 pandemic. I was stunned and appalled that many ulama had framed the issue simplistically around "It is Allah that we should fear, not Covid-19." They refused to follow the World Health Organization (WHO) guidelines to refrain from mass gatherings. They continued with their congregational prayers, oblivious of the grave dangers they imposed upon themselves and their congregation. And from there, to the general community and far beyond.

They are being irresponsible and their actions reprehensible. The recent four-day, 15,000-strong Tabligh gathering in Sri Petaling Mosque on Feb 27, 2020, triggered Malaysia's second and much bigger surge of Covid-19 cases. Those attendees have now spread the pestilence throughout Southeast Asia and far beyond. The first Covid-19 death in Malaysia was an attendee at that gathering.

This fatal ignorance and willful irresponsibility span faith and countries. White Christian pastors in America's conservative South openly defied the WHO protective guidelines, urging their congregations to shake hands and hug each other. At the Vatican in Covid-19-stricken Italy, Cardinal Burke called on the faithful to attend Mass!

Such determined defiance was not limited to God-fearing souls. The young in Florida and Australia flocked to the beaches, and in UK to mammoth concerts. At least there one could understand their psyche – the presumed invincibility of youth!

I found some solace in the pronouncements of the few wise, responsible ulama. Most welcomed and reassuring were from the incoming as well as outgoing Muftis of Singapore, Nazirudin Nasir and Fatris Bakaram respectively. Their sane, practical, and helpful advice was a much-needed antidote to the willful nonsense and dangerous rubbish emanating from the hordes of Muftis across the causeway.

We express our fear of Allah, Fatris reminded his flock, by following His teachings, as being grateful for the life and health that Allah has bestowed upon us. Nurture that precious divine gift so we could be of benefit to the community. In the current context, we must maintain our social distance and take all necessary preventive precautions to safeguard the health of ourselves as well as that of our loved ones, while at the same time not endangering others. Meaning, follow those prudent WHO guidelines. Fear of Allah also means that we should use our God-given intellect, not close our eyes and freeze our minds, he continued. Singapore was the first to close its mosques and canceled Friday and other congregational prayers.

Similar sentiments were expressed in Indonesia, alas by far too few. Among the rare precious sane voices was that of Imam Das'ad Latif. He went further and invited a physician to be on his podcast to discuss the pandemic and educate his listeners. Now that is an alim who is very much aware of the gaps in his own knowledge and goes out to find some experts to fill it. Alas, such humility is glaring by its absence among Malaysian ulama. They already know it all. In Zimbabwe, Imam Munk, a preacher whose views on other social issues I do not share, expressed similar sentiment. Like the Singapore Mufti, he cancelled his congregational prayers. Bless him!

Malaysia meanwhile continues as usual, oblivious of the turmoil and mortal danger. The former Federal Mufti and now newly minted Minister of Religious Affairs suggested that Imams shorten their sermons. The widely listened-to former Mufti of Perlis, Mohamad Asri (MAZA), continued with his mass gatherings, mesmerizing his listeners and himself with his exquisite and prolonged recitations of obscure ancient Arabic texts. He none-too-tactfully reminded the Minister of Religious Affairs that he had no authority over the states. Meaning, Asri was not bound by the ministerial edict. I would have thought that in a national emergency, with the virus not recognizing boundaries, Asri would gather his fellow Muftis to advise the Agung and his Council of Rulers on a national consensus.

If the Agung and his brother rulers could gather in short order to dismiss former Prime Minister Mahathir, surely this Covid-19 pandemic is a much more pressing issue.

Malaysian ulama behave like out-of-touch psychiatrists who in discussing depression would endlessly quote Freud, Jung, and Maslow, while remaining blissfully ignorant of such modern insights as neurotransmitters. In Brunei, the Sultan reminded his subjects that the virus is from Allah and that citizens must return to Him. No mention about washing hands or maintaining social distance.

With all those, I am blessed that my community here in Silicon Valley, California, has an enlightened Imam Ilyas as our spiritual leader. It was he, after consulting his brother Imams in the area, who first suggested closing our masjid. Our secular Board quickly endorsed that, and the message was sent out right away to all our members, well before the Governor's edict.

Though born in England, Imam Ilyas attended the local secular public school. He then pursued his Islamic education via the traditional route in India. He thus represents the best of Western liberal education and traditional eastern one, the former its inclusivity and open-mindedness, the latter, deference to precedents and traditions. He balances and synthesizes worldly knowledge and current insights with religious knowledge and spiritual values. That is the kind of leadership contemporary Muslim societies desperately need but are not getting.

Readers' Rating: * *

Sampling of Reader's Responses:

"Your piece ... says it all about what ignorance can bring about unnecessary calamity! I sincerely hope some of these people will take heed."

"It is not the fear of Allah or Covid-19 that should be our motivation to act responsibly but our respect and love for our neighbors."

"Which comes first: depression or neurotransmitters? Or perhaps both at the same time?"

"Too much faith can make one blind, deaf, and dumb to reason. And deadly too!"

"A small correction. The Mufti of Perlis was the first to prohibit Friday prayers and all *jamaah* [congregational] prayers in all mosques in Perlis a good two weeks before the Federal government acted."

"We need that kind of preacher in our society ... Allah did not ask us to just pray without taking any precaution to overcome diseases. What is the benefit of knowledge if we cannot use it wisely?"

X: VIRTUAL CONFERENCES

LeadUS Malaysia Zoom Conference
Does The Malay Mind Need To Be Liberated?

[Panel Discussion Via Zoom organized by LeadUS Malaysia in Kuala Lumpur on January 10, 2021, with co-panelist Professor Mohamad Tajuddin Rasdi. Moderated by LeadUS Malaysia's Dr. Rozhan Othman.]

Dr. Rozhan Othman: A mindset is more than just an opinion. It is a worldview that develops through experience, conditioning, and socialization. In some situations, social and political institutions are created to reinforce the mindset. The Malay mindset in Malaysia is distinctly different from that of the Malays in Indonesia, South Africa, and Sri Lanka. The mindset forms the *weltanschauung* or *tasawwu*r. When this is not questioned or subjected to periodical scrutiny, it becomes a dogma. What would you consider to be the key drivers that shape the Malaysian Malay mindset, and what aspects of the Malay mindset has become dogma? How does this shape how Malays behave?

Bakri Musa: You could cite three more groups of Malays who are nearby and thus more relevant examples – Malays in Singapore, Brunei, and Southern Thailand. Did you know that the first Malay with a PhD from Harvard was from Pattani (Southern Thailand)? Then consider this: At one time there were more Malays at UC Berkeley from Singapore than from Malaysia.

As for Brunei, I once met her Minister of Education back in 1970. I suggested to him that Brunei uses its vast oil resources to build a center of excellence for education in the Malay world (Nusantara). He stunned me with his answer. No point spending money on educating Malays, he assured me, for then they would become independent-minded, and you would have a revolt. Remember the deadly Azhari Rebellion of 1962 that nearly toppled the sultan, he reminded me.

Coming back to Malaysia, the drivers for the Malay mindset today are first, religion; second our medieval feudal culture; and third, the behaviors of others. Within Malaysia the others would be the non-Malays; abroad it would be the West. I would put the relative weightage as thus: religion at 75 percent; culture 20; and the third, 5. I would put education (specifically the national) system as a subset of culture.

The behaviors of others account for only 5 percent, but that obsesses Malays to no end. I could not care less whether Malaysian Chinese can speak Malay or if they are all rich. Imagine if they were to excel in Bahasa and the best Malay novels were to be written by them, what a slap in the face that would be for Malays! As for the West, look how obsessed was Mahathir with George Soros. This Malay obsession with the "others" within Malaysia is reflected on the negative, divisive, and destructive efforts at closing vernacular schools. Our fellow panelist Professor Tajudddin is a fine product of the Chinese school system, and you want to close it?

As for our culture, I worry less about the feudal elements in it. Feudalism will collapse on its own weight. The continued egregious behaviors of Malay sultans and orang *kayangan* (aristocrats) would only grease the slide. How long would Malays tolerate their sultans cavorting with foreign ladies and then be stuck with humongous alimonies, all paid for ultimately by taxpayers? The only aspect of our culture that worries me (apart from our entrenched feudalism) is our education system.

Religion is what I worry about most. Caution here before all hell breaks loose. I am not referring to Islam, rather the variety propagated in Malaysia which some critics have labelled as the "religion of the ancient Bedouins." Malaysian Islam now has state imprimatur. As such it is less religion, more massive bureaucracy, with one of the biggest budgets, personnel, and thus influence. It is also the driver of the Malay mindset and dogma. This however, is a recent phenomenon. A generation or two ago Malay leaders had no qualms in sending their children to such schools as St. Johns Institution and the Convent of the Holy Infant Jesus. Today they will hound Muslim women who do not don a hijab.

In its first few centuries Islam was a beacon for the world. Then a long decline. Only now are we seeing tantalizing rays of light emerging amidst the darkness. In part this is the normal trajectory with all civilizations. Ibn Khaldun wrote something about that. We see this thin ray of enlightenment beginning in the tiny Gulf States. Consider that three of the top 10 airlines are from this region – Emirates, Qatar, and Etihad.

Another is Turkish Airlines, another Muslim country. At one time Malaysia Airlines was considered among the tops. Not now. A not unrelated observation, those small Gulf States also have the highest number of branches of American universities.

The other source of enlightenment is the West. English is now the second most important language of Islam, next to Arabic. There are more English translations of the Qur'an in the last fifty years than in all previous 1400. The West is also the beneficiary of those enlightened Islamic scholars who had been driven out of their native land. A more tangible indicator is this. There are more new mosques being built in America than any other houses of worship. Even more remarkable, all are self-funded, with no state help.

An ahadith asserts that *nur* would emerge from the west. If you interpret *nur* to be light or enlightenment and not literally as the sun, there is wisdom in that. The finest Departments of Islamic Studies are at Western universities. Meanwhile the Islam in most Muslim countries, Malaysia included, is the sclerotic variety.

If we aspire to have *nur* emerging in our midst, then we must emulate the West, just as those early Muslims the Greeks. If that is too much, and we prefer the Arabs, then emulate the Gulf States, not Egypt or Saudi Arabia. Yet those backward countries are where we sent most of our students.

One way to change the Malay mindset is to bring in Western liberal education, free from the suffocating control of the Islamists. Malaysian public universities, where the faculty and students are overwhelmingly Malays, are the cause of the Malay mind being entrapped. Those pseudo-scholars are intent on indoctrinating their students.

I hate making that statement as it would offend those who are genuine scholars and researchers who toil hard every day, unappreciated, and underpaid to change the situation. I know many of them and I salute them for their dedication despite the obstacles thrown in their way. Unfortunately, they are not the ones elevated to the National Professors Council. Therein lies the problem!

Dr. Rozhan: Mindset change is a prerequisite to social transformation. In Japan, modernization became a focus of the Meiji Restoration. It dismantled the Shogunate, transformed the feudal agriculture system, and embraced industrialization. This transformation included changing values and mindset. Work in an industrial setting requires precise scheduling and punctuality, something that was not required in an agricultural setting. The Meiji Restoration instilled punctuality by introducing watches and organizing annual watch synchronizing events to ensure uniformity of time across the country as well as emphasizing punctuality.

South Korea's President Park Chung-Hee initiated the *Saemaul Undong* movement to bring modernization to rural areas. It also sought to dismantle the beliefs in superstition and shamans of rural dwellers. We see a similar change in China under Deng Xiaoping. He embraced capitalism and changed the Maoist attitude towards wealth and profit making. In all these changes there was a strong visionary leader driving the transformation. Do Malays need such a strong and visionary leader to liberate their mind or is a change led by strong leaders potentially problematic? Hitler was after all a strong leader who changed the German mindset.

Bakri Musa: In all those instances you mentioned there was a trigger mechanism, usually external, that toppled the comfortable coconut shell of that society and culture. How that society responded would be the determining factor. With Japan it was the blatant intrusion, unmolested, of Admiral Perry into Edo Harbor in 1853. With that the Japanese realized how impotent and far behind the West they were. That prompted them to learn from the West. The Japanese did not delude themselves into thinking that they were superior, or the best.

That is the first needed lesson, to recognize your deficiencies. That applies to society as well as individuals.

Realizing how far behind they were, the Japanese sent thousands of their teachers, professors, and administrators to the West, not for weeks or months of *culup* (quickie) courses as Malaysia does, but for years. When they returned, they were guaranteed their old positions. They were to stay abroad until they felt that they had learned everything they needed to in their field. When they returned, they put into actions what they had learned from abroad.

Among the five Charter Oaths the Japanese of the Meiji era adopted, one was to seek knowledge from around the world (echoing a familiar ahadith); another, participation of all classes in the administration of the state; and third, public discussions of all major decisions. No more top-down command or *titah* from the emperor. The most consequential Charter Oath was those evil customs of the past be discontinued to be replaced by new ones based on just laws of nature. Implied in that was their collective acknowledgment that some of their old customs were evil.

Granted, a few of those sent abroad learned only the superficial trappings of the West, as with their formal attires. One senior official took to dispensing with his erstwhile concubines (a Japanese tradition) and stuck with only one wife, trying to be "Western." Well at least that was a positive gesture.

Malaysia too sent thousands of her young abroad. However only a few appreciated and even fewer absorbed the ethos of what made the West advanced and brought those values home. Others were satisfied only with acquiring the colorful plumage of the Cockney crowd and other undesirable youth subculture of the West. No surprise there as most of those sent to America gravitated towards lesser institutions, its Creekside state universities. No wonder on their return home they had a warped view of America and Americans. One former Chief Secretary to the Government of Malaysia, Ali Hamsa, went to Oklahoma State. Any surprise that he could not stand up to little Prime Minister Najib?

By contrast, look at the previous Trump Administration. How many of his cabinet secretaries and other top officials had resigned in protest long before his debacle of January 6, 2021? They did not just resign, they criticized him publicly. In contrast, how many Malaysian top officials have resigned over Najib's 1MDB mess, much less criticized him?

With China, it was Deng who recognized the destructive madness of Mao's Cultural Revolution. In late 1970s when he came to power, the first thing Deng did was to ask President Carter to accept a few hundred Chinese students to top American universities. Today, Chinese students and scholars are a major presence at those places such that they are now viewed as a national security threat! American-trained Chinese scientists sequenced the Covid-19 genome within weeks. Fantastic! A generation ago Mao would have sent those scientists to the ulus for their "re-education," or even killed them.

Deng was a diminutive figure and far from being charismatic, yet he transformed China. Those American-trained Chinese scientists he sent abroad rebuilt the country's universities and academies that had been wrecked by Mao. When I first visited Beijing in the 1990s, most of the foreign passengers in the plane were teachers, lecturers, and professors. Today the greatest number of students sitting for American tests like SAT and GMAT are from China. A generation ago, none!

Mandarin is far more advanced than Malay, yet Chinese parents today rush to enroll their kids in English schools. Their leaders do not accuse them of not *mertabatkan* (respecting) their own language.

You are right. The danger or flip side to our yearning for strong leaders we could end up with a local Hitler or Trump. What we need instead is an environment where our bright young people could get or be enticed into positions of responsibilities in government. Strengthen our institutions by having these smart courageous people helming them. This is one reason I am cheering for Anwar's Parti Keadilan Rakyat. He attracted many smart young people like Rafizi Ramli, Nik Nazmi, and Sim Tze Tzin into his party. Rafizi excepted, they were all successful in the last election. The government had to arrest Rafizi so he could not contest in that election. Today he is out of politics. I do not blame him but what a loss for Malays, Malaysians, and Malaysia. Contrast the youthful vigor of PKR versus the sclerotic senescent UMNO.

Years ago I met a group of Malaysian government scholars here in America. Unlike the masses sent abroad, they were among the rare species to be attending elite universities. They were discussing how to "bomb" their interviews back in Malaysia so they would be denied a job. Thus freed of their scholarship bonds they could return to America where opportunities are so much brighter for them! Those are the very people Malaysia should attract and retain, not those from the Oklahoma State universities. Why did Malaysia not emulate Japan of the Meiji Restoration? Malaysia should have encouraged those bright students to stay back in America as long as they want in order to gain valuable experiences.

On the other side, I once met the Chairman of the Public Services Commission while he was on an official tour of America. He complained how unimpressed he was with Malaysians who graduated from American universities. Well, that chairman could not differentiate between Stamford College versus Stanford University. Where do you start to change things when you have those types in positions of high authority?

Dr. Rozhan: World War II was a tipping point in Western colonial history. The defeat of Western colonial powers by Japan, an Asian country, shattered the colonials' perception of their invincibility and superiority. That catalyzed the independence movement in many countries. One development not often mentioned is that the Japanese Occupation exposed the impotence of the traditional feudal elite. In Burma, India, and Indonesia, that contributed to the dismantling of the traditional feudal power structures. In Malaya, the traditional feudal elite quickly toed the British line after the war. The sultans supported the British-sponsored Malayan Union Treaty that would have made the country a permanent British Dominion. Despite that and unlike in other countries, the Malay feudal elite was maintained after Merdeka. What does this say about the Malay mindset then and how does this shape the current Malay outlook?

Bakri Musa: WWII was the tipping point not just for colonialism but also Malay culture. There were three other tipping points in our culture — the coming of Islam, intrusion of Western imperialism, and the path we chose towards independence. Each inflection points affected the collective Malay mindset. The true measure of a culture is how well it prepares its adherents to such major events, especially when unexpected and catastrophic. Compare the respective local responses to the Asian tsunami of 2004 versus the Katrina hurricane a year later.

To the simple, science-illiterate Indonesians the tsunami was not the result of some tectonic plate shifts deep beneath the Indian Ocean, rather Allah sending them a message. With that, the century-long Aceh rebellion, in effect a civil war among the Muslims there, ended in short order.

Americans are educated, sophisticated, and have vastly more resources. Yet a decade after Katrina the deep social and racial divide exposed by that tragedy have only worsened. Instead of effective rehabilitation, America was mired in endless lawsuits. Meanwhile the thousands of mobile homes built for such an emergency were left to deteriorate in warehouses, undistributed.

Culture explains the difference between the two reactions.

I would give an A+ grade for Malay culture for the path we chose towards independence. We did everything right. We chose the right leaders and they in turn picked the right strategy and perfect timing. As for the sultans, they were against independence initially. As it was not worth fighting them and dividing our society along the royalists and republicans, our leaders essentially bribed them with exalted titles, generous civil allowances, and other expensive privileges. Those costs, our wise political leaders decided then, were far cheaper had we remained colonized.

For one, had the sultans balked and our independence delayed, Malaysia would have been forced by the British to receive the millions fleeing Mao's Cultural Revolution in the 1950s. Instead, they landed on the then-British colony of Hong Kong. The impact of those refugees from Mainland China would have made the Vietnamese hordes a few decades later seem like a mere trickle.

As for the Japanese Occupation, well, we are still here and intact. That says something about our culture. An interesting aspect to the Occupation was first, there were no lazy Malays then. Second, how easy the Japanese disposed of the Malay sultans. They were simply ignored, and Malays did not miss their sultans. Today when I see Malay sultans acting up, I wish someone would show them pictures of them genuflecting to those Japanese soldiers back during WWII. Fast forward to the present, these Malay sultans put themselves in the same league as Queen Elizabeth and the Japanese Sun Emperor. To put Malay sultans on par with them would involve considerable "concept stretching," to quote Clifford Geertz. Instead, Malay sultans have more in common with Papua New Guinea tribal chiefs.

I remember my mother telling me stories of fishing in Sri Menanti River with the future Queen of Malaysia during the war. There was nothing regal about her in tattered sarong. A few years later there she was being *sembah* on the throne. We the rakyat put her up there.

Third, the Japanese recognized the talented amongst us. P. Ramlee was discovered by the Japanese. So was Ungku Aziz and Tun Razak. Today our culture and our sultans instead honor plunderers and thieves.

As for the coming of Islam, I would give a B grade for our collective response. We accepted the faith willingly but only the theology part. We learned nothing from the Arabs about trading, the activity that brought them into our world in the first place. We translated only the religious texts and *hikayats*, none on the sciences. Nonetheless the greatest benefit to our society was that those early Muslims introduced the written word into our culture. Anytime that happens it gives that culture a quantum leap in advancement. If only our forefathers had gone beyond and learned something from those polymaths of the ancient Arab world!

By contrast, I would give only a passable grade to our response to colonialism. We failed to differentiate between the hideousness of the Portuguese and Dutch versus the less malevolent British variety. There was a thing or two we could have learned from the culture that brought in the Scientific Revolution and ushered in the Industrial Age. As our Munshi Abdullah noted, we were not even curious to learn from a society that could make steel float, referring to the warship *Setoris* that the British had anchored off Singapore harbor.

The consequential difference between the Dutch and British as colonizers is this: Today Malay elites still look fondly to the Brits. Having a condo in London is still the supreme bragging rights among Malays. The Indonesians however have nothing but contempt for the Dutch. Today's Indonesians are learning English, not Dutch.

Had we accepted what little the British had afforded us, as with sending our children to the few English schools, imagine how far ahead we would be today. Think of the few Malays who bravely broke that negative trend – Ismail Ali, the brilliant (and honest) first Governor of Bank Negara; Tun Suffian, first Chief Justice and one still held in high regards; and Majid Ismail, orthopedic surgeon, all Queen scholars. Think of Za'aba. He attended St. Paul Institution in Seremban, a Catholic missionary school, despite his father forbidding and subsequently disowning him.

The cultural hypocrisy of our sultans and leaders was that while they were (still are) Anglophiles, sending their children to English schools, or today, International Schools, they exhorted the masses to do otherwise. This glaring duplicity is missed by many.

An unexplored enquiry remains. Why did our culture readily embrace the then new and alien influences when those were brought in by Muslim traders, and then once we became Muslims, we remained closed or even hostile to later foreign cultures? Was the West a crude and thus ineffective colonizer or were the early Arab traders subtle and more sophisticated in influencing us? It seems that way today what with Malays unabashedly embracing Arabism.

Despite independence and we are in charge, Malays are fast being left behind. This time we cannot blame the colonials. To catch up we must change our mindset. Begin by holding our leaders accountable. If we cannot do that or fearful of doing so, then ignore them.

My parents did exactly that with respect to my education. They noted that while the Minister of Education when I was young, Tun Razak, was exhorting Malay parents to send their children to Malay schools, he was surreptitiously sending his – all five of them – to English schools, and in England to boot! My late father decided that until Malay leaders heed their own advice, he would ignore them. He was right then and even more so today. My father was definitely in the minority, then or now.

We see this hypocrisy even with religious leaders. They pray, fast, undertake Hajj umpteen times, and adorn themselves with overflowing robes. Then when given illicit funds *aka* bribes, they consider that to be *borkat* – gift from Allah!

The most effective way to liberate the Malay mind is to ignore current Malay leaders of all varieties and begin thinking for ourselves.

Dr. Rozhan Othman: In your book *Liberating the Malay Mind* you quoted from *Nahjul Balaghah* an incident involving a mullah, his donkey, and his neighbor. For the benefit of the audience, can you describe the incident and explain the point you are trying to make. Does this incident illustrate the harm of dogmas in people's mindset? Specifically, how do you relate that to the quest to liberate the Malay mind?

Bakri Musa: That mullah was fed up with his neighbor forever borrowing things from him and not returning them. One day this neighbor came to borrow the mullah's donkey. Anticipating the request, he had earlier stowed the animal away in the barn and out of sight. So when the neighbor appeared with his expected request, the mullah was ready his sharp retort.

"I am sorry, my brother has borrowed my donkey earlier."

As the neighbor prepared to leave, disappointed, the donkey brayed in the barn.

"I thought you said your brother had borrowed your donkey?"

To which the mullah replied, "Do you believe the braying of a donkey over the words of a mullah?"

If you have a critical mind, you believe the truth even if it were to be revealed by a donkey over the falsehood of a mullah. If you do not have a critical mind you could fall for the lies perpetrated by those in power. Soon you would believe the "big lie." In America that resulted in the deadly storming of the US Capitol on January 6, 2021, by fanatical Trump supporters. America is lucky in that she has strong institutions and enough courageous people who can think critically. Not so in Germany of the 1930s. Or Malaysia today; hence the 1MDB and other expensive and destructive debacles.

I have a more relevant, relatable, and more contemporary example for Malays than that donkey story. Consider this scene. The Agung stepped out of his grandiose palace sporting his latest model Giorgio Armani sunglasses.

"It's dark today!" he *titah*, as he looked up to the sky.

His ADC immediately instructed his aides. "Our Agung is smart! He can forecast the weather. Go quick, grab some umbrellas."

Not to be outdone, his second underling added, "Oh, our Agung is thinking of his subjects in Pahang, what with the recent devastating floods. We must warn the rakyat!"

At least that second aide was thinking of the welfare of the citizens.

Then the third added, "It's actually very nice, your Majesty. Just take off your sunglasses!"

Among the three aides, who was thinking critically? If you are a leader, who would you choose to work with you?

You can tell much about leaders by those they keep around them. That is why I am impressed with Anwar Ibrahim; he attracts many bright young talents into his party.

In my *Liberating The Malay Mind* I addressed the challenge of critical thinking at the societal level, as with modernizing the school system away from rote memorization and mindless regurgitations at test times. My forthcoming book addresses how we could improve our critical thinking skills. Don't count on our schools and universities to teach that! Tentatively titled, *Qur'an, Hadith, And Hikayat: Exercises In Critical Thinking* [2021], I use examples familiar with and relevant to Malays. Once we can think critically, then we can decide whether to believe the mullah or the braying donkey.

The best antidote to the current corrupt Malay leadership is for individual Malays to exercise critical thinking. The American writer Suzy Kaseem put it best. "Nothing threatens a corrupt system more than a free mind." Our own Usman Awang was even sharper. *Jika hidup berjiwa hamba, pasti tetap terjajah abadi.* (A slave mentality ensures a life of endless servitude). A critical mind is the best defense against *berjiwa hamba* (slave mentality).

One example of an exercise in critical thinking I took from the Qur'an was Ayat 7 of Al Fatihah, (approximately translated), "Guide us along the path of those you have blessed, not those who have incurred your wrath." I challenge readers to cite examples of contemporary individuals whom they considered to have earned Allah's blessings and why. Another is the familiar ahadith, first tie your camel securely, only then pray it does not escape. I use that to counter the current preoccupation of Muslims to just pray so their camels would not escape.

In another example I use the stunning difference in responses of American versus Malaysian students to the folktale "*Batu Belah Batu Melangkup.*" To Malay children that story is a lesson on obedience to mothers as encapsulated in another ahadith, "The door to heaven lies at a mother's feet." To American children however, the mother's behavior was the height of maternal irresponsibility. Same facts, radically different interpretations!

Those are some of the exercises I will use in my forthcoming book.

Dr. Rozhan Othman: What role has higher education played in shaping the Malay mind? Is there a difference in the kind of a mindset developed in our public universities compared to private universities? Are our public universities part of the solution or a part of the problem in the development of the Malay mindset?

Bakri Musa: Let's talk about education in general. Munshi Abdullah likened a child's brain to a *parang* or machete. Teachers and educators are to sharpen that parang. With a sharp parang you could hack your way out of a jungle. To a surgeon, a sharp knife is an instrument to treat cancer; to a sculptor, to create exquisite works of art. To a thug on the other hand, it is a lethal instrument. Hence the need for the moral aspect to education.

What we have in Malaysia today is not education but indoctrination masquerading as one, more so in religious schools but also now in the national schools. To me that would be the *tong sampah* or garbage bin model. You throw in everything and hope to retrieve some of it later. The rest would rot or be stuck to the bottom of the bin. The Portuguese educator Paulo Freire used a different metaphor, the bank account model. At least there is the potential element of internal increment, as with the interests accrued.

To be considered educated today, one must be familiar with great thinkers of the past, not just the philosophers but also the literary and creative giants. One must also know what a virus or atom is and have basic knowledge of the cosmos. If we know something about our solar system, then we would not argue when Ramadan starts. In addition, one must have some mathematical skills, at least algebra if not calculus so you could think quantitatively and be more precise. Otherwise it would be *agak agak* (guess work). I once met a senior Malaysian economic planner who was unimpressed when I compared Singapore's growth of 5 percent versus Malaysia's 4. It was only 1 percent difference, he told me. What's the big deal! And this guy had a PhD!

The difference between 4 versus 5 percent growth rate is 25 percent, not 1 percent!

In good American universities with their broad-based liberal education, students must take science, mathematics (or statistics), and an Arts course, and a second language regardless of their majors. Of course, the math for a future engineer versus an English major would be very different, as encapsulated by such courses as "Physics for poets!" In addition, you must have written at least 30 major essays by the time you graduate. By contrast in Malaysia, to ask the students to take English would cause a national uproar among Malay educators.

That is my long way of saying that Malaysian education at all levels is part of the problem, and a very major one at that, and thus cannot be part of the solution.

Islamic Renaissance Front Seminar
Promises and Challenges of Digital Technology In Distant Learning

[Presented in part at a webinar sponsored by the Islamic Renaissance Front (IRF), Malaysia, Saturday January 31, 2021, together with fellow panelist Dato Dr. Madeline Berma, and Encik Shamshir Alam moderating. I thank IRF's Dr. Ahmad Farouk Musa for the invitation.]

Digital Technology – The Great Equalizer

First of Four Parts

The development of any nation or society rests not on the richness of its natural resources, fertility of its soil, or salubrious climes rather on the quality of its human capital. That in turn is dependent on two pillars – the quality of its education system and health of its citizens. The current Covid-19 pandemic only aggravates and exposes the current weaknesses.

The deterioration of Malaysian education is now beyond dispute. According to Program for International Student Assessment (PISA), Malaysian high school students lag by at least two years their peers in Singapore and South Korea. As for citizens' health, the obvious weakness with the health system is exposed by the current pandemic which is still not under control. The country has yet to initiate mass vaccination.

This Covid-19 pandemic also exposes the glaring weaknesses of the nation's education system as a whole and in particular the gross inequities between urban pupils versus their rural counterparts, as well as between the rich and poor. All ultimately translate between Malays and non-Malays. This problem of educational inequities is not unique to Malaysia. Even advanced nations like America are not spared.

I will examine the promises and challenges of digital technology (DT) in education from three perspectives. First, DT's role in general; second, the broader issue of how societies or nations deal with inequities within them, and third, the role of DT not only in elevating the quality of education but also in economic development and the unshackling of citizens' mindset and thinking. I will compare and contrast the role of DT in education in Malaysia (especially during this Covid-19 pandemic) with other countries.

Malaysians have long been familiar with DT through such ubiquitous devices like smartphones, computers, and the Internet. DT is one invention with unlimited potential, much more than the invention of the wheel or electricity. It could elevate the conditions of humans and with that, reducing the glaring current obscene inequities. DT enables a poor Aborigines boy in Gua Musang to communicate with a millionaire's son in New York City. They both could watch the same movie, hear the same songs, and converse virtually through Skype and Zoom. DT touches every potential sphere of human activities, not just education.

Going back to inequalities and inequities in the human condition, Stanford historian Walter Scheidel wrote in his book *The Great Leveler: Violence And The History of Inequality* that throughout history, when a society has such gross inequalities there are only four avenues to ameliorate that. First, war; second, revolution; third, pandemic; and fourth, breakdown in the governance of the country that resulted in chaos as in war. As demonstrated by this Covid-19 pandemic, it exposes as well as aggravates the inequalities within a society. This pandemic would also test Scheidel's observation.

DT could potentially replace pandemic or be the fifth factor that could bring equity among humans without the associated death and carnage as with war, revolution, or collapse of governance. DT could enable a backward society leapfrog to advanced status in short order. Conversely, the deepening digital divide could rapidly become a digital chasm, further pushing developed societies that much further ahead of undeveloped ones.

Malaysia is fortunate in that it is not experiencing war or revolution, but like the rest of the world, it is still gripped by the Covid-19 pandemic. The country's administration lacks efficiency and competence while being afflicted with corruption and breaches of fidelity among her leaders and administrators. This is the opportune time for the nation to adopt and embrace DT in all areas and not just in education so we could leapfrog all those obstacles.

When discussing DT, two issues immediately crop up. First is equipment or hardware; second, content or software. With hardware, the factor there is cost. Building a 5G tower in Ulu Kelantan for the rural folks there would require associated infrastructures like electricity and internet channels. In America, one tower could cost US$50K in addition to operating and maintenance costs. In India, Sugata Mitra built his "Hello Hubs" and "Schools in the Cloud" costing about US1 million each. Expensive propositions!

I digress here to discuss "costs" and the meaning of "expensive." Consider the washing machine. The cost of the first one could be a million, what with cost of building the factory as well as the engineers to design and build the machines. However by the time the millionth machine is being built, the cost would have dropped as all those expensive start-up costs had been amortized over the years and among the million machines built. Now it would only be the costs of labor, materials, and marketing. Competition would further lower the price per unit such that today a machine would retail for only a few hundred dollars. Meaning, technology costs always fall.

The barrier of costs is quantifiable and as such surmountable. That which we cannot measure is much more difficult to overcome. Further, if we were to have open tender, through genuine competition and avoiding companies associated with Rosmah Mansor [Prime Minster Najib Razak's wife who was later convicted of corruption with respect to the contract for supplying solar power to rural schools in Sarawak], we would further lower the price. We can and must give every school child in poor rural areas a free or subsidized laptop and broadband access.

The government is working with neighboring countries to blanket the whole of Southeast Asia with satellites. This is fantasy considering the many nations that would be involved and their conflicting priorities and national interests. Instead it would be better to focus on our giant maritime neighbor Indonesia and possibly the Philippines. Besides, their scattered islands and communities are perfect for wireless communication. Laying undersea cables and across thick jungles would be prohibitive. If you were to include other mainland nations like Burma and Thailand into the network, that would only complicate matters.

The cost of satellites including its launching is coming down fast. Malaysia now has five satellites. I am certain that they have not reached their full capacity with channels still open to provide broadband services to the interior and other areas. The issue there is one of engineering and administration, in particular current statutes, not with costs as those satellites have already been paid for.

The costs could be further reduced if we were to have open international tenders. China's Huawei is already building satellites for poor African nations. Likewise with giving computers to school children. We do not ask parents to buy desks and chairs for their school children, so why not extend that to laptops? In short, the hardware cost is surmountable. Sell the national airline if need be, to fund the project!

There is yet another angle with regards to cost. That is, how much more expensive or what greater price would we have to pay later if a major segment of our population especially the poor who are mostly Bumiputras were to be left behind in this field? We cannot even begin to quantify that. Worse, their disadvantage would continue to be amplified with time, and with their children and generations to come.

Issue of Content and Software
(Second of Four Parts)

With hardware, the principal issue is of costs. With software and content, we already have many excellent programs available in the public domain or cheap proprietary ones. There is no need to reinvent the wheel, only to modify them to fit local needs. Malaysia is fortunate to have many imaginative educational local contents created by enterprising teachers such as Norhailmi Abu Mutalib and Samuel Isaiah, both finalists in the Global Teacher Prize award. In Sarawak we have Cikgu Nazmi Rosli, winner of the Golden Hearts Prize. There are many others who have created attractive contents for their students. We must honor and recognize these teachers by giving them grants so they could expand their work. We do not need to wait for them to receive foreign recognition before supporting them.

Malay language is fortunate that its script is romanized; we are thus spared the burden of the Thais, Chinese, and Tamils. Yet we do not appreciate this significant advantage. Many in particular the nationalists want to revert to *jawi*.

There is one issue with respect to current content. Eighty-five percent of the Internet content and the language of DT generally is English. That is a big obstacle with Malay students as they are severely deficient in that area. We do not emphasize English as a matter of policy in the mistaken belief that learning English is tantamount to not respecting our national language. That erroneous conviction destroys our education system, and with that, our young and future community.

To benefit maximally from the Internet, Malaysian students have to be facile with English. This is the biggest handicap, again self-created by our policymakers, facing Malay students. That need not be. Sugata Mitra showed in his studies with rural students in India that this problem is readily remediable. With his innovative on-line programs in English like "Granny in the Cloud" and "Schools in the Cloud," those students could learn to converse and understand spoken English in a matter of weeks.

A year or two ago there was the sensational story of a seven-year-old Malay girl. They call her Aisyah London because of her fluency in English even before she entered school. More impressive, her English was not the typical rojak Manglish of locals with their peculiar singsong intonation, but the crisp BBC variety. She achieved this because her parents let her listen to BBC and Youtube. That is the same phenomenon Mitra discovered with his Indian rural students. For Malaysia, going by Mitra's experience in India, it would be better to build 5G towers and give free broadband access to rural students than to send ill-trained local teachers to teach them English, or Manglish.

In his "Hole in the Wall" experiments in India, Mitra placed a computer in a space (hole) in a wall. There were no instruction sheets or prior lessons given to the students on how to use it. He then videotaped the students' reactions. In just a few weeks the students had self-taught themselves how to surf the Internet. Indeed they in turn taught their teachers! This experiment has been repeated elsewhere outside of India, and the results were the same. Visit any kampung and you will find students already facile with using smartphones without having been formally taught.

Mitra concluded that children, whether in India, Sweden, or United Kingdom, can spontaneously organize themselves to learn on their own and to teach their fellow classmates without there being any specific instructions or directions from their teachers. With that, Mitra spawned such programs as "Self-Organizing Learning Environment" (SOLE) and "Hello Hubs."

To recap, first, the issue of costs with hardware is surmountable. Indeed the cost of not supplying hardware and broadband access to our rural students is many times more. Second, content is not an issue. We should count ourselves lucky in that our national language uses the romanized script, the script of the Internet.

There is one other factor that is often forgotten or ignored. The term I coined for this is "culture-ware." That is, those elements in one's culture and values of one's society that would encourage one to accept new ideas and technologies, or conversely, oppose whatever is new and novel, except for cars and wives. This is especially so when it comes to ideas.

Referring to my earlier example of that Orang Asli son in Ulu Kelantan. Yes, he could converse with the daughter of a billionaire in New York through Skype and Zoom, but will their respective parents as well as societies allow and condone that, or conversely put obstacles in their path? This is what I meant by culture-ware, one that is difficult to overcome. At another level, should we encourage our young to learn English so they could surf the Internet? Likewise, would our religious bureaucrats feel comfortable letting local Muslims listen to sermons given by such enlightened ulama as Syamsul Ali of New York or Ulil Abdalla in Jakarta?

In her signature song Judy Garland croons, "How are you going to keep them on the farm once they have been to Gay Paree?" Today, digital technology brings Gay Paree to the kampungs!

This is the biggest quandary referred to by my term culture-ware. There are many studies on the benefits to students who are comfortable with the Internet. First their English fluency shot up. Best of all theirs is not pidgin English or local singsong Manglish that is the consequence of local teaching, but standard English. Beyond that, they could quickly be on par with those students in the First World. These advantages spill over onto the greater community, as with accessing the vast Internet to help local farmers and traders.

On the flip side, there are many hidden sinister components with DT. Among them, on-line gambling, pornography, and cross-border money laundering. Then there is "face recognition" technology. On one hand, it allows the rapid detection of missing children. On the other, it allows a repressive government to violate their citizen's rights, as is happening today with impunity in China and elsewhere.

That reflects a general truism in science. That is, all human inventions have this dual and contradictory potential. Nuclear technology allows us to have cheap energy but at the same time it has the potential to destroy mankind. DT is no exception. That is the daunting challenge. DT affects all aspects of our lives, from trade and the economy generally to liberating the human mind. We cannot afford to ignore it. We must give it top priority. It is the technology for the present as well as the future, one that could enable us to leap forward to join the ranks of the developed world.

Digital Technology In Rural Education: The Experience of Malaysia and Elsewhere

(Third of Four Parts)

Even though DT has been used in education at all levels worldwide, the final treatise on how best to maximize its utility has yet to be written, and possibly could not be. The model that works for one nation in a particular instance would not be suitable elsewhere within that country, much less beyond. The model that works in rural Gua Musang in Peninsular Malaysia would not necessarily be suitable for the interior of Sarawak or urban Kuala Lumpur. Differences also occur at the primary, secondary, and tertiary levels. Likewise with specialized fields as with music and special-needs education.

The "One Laptop Per Child" (OLPC) program was less successful in Africa than in India. Meanwhile Uruguay could leapfrog the achievements of her rural pupils to match those in urban schools, as well between the poor and the rich through the use of DT. Beyond that Uruguay's OLPC program was able to, as a collateral benefit, increase the overall use of and familiarity with DT in the general community as a consequence of the diffusion of skills from those school children to their parents. In Kenya on the other hand, the computers given to those children would be lost or not working, resulting in their becoming useless ornaments.

The Malaysian story is more encouraging. There now appears contents that are suitable for local use. Earlier I referred to the contributions of teachers like Nazmi Rosli, Norhailim Mutalib, and Samuel Isaiah. That is the beauty of DT. It stimulates the growth of local talents and entrepreneurs in places and individuals you least or not expected. The responsibility of those in the Ministry of Education and others in authority is to support such efforts and individuals not just through recognizing them with prizes and honors but more usefully with grants so they could expand their contributions.

Three cautionary observations are pertinent here. First, here in Silicon Valley, California, the Mecca of DT, there now appears schools that are attracting much attention because they take a contrarian path. That is, those schools are banning computers, smart phones and other digital gadgets in the classrooms. DT like computers are used only in administration, not classroom education. These parents are very much aware of the importance of DT as they work in the industry, but they do not wish their children to use DT in their education. At first glance this may appear puzzling as it is counter to the trend in the greater society.

On close examination it is not. Those children are atypical. They are already familiar with modern digital gadgets at home and outside the classrooms. Their parents want their children's education to focus on social, creative, and emotional skills, meaning, those that cannot be taught through DT.

What does it mean when in Silicon Valley parents do not allow computers in their children's classrooms? Those parents wish to go back to basics and the old style, that is, education is an endeavor between a teacher and her students, using only the old chalk and blackboard. This is the exception that proves the general rule. Their children are already facile with DT outside the classroom. As such their teachers emphasize those elements that cannot be taught or emulated through DT, such matters as manners, working in cooperative manner, and helping each other. This Covid-19 pandemic does not in any way hamper their education; they only had to adjust to the e-learning component.

My second observation is that in any district there would be schools where teachers are reluctant or not fond to serve for a variety of reasons. To attract teachers, these schools do not have to depend on having DT and computers but on more mundane factors as with increased salary, additional allowances, and other incentives as with providing living quarters. Those other factors could be more decisive. That was how the colonial government could entice graduates of Oxford and Cambridge to teach at my small-town school of Kuala Pilah back in the early 1950s. Yes DT would ease teachers' burden but by itself would not attract teachers to Kapit or Gua Musang.

The third observation is that those schools that are successful, whether in Malaysia, Finland, or America, share many commonalities. Among them, their teachers, parents, and local community are all on the same page in supporting the goals of that school. In short, it would be difficult for a school and its students to excel if the teachers do not get the support of the parents and community. DT will not alter those critical and central dynamics.

Malaysia is fortunate in that education at all levels are under the jurisdiction of the central government, unlike in America. That however, could also be a curse. With central control, inequities in funding between schools could be readily solved or ameliorated. Local control is the factor for inequities between schools in America. This difference could be as high as four-fold. Finland is like Malaysia in having central control. However, Finland controls only the funding; in Malaysia the control is total, from textbooks, curriculum, and teachers' pay as well as promotions. As a result in Finland there is little difference between the lowest versus the highest performing schools and patents are not consumed with looking for "suitable" schools for their children, only one that would be convenient to them, location and transport-wise. By contrast, Malaysian parents, like their American counterparts, are consumed with searching for "good" schools for their children. Consider the intense competition among Malay parents to send their children to residential schools. By right such schools should be only for the poor and those in remote locations.

Educational achievements, whether pre-DT or now, are linked closely with the development of a society and inversely related with poverty. This is a worldwide observation. In turn this is related to the quality of human capital alluded to in my introduction. According to a study by the economist Muhammad Abdul Khalid, 100 percent of children in the public housing in Kuala Lumpur are in the "poor" category. Poverty encompasses both urban and rural areas.

According to KS Jomo, another economist, 90 percent of pupils in Malaysia do not get access to DT, a rather high figure. According to the Hasanah Foundation, only 37 percent. In America the comparable figure is under 15 percent. Jomo suggested that the old radio and television educational channels be resurrected as rural schools could access those much easier than getting broadband signals. I agree but only as a temporary and stop-gap measure. The goal should still be broadband access for all especially poor rural students. There are many weaknesses with the old educational radio and television channels. The chief being that the traffic is only one way, with no immediate feedback from the listeners. The teachers thus could not gauge their effectiveness. Besides, rural pupils in Malaysia must get the same digital and other facilities as those in urban areas and elsewhere in the developed world.

It would be much more fruitful if we were to adapt the existing television bandwidth to carry wifi (internet) signals. This is not an engineering issue (that can and has been overcome as in parts of Africa) rather administrative or legal. Giving broadband access to rural areas, whether by cable, satellite, or using existing phone lines, is an engineering issue taking into account local physical (as with hills, jungles, and other barriers) and other factors. The choice that would be best for interior Kapit would not be suitable for flood prone coastal Kemaman, or the jungle of Gua Musang and public flats of Kuala Lumpur.

Digital Technology in Rural Education: The Experience in Malaysia and Elsewhere

(Last of Four Parts)

Educational achievement, with or without Covid-19, then or now, is directly correlated with the development of a society, and that in turn is inversely related to the level of poverty. Whether this relationship is spurious, meaning not related or meaningful, could be debated; likewise in determining whether it is the cause or effect. It could very well be that rich countries have the resources to spend more on education. Meaning, the relationship is consequential not causal. Nonetheless there are enough examples where wise investments in education would benefit society. In Europe, there are Finland and Ireland; in Asia, Singapore, Taiwan, and South Korea. The latest example is Rwanda, as reflected in, among other things, its capital city Kigali being the cleanest city in Africa. Superior education there relates to that nation's rapid enhancement of the quality of its human capital.

Whatever model is chosen for a particular nation, be prepared to study and monitor its effectiveness. The initial choice should be just the beginning of the effort. This is where Malaysia fails. We assumed that we have designed the perfect system and that it will work now and forever. Thus we do not study its limitations, effectiveness, and thus acceptance. Even if it were to be successful, we still need to study it so we could continually improve on it and modify it for possible applications elsewhere.

Consider what Sugata Mitra did in India with his first "Hole in the Wall" experiment in 1999. From there he improved on it to develop his "Schools in the Cloud," "Learning Hubs," and "Granny in the Cloud."

In 2003 I visited a school in my old village where the teachers had each been given an expensive Apple laptop. However, when I asked them, they were all disappointed. They could use those computers only at school. When school was over the computers would be locked up in the headmaster's office. Those teachers had barely enough time to teach their classes let alone learn new skills. The result? The computers gathered dust in the cupboard and the cables chewed up by rats.

Contrast that with the experience in Uruguay. The schoolchildren there were also each given those computers to take home. There they could teach their parents how to use them for their little "mom and pop" businesses. As a result, computer literacy in the village soared from such informal diffusion of computer skills. Because the feel that they "owned" the computers, they took good care of it instead of treating it as a "government property."

To conclude, my takeaway points are first, all children rich and poor, rural and urban, must have broadband access for free. DT should be basic and an integral part of education, as with desks, chairs, and blackboards, as well as electricity and potable water. With DT schools could become the villagers' or community's hub for broadband access. Choose one of the many proven models as OLPC or Learning Hubs and modify them for local use.

Second, because of the current limited access to broadband, e-learning should be confined to subjects that could not otherwise be taught, meaning STEM. Others like history, civic classes, and religious studies should be deferred. Third, use the old educational television should only be as a stopgap measure. Fourth, try the different models and study them so we could improve on them. Establish local champion leaders and give them the necessary training. Continue collecting data as to use, efficacy, and problems associated. Fifth, DT is now an integral part of education at all levels. With that comes a fundamental change in the role of teachers and educators. They are now less the "sage on the stage and more a guide at the side."

Islamic Renaissance Front Zoom Conference
Is Malaysia Becoming The 'Sick Man of Southeast Asia'?

[Presented at a webinar sponsored by the Islamic Renaissance Front, Saturday March 20, 2021, with Najeeb Gounjari as moderator and fellow panelist Universiti Kebangsa'an Malaysia's Dr. Sharifah Munirah Alatas.]

Thank you, Dr. Ahmad Farouk Musa and the Islamic Renaissance Front (IRF) for inviting me. I am supportive of IRF's continuing and tireless efforts to present a more inclusive and progressive brand of Islam. That version is so much more beautiful and meaningful in contrast to the faith's current jarring and trivial manifestations in much of the Muslim world, Malaysia included.

The irony does not escape me. While I enjoy much religious freedom in a secular society here in America, for many in the Islamic world, Malaysia especially, this fundamental right that is so cherished in Islam is treated with contempt and denied to far too many.

Inappropriate Metaphor

To the topic at hand, that is, characterizing Malaysia as the sick man of Southeast Asia, I put forth four propositions.

First, this Covid-19 pandemic is an outlier, a far out-of-the-ordinary event though not quite to the level of Nassim Taleb's "black swan." In statistics we ignore those outlier data. Meaning, such traditional figures and indicators collected during this period would not be accurate and have low if any predictive value. Caution is thus needed in using them to paint grand pictures. For another, we do not have a long enough series, and for another, Malaysian statistics, like all Malaysian figures, are suspect. Besides, economic indicators like Foreign Direct Investments (FDI) and income distributions are the result, not the cause of sound governance or effective socioeconomic policies.

Back to extraordinary or outlier event, one would not judge someone's swimming skills in a tsunami; even champion swimmers would get swamped. America, the richest nation, and Sweden, the most enlightened, both stumbled during this Covid-19 pandemic. Likewise, hitherto well-run corporations headed by iconic chief executives have been battered and report horrific figures during this period.

The 'sick man' is not an appropriate metaphor because sick implies that you were once robust and healthy. Malaysia was never that. She was never a roaring tiger as painted, not even a potential one. A paper tiger perhaps, with canned or recorded cheers in the gallery and echo chamber as in a football game on radio. My preferred metaphor is that Malaysia is the scrawny stunted kid, and not just of Southeast Asia. Picture a youngster with bloated tummy full of worms, has poor personal hygiene, and not well tutored, or *kurang ajar* as we put it. That represents the quality of our human capital. To put in the language of the alley, it sucks. That is Malaysia's foundational weakness.

The sick metaphor also implies that with appropriate remedies Malaysia would be back to her previous healthy robust self. With the scrawny stunted kid however, that would require a long intensive process beyond the clinical remedies. You would have to first focus on the basics, as with changing lifestyles, eating healthy foods, and nurturing good habits. Once healthy and full of vigor, you would then be ready and eager to learn. The government's job would then be to provide good schools and trained teachers. Only then would employers local and foreign be eager to hire your citizens, or they could start their own enterprises. From there, all subsequent positive socio-economic indices like FDI, GDP, and income distributions would emanate. Those are derivative figures, the result not the cause.

This scrawny, stunted kid metaphor is appropriate for another and more significant reason. An insight of clinical medicine is that children who had adverse childhood experiences (ACE) encounter many other difficulties later in life beyond merely medical, as in learning and social adaptations. Worse, they would in turn transmit those vulnerabilities onto their children, partly through their own inadequacies as parents in nurturing the children, and partly because ACE also affects their gene expressions, a phenomenon referred to as epigenetics.

Transferring this observation to nations, it explains why dysfunctional young nations like Pakistan and Lebanon continue with their destructive downward spiral. Their incompetent leaders breed ever more dysfunctional successors. That is also true with Malaysia under long-time leader Mahathir. Look at the quality of all his successors, each competing to be even more dysfunctional than him and their immediate predecessor. UMNO Youth was once characterized as *halia* (ginger) group because of its pungent criticisms of the party's top leadership. In contrast, today's UMNO Youth is mousy, satisfied with the crumbs falling off the party's dining table.

Dispensing with metaphors, Malaysia is more the Ireland and Quebec of pre-1960s. The political, demographic, and other dynamics are eerily comparable. In Malaysia, there is the numerically dominant Malays versus non-Malays; Ireland, Catholics, and Protestants; while Quebec, Francophones versus Anglophones. The political, socioeconomic, and other cleavages parallel those same dangerous fault lines of identity.

Like those Irish and Quebecois of yore, Malays today also endure our own share of ugly stereotypes hurled at us not just by non-Malays. Read and listen to Mahathir's ugly ranting and insensitive caricature of the "lazy and *mudah lupa*" (forgetful) Malays.

Like Ireland and Quebec then, Malaysia today is often viewed as one entity. In reality there are two, separate and distinct. National data must therefore be teased into the two distinct components. Statistics on non-Malays resemble First World; for Malays, very much still Third World. For example, fertility and birth rates as well as poverty rates among Malays are closer to the pattern seen in Indonesia while those of non-Malays, Japan, America, and Western Europe. Jumbling those figures and treating them as representing one homogenous group would only mislead one, professionals and others alike; likewise if we were to apply the same remedy to both. That would be a recipe for failure. Worse, it could be disastrous.

A developed Malaysia would not necessarily produce a developed Malay community. The economic wisdom that a rising tide would lift all boats is true only if they were all free to float. Those tethered to docks, have short anchor lines, or stuck under bridges would be swamped. That is a crucial caveat. The last six decades have proved that tragic reality in Malaysia. On the other hand, if we were to succeed in developing Malays, then Malaysia would automatically follow suit. For Malays, this would mean freeing us from the yoke of our feudal culture, adopting a more progressive brand of Islam, and modernizing the education system, among others.

You could imagine Malaysia's two societies as two jet planes. One is already comfortably at cruising speed high in the clouds at 35,000 feet; the other is still struggling to take off and facing severe headwind. With the former, all you have to do is not interfere or distract the captain. The plane could fly itself. With the second, you would need frequent communications and feedback from the Tower as well as an alert, skillful, and attentive captain. Unfortunately, Malay leaders are anything but.

My final point is that Malaysia does not need another New Economic Policy with its endless iterations or a grandiose Vision 2020 (nobody talks about that anymore) with its endless slick sloganeering and threatening *keris*-wavings *a la* Shahnon Ahmad's main character in his novella *Unggapan* (Sloganeering). Instead, we need to emulate Ireland and Quebec of the 1960s. That is, undertake our own Quiet Revolution. No loud hurrahs or blasting *kompang* (drums) to announce it. Just buckle down to undertake the much-needed hard work in executing fundamental changes.

The immediate obstacle towards that path would be to confront the evil trinity of endemic corruption, rotten education, and entrenched Islamism. On reflection, I should put the last first, as Islamism has now infiltrated all sectors and destroyed the nation's entire affairs and structures. Caution here before all hell breaks loose. I use the Turkish scholar Soner Cagaptay's definition of Islamism. It is "a political ideology that strives to derive legitimacy from Islam." I have no problem with "strives to derive legitimacy from Islam," rather its malignant strain, the jihadists who exploit the faith to further their personal and political agenda. This is reflected in the current destructive Malay thinking that it is better to endure a corrupt and incompetent leader as long as he (always a he) is a Muslim instead of supporting a competent and honest but non-Muslim one. What perversion!

Back to my original point, once we have succeeded in dealing with that basic destructive trinity of evils, only then could Malaysians, Malays to be more specific, contemplate and embark on modern development.

That in brief is my presentation. What follows are but illustrations, amplifications, and reiterations. Time permitting, I will discuss Malay capital formation. Capital formation is the driver of economic growth and wealth creation. The accepted wisdom is that Malays are backward because we lack capital. I argue the opposite. Malays do not lack capital, rather that Malay capital, be it physical, human, or social, is trapped. As such we cannot leverage it. Worse, those traps are of our own making.

Crises Reveal A Society's Strengths And Weaknesses

Crises reveal a society's innate strengths and expose its weaknesses. With this Covid-19 pandemic, it is worthwhile to be reminded that while it is devastating, it is not the Depression, much less the Japanese Occupation. Not even close. This is reflected in the world's major stock market indices remaining robust.

For Malaysia, the disastrous economic figures during this period are but unneeded reminders of the corruption and incompetence of Malaysian leaders. Pandemics, like wars, will end. Unlike wars and revolutions where lives would be lost in addition to the physical losses, there would be no destruction of physical infrastructures with this or any pandemic. This Covid-19 could be likened to a biological neutron bomb, except that it does not discriminate between friends and foes. As such the recovery should be easier. I am not being callous here. Corruption and incompetence on the other hand are not so readily remediable; they only get worse unless tackled with vigor head-on.

That pot-bellied scrawny kid full of worms is a good metaphor for a corrupt nation like Malaysia. Tapeworms measure in feet. That would be Najib Razak and his 1MDB. Tiny pinworms are no less destructive. They are the constables extracting a few hundred ringgit in lieu of your traffic summons. In their aggregate they are just as corrosive and destructive.

Host-parasite relationships are delicate and well-tuned. Too many worms and you kill the host, and with that, the worms too. Termite infestation is a better metaphor. Termites destroy the foundation until it collapses, and then some. To prevent or reduce the infestation, eliminate damp hidden areas. Then with the first telltale trailing, initiate immediate actions. Making public tenders and contracts open and the bidding process transparent would be the equivalent of airing damp hidden places. Getting rid of GLCs would eliminate those damp dark places. 1MDB, Tabung Haji, and other government-linked companies are Exhibits A in this regard.

Where damp hidden areas cannot be avoided, use concrete instead of wood. If wood, only hardwood like *meranti*, or pretreated ones, not raw *rantings* (twigs). Meaning, appoint only those with proven ability and unquestioned integrity. Endless exhortations to be honest would not do it. When the late Bank Negara Governor Ismail Ali, the first native to be appointed to that august position, was asked how he dealt with corruption, he replied that it was not an issue with him as no minister would even dare approach him for favors. Even his brother-in-law Mahathir was intimidated by Ismail's legendary integrity. That's *meranti* quality in action!

Corruption is a huge and complex problem. One could easily get overwhelmed by its immensity and intractability. Three key positions have the greatest impact on the fight against corruption: Attorney-General (AG), being the principal prosecutor, Chief of Police, the main investigator, and Chief of Anti-Corruption Commission. Following the

2018 General Election I urged the incoming Pakatan Harapan to recruit from the FBI, Scotland Yard, or some such agencies for those three pivotal positions. Not because of the lack of local talent rather that Malaysians have been hopelessly and deeply polarized that it would be difficult to find someone who could be seen as neutral or to have general acceptance.

However, when Latheefa Koya was appointed Anti-Corruption Chief and Tommy Thomas AG, my initial skepticism vanished. Latheefa exhibited extraordinary courage and steely tenacity, as when she released those infamous taped conversations of Rosmah Mansor advising her 'honey' (Prime Minister Najib Razak).

As for Thomas, I too had high expectations but that vanished with his first public press conference where he struggled to speak in Malay. This character was born, educated, and lived all his life in Malaysia! My hopes on him were later resurrected when he filed those major criminal charges against Najib and his gang.

Then when Thomas resigned, my initial disappointment with his inability to speak Malay turned to horror with the release of his memoir where he related his experience dealing with the Malay civil servants in his department. Having spent some time with the Malaysian Civil Service, I share his observations about its work culture and ethos. His error however, was in equating that with Malay values. Thomas should visit his ancestral homeland and spend some time with the Indian Civil Service to broaden his perspective! His belittling and stereotyping those Malay civil servants, and Malay culture generally, was not a class act, more so as he reveled in his newly acquired glittering Malay Tan Sri feudal title. He was but another Malay-knight wannabe!

At one level, his memoir effectively blocked the future path for any capable non-Malay ever to be appointed AG again, or any senior position, at least for this generation. He had poisoned the well. Far more consequential, with his memoir Thomas had turned the current criminal trials against Najib and other corrupt UMNO leaders as but attempts by non-Malays to do in Malay leaders. That is lethal poison in the Malaysian body politic. As for a Malay chief, the current Chief of Police Hamid Bador recently admitted that there are groups within the police force out to oust him. That speaks volumes of his command ability.

There will be hue and cry among Malays and the Council of Rulers to having foreigners in those top key positions. However, only by getting rid of the raw *rantings* and replacing them with *meranti* even if imported could Malaysia make a dent on this fight against the twin blight of corruption and incompetence. Give those foreigners a mandate to groom capable locals from among their subordinates within a specified time.

As for education, my remedy would be to dispense with endless Blueprints and expensive Finnish or World Bank consultants. Again, focus on the basics. Make Malaysians bilingual (Malay and English), mandate 13 years of schooling, and increase the hours devoted to STEM. Challenge public universities and their scholars to study and solve local problems.

There in a single short paragraph my remedy for Malaysian education. The crux is not with recognizing the problems or coming up with the solutions (those are obvious), rather the political gumption to undertake those much-needed changes.

Education gets the biggest budget allocation every year. However, consider two big ticket items of wasteful expenditure that are a matter of policy: residential schools, and overseas undergraduate scholarships. That is quite apart from such scandals as the bloated over a billion-ringgit contract with Rosmah Mansor's company to supply solar panels to rural schools in Sarawak. So far, no panels despite the massive funds expended!

These residential schools consume a disproportionate share of the funding. Most of that is spent just to feed and house the students, not for education. The 100th residential school would be built and run in the same manner as the first, with no innovation. I am reminded of the observation the American surgeon William Mayo. A surgeon repeats the same mistake a hundred times and calls that experience!

Of the hundreds of residential schools, I would expect that a few would emphasize sports, foreign language, or fine arts. More than a few could be partially residential or even day school, thus dispensing with the huge hostel costs. Or the rich be made to pay their share of the costs. Only in 2020 did the government reserve 60 percent of residentials school slots for B40 (the bottom 40 percent in poverty level) students. I would make that 100 percent or at least 80, and have the rest pay full fare. If rich

Malay parents were made to do that, they would think twice or many times before sending their children to such schools.

I once asked the headmaster of Malay College (MCKK) how the school budget is allocated to academic and teaching versus hostel and feeding components. He could not answer me. The budgeting is so convoluted and opaque. On purpose, of course, as all the food contracts would be handled by the Ministry to be given out to the Minister's cronies.

I am shocked that many well-to-do Malays still brag about their children attending Malay College and similar schools when they should be embarrassed. Mahathir had all his children in residential schools, in short, being made wards of the state. They are now all successful. Have many of them if any, or Mahathir himself, have reimbursed or donated to those schools?

On the academic side, I am pleased that MARA residential schools now offer International Baccalaureate. Malaysia's brightest should be assessed and compared with their international peers, not with those from Sekolah Kebangasaan Ulu Kelantan.

Yet another way to cut costs would be to eliminate the lower forms at these residential schools and focus only on the last four years: Form IV to Upper Six. Besides, children at the lower Forms (I to III) are too young to be separated from their parents. At that tender age they need their parental guidance the most.

As for overseas undergraduate scholarships, dollar for dollar, for the cost of sending two students (at US$60K each) abroad a year we could recruit one Berkeley professor at US120K. That professor in turn would a spend about US$100K locally for housing, living expenses, and income tax. He would be lucky to have $20K to repatriate at the end of the year. Thus in terms of actual outflow of precious foreign exchange, spending on one student abroad equals (in cost) the hiring of three American professors. Imagine the impact! The $120K sent abroad for the two students would be lost, with zero local economic multiplier effect. Worse, most Malay students sent abroad would end up at marginal institutions like the Creekville State Us, not the Berkeleys or Ivy League. Many were also sent abroad to do essentially Sixth Form, another colossal waste of funds.

The motto and premise should be: Malaysia sends her best only to the best.

Then consider the deteriorating standard of English. Yet not a single university in the country has a dedicated Department of English. Nor does Malaysia have a single English-medium Teachers' College. This stunning disconnect between policy and reality is obvious to all except Malaysian leaders and policymakers. Contrast that to Japan. Japanese is a far more advanced language than Malay, yet Japan recruits thousands of native English-speaking teachers through its Japan English Teachers Program (JETP); likewise Taiwan and South Korea. Malaysia gets a dozen teachers through the Fulbright Program and makes a huge fuss over that.

Malaysia must try different models and evaluate their effectiveness. No one school system would suit or best serve a particular community. If we have one system and have an idiot in charge of it, then the whole nation would suffer. I am a biologist at heart. The lesson of biology is that diversity is the best assurance for the survival of a specie.

Some of the models would include bringing back the old English schools of the colonial era, but with a twist. Locate them in the kampungs where the need is greatest as there is a low level of English spoken in the community. Likewise, as the Islamic cachet sells with Malays, we should have English-medium Islamic schools. The Al Junid Islamic School in Singapore uses the International Baccalaureate curriculum, likewise many Islamic schools in America. The science that these students study is real science, not the bastardized "Islamic" version, the sequalae of the ill-advised Islamization of Knowledge fad.

As for the poor performances of rural students *vis a vis* urban ones, the MIT economist Esther Duflo and her husband fellow economist Abhijit Banerjee conducted the equivalent of clinical trials in East Africa with respect to finding the most effective intervention to improve students' educational achievements. It turned out the most enduring and effective was to regularly deworm poor rural children with cheap anti-helminth pills. In the 1950s our own economist Ungku Aziz suggested exactly that with respect to kampung students in Kelantan. I do not know whether anyone did that and studied the impact.

That issue with Ungku Aziz's findings reflects another lapse with Malaysian actors. There is little follow-up on any good ideas or initiative.

We are satisfied with the first positive results without exploring their further potential or improving on it. Nobody carries the ball forward.

Consider another of Ungku Aziz's innovative idea, Tabung Haji, the huge modern financial vehicle to mobilize Muslims' savings. It was immediately and hugely successful, but nobody improves on that since its inception in the 1960s. I would expect Tabung Haji today to have expanded in other Muslim countries and have its own hospitality subsidiaries and other investments. I would also expect it to be a full financial services enterprise.

My third thrust is to curtail if not eliminate Islamism in state affairs. This should be top priority as Islamism now is the factor contributing to corruption, incompetence, and rotting education. With that, the community. That what keeps Malays backwards. This however has to be done adroitly. Carelessly executed and you would have religious riots. To the jihadists those would be but opportunities to get their express tickets to Heaven.

Muslims consider pork *haram* and would not eat or touch it without there being any official sanctions or prohibitions against that. We have internalized that. However, corruption is also haram, but Muslims have found ways to make it acceptable. It also reflects the perversion of Islam's core values that to these Islamists a corrupt, incompetent but Muslim leader is preferable to an honest, competent but non-Muslim one. Further, to these Islamists the loot of corruption is but bounty from Allah (*borkat*). Another has it that cash given at election times to garner citizens' votes is but *sedekah* (charitable gifts). As for education, the Islamists' version is nothing but catechism and indoctrination. They have little inclination to acquire critical thinking or useful worldly skills.

The influence of these Islamists at the top is deep and pervasive such that any attempt to cut their funding has to be done adroitly as that would be met with instant resistance and viewed as an assault on the faith itself. One approach to circumvent this would be to cut down all ministries' budgets by 10 percent annually for the next five years, except for key ministries like Health, Defense, Education, Rural Development, and Internal Security. You do not need ministries for Tourism, Women's Affairs, Youth and Sport, or Federal Territory. You have a mayor for that, far cheaper and closer to citizens than a minster. With those wide cuts, the religious department would not feel as if it is being unfairly targeted or singled out.

Peruse the expenditures of the religious establishment at both federal and state levels. Grandiose headquarters and ever-expanding moral squads. Islam is not so much a religion but a giant bureaucracy. At another level it is but a massive public works program for otherwise unemployable Malays who are the products of these rapidly expanding religious schools. These religious functionaries and the nation would be far better off if they were to clean up the mosques, rivers, and public parks instead of hounding people for not fasting or holding hands in public.

The negative impact on Malays for this huge diversion of human capital is immense. Consider that for every Malay pursuing revealed knowledge and prophetic traditions, there would be one fewer to take up virology and produce our own vaccine against Covid-19 and dengue.

This blight of Islamism is the toughest nut to crack. Failure to do that would doom Malaysia, and Malays in particular, to beyond redemption.

I should clarify that statement. As alluded to earlier, Malaysia is two nations. My "beyond redemption" prognostication refers only to Malays. Non-Malays have long ago tolerated if not bypassed the government. To them, it is but a place to renew their passports and driver's licenses. Malays are the ones who bear the heaviest burden of a corrupt and incompetent government.

Lessons From Ireland and Quebec

As with the Irish and the Quebecois of the 1960s, Malays today are in desperate need of our own Quiet Revolution.

During the first half of the last century, Ireland's biggest "export" was her people desperate to escape their wretched homeland. Today, Irish émigrés are returning to the republic's booming hi-tech and biotech industries. Ireland too had her obligatory "war of independence" in 1921, but her colonized mentality and the consequent excessive nationalism persisted long after; likewise old prejudices. In the movie "Titanic," the rough uncouth Irish hero was confined below deck with the rest of his countrymen. The cultured heroine and her fellow English aristocrats were ensconced on the luxurious upper decks, separated physically and upwind from the messy crowd below.

Post-independence, the Irish became inward looking and stagnant allowing the ever-dominant Catholic Church to become even more entrenched. It is said that Ireland suffered under two colonizers: London and Rome. When the Irish got rid of the first, the second became unchallenged. A 1937 constitutional referendum made blasphemy a crime, reflecting the Church's supremacy. Sounds familiar to Malaysians! As a result, the few remaining Protestants felt out of place. They too emigrated, taking their skills, capital, and enterprising spirit. That too should sound familiar to Malaysians.

Ireland's remarkable transformation, and with that its moniker Celtic Tiger, came within the memories of some still living today. Sean Lemass began by clipping the Church's influence in state affairs and citizens' lives. Contraception was legalized despite heavy Church opposition. With that, women participation in the workforce increased, and Ireland's former dizzyingly high birthrate declined. Contraception, like divorce, is women's rights issues. The old constitution required women to give up their civil service posts upon marriage. By the end of the 20th Century, Ireland had elected its first woman president, Mary Robinson. Remarkable! When Robinson, raised a strict Catholic, married her Protestant husband in 1960, her parents refused to attend her wedding. And they were both doctors!

Liberalization went beyond. The most dramatic was in education. The Church's role was clipped, and education secularized. Prior to that, despite or perhaps because of heavy Church influence, Protestant schools and colleges attracted many Catholics. However up till 1970, for Catholics to attend Trinity College, a Protestant institution, that was deemed a mortal sin, deserving excommunication! Despite that, in the 1920s a fifth of Trinity students were Catholic. They are now no doubt doing time in purgatory! By the 1990s the majority of Trinity's students and many of the professors are Catholic. Education continued in English. Lemass did not succumb to the prevailing nationalistic impulses to use Gaelic.

Malaysia is obsessed with developing Malay language even at the expense of handicapping her citizens. A language is more likely to thrive if the nation or race behind it is successful. The decline of Gaelic coincided with the economic eclipse of the Irish. Today however, with a new prosperous Ireland, Irish politicians liberally sprinkled their speeches with Gaelic; the language is now chic. A point for Malays to ponder!

These radical changes did not occur in isolation but in tandem, one reinforcing the other. The secularization of the education would not have occurred without the corresponding decline in Church influence; likewise, social and political reforms like legalizing contraception.

Any change in the social order can be disruptive and destabilizing, creating a moral vacuum. With the decline of the Church, the old certitude is gone and with it, for some, the sense of security and anchoring stability. It is a challenge to come up with alternative value systems. However, such challenges are more likely to be solved when the nation is thriving than when it is economically declining. Substitute Irish for Malays, English for non-Malays (Chinese specifically), and Islam for Catholicism, and you have the same dynamics in Malaysia today. The solution is obvious — emulate the successful Irish.

In Quebec of the 1960s, it was the Anglophones versus the Francophones (the majority). McGill University prior to the 1960s was essentially an English institution. By 1970s it had more than its share of French Canadians on the faculty as well as student body. Substitute Catholicism for Islam, francophone for Malays, and anglophones for non-Malays, and we have today's Malaysia. Quebec even had its own version of May 13, 1969 "incident," its October 1970 Crisis that saw tanks and soldiers deployed on the streets of Montreal. It was my misfortune to witness both needless tragedies.

Quebec's Quiet Revolution replicates the Irish one — clipping the role of the Church in matters social as well as in secularizing the education system and opening up the society to the world.

When I was at McGill in 1970, I heard the same stereotyping of the French Canadians that I hear from Mahathir and others about Malays today. That they were lazy, obsessed with religion and the Hereafter, did not save or value education. On Saturdays they get drunk and then redeem themselves in church on Sunday, the French-Canadiens that is. Today no one ever refers to them in those derogatory terms. Stanford's current President is a French Canadian who came from one of those families caricatured in the 1970s.

The two pivotal Quebecois leaders at the time were Jean Lesage, a brilliant lawyer before he entered politics, and his successor Robert Bourassa, with degrees from Oxford and Harvard. Lesage with his *l'equip de tonnerre* (terrific team!) executed his message of *C'est le temps que ca change* ("It's time for a change"). As in Ireland, both these leaders clipped the powers of the Church in state affairs, especially education. Whereas before young Quebecois flocked to convents and seminaries, now they attend junior colleges to prepare themselves for universities as well as to be trained as mechanics and electricians. Lesage mobilized Francophones' savings and invested them in Quebecois enterprises. That would be like Tabung Haji investing in small Malay businesses instead of luxurious hotels, multinational corporations, and money losing GLCs.

The Irish and Quebecois had leaders who dared take on the powerful and entrenched religious establishment. Malay leaders on the other hand, from Mahathir to Muhyiddin, are intimidated by the ulama. Mahathir tried to ride the Islamist tiger and was nearly devoured. Malay leaders are scared of the ulama class, fearful that they would side with the sultans in the old ugly, destructive triangulation game. In the 1980s it was the ulama and the politicians against the sultans.

Many fear that Malaysia would degenerate into a failed state *a la* Pakistan. That is misplaced anxiety. Unlike Pakistan, Malaysia has a substantial, dynamic, and enterprising non-Muslim population immune to the Islamists' influence and strictures. These non-Muslims would carry Malaysia forward. Malays as a community however could degenerate like the Pakistanis, wrecked by eternal intra-ethnic conflicts and consumed with "out-Islaming" each other. Worse, Malays could be like the Iranians under the Ayatollah. Khomeini drove more Muslims out of the faith than Stalin or secularization could ever hope. A more likely scenario would be for Malays to be disillusioned with the faith, realizing that these Islamists have been selling us a bill of goods. Ever accommodative as per our culture, we would not renounce our faith but just give it lip service.

Should such a miracle were to happen in and Malaysia be blessed with her own Lemass or Lesage as a leader, then we could raise the bar and embark on a more ambitious goal of modern economic development that would usher us into the exclusive First World club. Until then, discussing issues as attracting foreign investments and income inequities would remain just that – talk.

Assume for now that Malays and Malaysia have successfully executed our own Quiet Revolution and thus ready to partake in some serious economic development. What next? Again, there are many ready successful models to choose and there is little need to reinvent the wheel. Emulate current successful societies but make the necessary innovations to suit our particular circumstances. Back to the tire metaphor, we could make it tubeless, be of bulbous lightweight plastic so they could float in rice fields or have skid tracks as with tanks to drive over muddy roads.

The core of or fuel for economic development is capital, defined as something that could produce wealth. A piece of rock remains but a rock until chiseled into a sharp arrowhead. Tied it to the end of a pole, and with a modicum of skill, it becomes a piece of capital equipment capable of bringing wealth, as with venison on the table.

The long-accepted wisdom is that Malays lack capital, the principal reason of why we lag economically. I suggest otherwise. Malay capital is there and plentiful but trapped and not mobilized efficiently or invested prudently. We have plenty of sticks and stones, but they remain as just that. We do not sharpen and tie them together to form arrowheads. We also refused to learn to be skillful spearmen. Then we wonder why we have only ferns and mushrooms on the table, but no venison.

Trapped capital remains the biggest impediment to progress and economic growth as we cannot leverage that capital. The Peruvian economist Hernando de Soto noted in his *The Mystery of Capital. Why Capitalism Triumphs in the West and Fails Everywhere Else* that the West have created the legal structure of property rights. That allows property owners to leverage those assets into wealth, in contrast to the largely extra-legal arrangements in the developing world that resulted in their capital or assets being trapped. The importance of capital is encapsulated in Thomas Piketty's Einstein-like formula, $r>g$, where "r" refers to the return on capital and "g," the growth of the economy. It is this "r" that contributes to societal inequalities more than anything else. That simple formula is the summation of that wise observation, "The rich get richer while the poor remains poorer."

Likewise with human capital, the most important form of capital for a society or nation. Malays constitute over 60 percent of the population of Malaysia, but we lack quality, and that in turn relates directly to our education system. Fix that and we would release or leverage our human capital for wealth creation. Those in the moral police squad is an example of trapped human capital, a part of the massive Islamic bureaucracy that disincentives Malays from pursuing other employment endeavors. If more Malays were to pursue virology and biotechnology generally, we could come up with our Covid-19 vaccine instead of forever arguing whether the ones made in the West are halal. That is what I would call the trapping of our capital, in this case intellectual capital.

When I see pictures of or read about these *khalwat* (adultery) raids on hotels, I am reminded of a story attributed to the legendary Caliph Omar. On one of his famous walk-about management rounds he spotted an amorous unmarried couple in their apartment. He barged in and pronounced them guilty of *zina* (illicit sex), and thus would be punished by stoning to death. The gentleman admitted that he had indeed committed a sin but against Allah. The Great Caliph on the other hand had invaded their privacy and thus sinned against them. At which point, the great Caliph admitted his error and withdrew. Regardless of the authenticity of that anecdote, it reveals two things. One, the primacy of privacy in Islam; and two, even an ordinary citizen had a right and was not afraid to confront and challenge his great leader.

Human capital is also related to social capital – a society's values and institutions. This is best illustrated through personal anecdotes. The late Jamaluddin Jarjis, who once served as Ambassador to US, received his engineering PhD from McGill at about the same time I qualified as a surgeon. This was also at a time when the number of Malays qualified in the sciences were as rare as a banana plant amongst *lalang*. When few years later he wanted to set up his own consulting firm, not one Malaysian bank would lend him the money, not even Bank Bumiputra, an institution set up specifically to help Malays in business. Instead Jamaluddin had to go to Singapore. That difference between Malaysia and Singapore reflected the quality of their respective social capital. That banker in Singapore saw the value in Jamaluddin's potential; the Malaysian counterpart did not.

Likewise, when I came to America nearly 50 years ago I too had little money to start my own private practice. Unlike Jamaluddin and Bank Bumiputra, I had no difficulty securing a loan from the local bank. The difference? Enhanced American social capital. The bank manager knew the value of my human capital (a trained surgeon). As for the quality of social capital, he could phone my hospital CEO to verify that I am indeed a genuine surgeon. By ordinary and other measures, I would be considered as high risk: a recent immigrant, no tangible assets as collateral, and no local ties to act as guarantors. However, I had the one quality most valued – my enhanced human capital with my surgical skills.

Going back to the claim that Malays lack capital, referring specifically to the financial variety, there are at least three classes of Malay physical assets, all mega sums in value, that are trapped through our own making. First, those assets trapped under Muslim probates (*faraid*); second, *zakat* funds and *waqaf* (endowments); and third, land under Malay Reservation Act. In 2020, over RM70 Billion worth of assets belonging to Muslims are trapped in probate, some for decades. Yet the Islamic establishment, including the legends of scholars and Syariah lawyers, ignores this huge problem and the accompanying untapped and trapped potential.

Islamic inheritance is bewilderingly complex. Al Khwarizmi invented Algebra just for that. However, the solution is simple—avoid probate or *faraid* by not dying inter-state. Give away your assets (*inter-vivo* gifts —*hibah*) while you still have your wits with you. Or have a modified family *waqaf* (endowment) – revocable trusts. It is tragic that nation-wide *hibah* numbers only in the thousands when it should be in the tens of millions.

Few have mentioned this ready and much-needed simple solution. Many a tragic family squabbles could have been avoided by *hibah* and family trusts. This is also a major reason why Malay enterprises rarely survive beyond their founders. Back to Jamaluddin Jarjis, it is sad to read of his family squabbles over his assets after his untimely death as he had no effective state planning in place.

In Kuala Lumpur, under the shadow of the glittering Petronas Towers, is the odious eyesore and a perennial embarrassment to Malays – Kampung Baru (lit. new village) left as an urban slum for generations. The solution there is not more money, as is endlessly offered, but intellectual, to sort out the huge inheritance mess and associated tangled land titles.

Zakat (tithe) is another huge trapped Muslim asset. It is managed by the Islamic Department with its math-challenged, financial-illiterate personnel with zero management skills to boot. Of the eight criteria for *zakat* distribution, five could be considered as charity while the remaining three could be leveraged into investments in human capital. *Riqab*, the freeing of slaves and those in bondage, is irrelevant today. Interpreted broadly, it could instead mean emancipating people, as with funding scholarships or building factories and marketplaces to provide jobs.

The Prophet, *s.a.w.*, did exactly that in Medinah, to encourage trade and thus integration among the plural residents, quite apart from enhancing economic activities. The first structure he built when he established his community in Medinah was not a mosque but a marketplace. Ponder that! Thus local *zakat* funds could be used to build modern hawker stalls like those found in Singapore. Those are now major tourist attractions. Just provide power and potable water, plus amenities like bathrooms. Then provide cheap loans to those would-be entrepreneurs.

Likewise with *ibnus sabil*, helping travelers. *Zakat* funds could be used to build lodging facilities on urban mosque lands for visitors from the villages who are uncomfortable with modern hotels. Imagine the ensuing economic activities. Last, *fisabilillah*, jihad in the cause of Allah. Creatively interpreted, that could mean supporting those fighting corruption, injustices, and poverty. Meaning, use *zakat* to fund the activities of the Islamic Renaissance Front, Sisters in Islam, and Siti Kassim's crusade to help our Orang Asli.

Zakat is also mismanaged in another major but hidden way. Islam forbids *ribaa* (interests). As such those banks holding those assets get a huge bonanza – essentially free deposits of money. No surprise then the intense and aggressive competition to secure those funds. Ever wonder why Islamic officials go first class on their Hajj and other overseas junkets, courtesies of these banks. Those ulama do not consider that as corruption, however. That is the real corruption of the faith in Malaysia. If only *zakat* were to be professionally managed with respect to its investments!

At another level and viewed more broadly, *zakat* is the economist's ideal tax system – wide base but shallow rates, only 2.5 percent on the value of your assets annually, comparable to America's property tax. Also in America, this is tax-deductible on your income tax while *zakat* is income tax credit in Malaysia. Meaning, if you pay RM1K towards zakat, that will reduce your income tax by the same amount. In America if I give $1K to my masjid as zakat, it is only tax deductible. If someone at the 40 percent marginal tax bracket for example, then that $1K donation would cost only $600, with the government paying the other $400. Besides, with zakat's low base rate, it would not be worthwhile nickeling and diming your assets' values. For every dollar in reduction, you would save only 2.5 cents in tax, not enough to pay the accountant's creative efforts.

There is surprisingly very little comparative study of *zakat* versus income tax with respect to compliance, efficacy, efficiency, and most important, impact on society and citizen's economic behaviors. Thomas Piketty in his tome, *Capital and Ideology*, suggested a comparable global surtax on wealth (not income) to combat the growing global inequality. Unlike zakat, his would apply only to the super rich.

When the Malaysian Income Tax Act was amended in 1967 to make zakat a tax credit instead of just being tax deductible, I was surprised at the lack of howling protests from non-Muslims. Income tax is spent on all Malaysians while zakat only or mostly for Muslims. The amendment was made in response to Muslims' protests of double taxation. Like everything else, Muslims have failed to capitalize on this significant amendment, one worth considerably more, money-wise, than the monetary value of all the current Malay special privileges.

While few Muslims pay their zakat in full, they all faithfully do their income tax, as required by law. I do not think that they are being stupid or uninformed. Rather that they are being fair to their fellow non-Muslim citizens. Seeing how zakat funds are being misspent, they would rather pay their income tax instead of zakat.

The next major community asset trap is land held under the Malay Reservation Act of 1913. Today there is a huge cry and misplaced concerns among Malay leaders on the dwindling size of land under that statute. However, consider that one luxury condominium at The Pavilion costs much more than a hundred acres of Malay Reservation Land in Ulu Kelantan. Malay Reserve land is but another barnacle on Malay economy. Properly harnessed as per native trust land in Hawaii, it could trigger an economic boom among rural Malays.

The trapping of assets (in this case, land) under Malay Reservation automatically reduces their values. It is a marketing axiom, niche markets excepted, that if you restrict your potential buyers, you reduce the value of your asset. This fact is exploited by Malay government officials. They expropriate Malay Reservation land at a huge discount and then inflate the value to sell it to others, the typical rent-seeking maneuver.

It is also an accepted economic wisdom that development begins with capital formation. From its creation, mobilization, and investment would come economic growth, or creation of wealth. The ongoing tragedy for Malays is that we have imposed upon ourselves self-created and needless obstacles as well as burdens at each of these critical stages.

I began my presentation by putting forth five propositions. One, this Covid-19 pandemic is an outlier event and as such we have to be cautious in interpreting data from this period. Two, Malaysia is less a sick man, more the scrawny stunted kid. Three, Malaysia today resembles more of Ireland and Quebec of pre-1960s. As such we can learn much from them in executing our own Quiet Revolution to deal with the triad of our current curses of endemic corruption, rotting education, and unbridled Islamism. Last, Malays do not lack for capital, rather all of ours, including physical, human, social, financial, and intellectual are trapped. The tragedy is that those traps are of our own making.

There is little chance of Malaysia becoming a failed state, either Islamic *a la* Pakistan or secular, Colombia. The significant non-Malay presence, more so in the vibrant private sector, is an effective buffer against that eventuality.

Malaysia however is in desperate need for her own enlightened leaders in the molds of Ireland's Sean Lemass and Quebec's Jean Lesage. There are many potential ones in Pakatan Harapan. As for UMNO, Mahathir has introduced a lethal disease into his old party UMNO as well as the new ones he had formed such that those leaders would be but corrupt duds that would last for generations.

Back to the central question posed in the preamble to this webinar, Malaysia does not suffer from a benign cold nor an incurable cancer. Instead, she suffers from the metaphorical massive worm infestation. The cure there is an equally metaphorical lifestyle modifications and prudent regular deworming.

Comments And Questions:

Q: What role can non-Malays play?

MBM: The good news is that the presence of a significant and vibrant non-Malay community committed to Malaysia is the best buffer to prevent the country from sliding into a failed state, secular or Islamic. The operative word there is committed. The bad news is that if non-Malays were to consider Malaysia only as an immigration steppingstone while awaiting their (or their children's) Australian PR or American "Green Card," then they are not doing themselves or Malaysia a favor. If you still have that *pendatang* (immigrant) mentality, and with that the temporary abode mentality despite having lived in the country for generations, that would be the surest way that you would forever be treated as one. To avoid that, at the simplest level, would be to make yourself fluent in the national language and familiar with our history. One of the biggest beef Americans (or Australians and Swedes) have of immigrants is that they do not speak English (or Swedish) and do not adapt to their local culture. Muslims in America adapt to local ways as for example by not blasting the *azzan* in deference to our neighbors, and we do not feel less a Muslim for that.

In this regard I am impressed with the new non-Malay leaders in the Democratic Action Party like Anthony Loke who are fluent in Malay and comfortable in the culture of the majority. That speaks volumes of their commitment to the nation. I have been in America far shorter than many non-Muslims in Malaysia, yet I do not consider myself a *pendatang* in America, likewise my children and grandchildren.

Q: How much is too much Islamism in our schools?

MBM: There are only so many hours in a school day. If your reserve four for English, Malay, Mathematics, and Science, the key subjects I suggested, then Islamic Studies together with History and Geography would have to compete for the remaining time slots. Further, Islamic Studies should be taught as an academic subject, not theology. Reserve the teaching of religious rituals during extracurricular activities. For heaven's sake, do not teach the young on how to deal with dead bodies.

Use the rich materials in the Qur'an and hadith to teach critical thinking. I advocate this in my forthcoming [October 2021] book, *Qur'an, Hadith, And Hikayat: Exercises In Critical Thinking*. What does it mean when that *ayat* in Surah Al Fatihah says to keep on a straight path? Likewise with my favorite hadith, "First tie your camel securely only then pray to Allah that it does not escape." The beauty to such an approach to teaching of Islam (or any subject) is that you can then have an "open book" or take-home test. We should be interested in the students' thinking process, not their memorization prowess or exquisite *tajweed* (recitation).

Q: Does religion have a role?

MBM: Absolutely! As per the Iranian scholar Abdolkarim Soroush, religion should act more like the light on a car and not as its brakes. Religion or faith was what kept my parents and grandparents sane during the deprivations of the Great Depression and the horrors of the Japanese Occupation.

The central message of our Qur'an, like all the Holy Texts before it, is "Command good and forbid evil," (*Al-amr bi-l-maʿrūf wa-n-nahy ʿani-l-munkar*). Earlier scriptures may state it differently, but the theme is the same. As for the rest of the Qur'an, it is but commentary on that central theme. I could not care how often a leader has undertaken his Hajj or how diligent he is in his prayers, but if he steals people's money and breaches their trust, he should be jailed regardless how Allah would treat him in the Hereafter. That would be His prerogative, and only His.

As for the rituals of our faith, Ramadan is my most productive month. It is amazing how much time we spend on lunches. I have gone beyond in the past few years and have skipped my lunches altogether. If we do not mindlessly perform our rituals but instead ponder its greater meaning, then we would get much more out of it. During Friday prayers at my mosque, the crowd would linger long after the Imam had said his "Ameen!" To me that is the value of congregational prayers, to enhance community bonding, not how many points you would get in the Hereafter. However this aspect is often lost in our mindless pursuit of rituals. Picture the mass exodus right after Friday prayers in Malaysia.

How often does one ponder on the meaning the Al Fatihah, the verse most frequently recited during our prayers? What do we think of our leaders when we recite the Ayat, "Guide us along the straight path and not the path of those whom Allah has led astray?" Would you consider Najib Razak as a leader whom God has guided along the straight path and as such we must emulate?

Prayers when not just mindlessly recited provides us opportunities for reflection and contemplation.

Q: Why not abolish vernacular schools?

MBM: I am a surgeon, a biologist essentially. The greatest lesson in biology is that diversity is the best protection against extinction. Imagine if we were to have only one school system and we have an idiot or ideologue (they are the same) as the Minister of Education, a very high probability if not certainty in Malaysia, then the whole nation would suffer.

As for vernacular schools, Chinese-type national schools in particular, the fact that an increasing number of Malay parents are opting for that stream means that those school are doing something right. If those championing Chinese vernacular schools wish to have their schools be the first choice for Malaysians, especially Malays, then I suggest changing the name to Mandarin-medium schools. Emphasize the language, not the race. Then have halal canteens and recruit Hans Muslims from China to teach.

Q: What do you think of the nation's brain drain

MBM: Every nation suffers from brain drain but only developing ones worry about that. Brain drain is a barometer of what the smart ones think of their own country, or to be more specific, its future. I have no problems with someone leaving his or her country. That is an individual choice or freedom. I would not infringe on that. The Qur'an says it is our duty to emigrate (undertake our own *hijrah* – migration) if that what it takes to avoid a life of sin. Besides, a nation's concern should be to attract the best talents. Most of the teachers I had growing up were not native-born, and I did not turn out too badly. Earlier I mentioned about having the Chiefs of Police and Anti-Corruption as well as the Attorney-General be foreigners. I prefer that over a local or even a Malaysian émigré, as both would have their own prejudices about Malaysia. The pure foreigner would have no such baggage.

You know that your country is really developed when the emigres begin to return. By that criterion, none of the ASEAN counties is developed. A few decades ago Chinese students in America were consumed with securing their Green Card. Not so today, reflecting how far China has advanced in just the last few decades.

Q: Why not more meritocracy in Malaysia?

MBM: Meritocracy is like virtue; who would be against that? I am all for it. However, some necessary caveat. The ancient Chinese used their famed and grueling civil service tests to pick their brightest and talented to serve in the Imperial Palace and the civil service. It was a much-vaunted system. However, "merit" as measured by such tests refer to those qualities and attributes that are sanctioned or valued by those test makers. When Western colonials entered the world of those mandarins, they could not deal with the novel phenomenon or associated challenges as that subject (foreign domination) never appeared in the minds of the test designers, and thus not tested. The result? A puny county like Britain could humiliate the whole continent of China with its hundreds of millions of Chinese.

The issue with the current meaning or interpretation of meritocracy, as in China of yore, is that those in power get to decide the criteria of merit! In my medical school in Canada back in the 1960s, our farsighted dean was concerned with the lack of graduates interested in general practice specifically in rural areas. So he changed the composition of the admission committee to include rural practitioners instead of the usual crop of specialists on the faculty. The result? More subsequent graduates opted for rural practice!

The human capability is infinite. When merit is assessed by tests, remember that those tests are designed by humans with their own concept of what is meritorious. Therein is the danger.

Do Malaysian Universities Need Revamping?

[Presented at a webinar organized by the Islamic Renaissance Front (IRF) on October 30, 2021. I thank Dr. Ahmad Fariuk Musa for inviting me, the moderator Nageeb Gounjaria, and my fellow panelists Dr. Sharifah Munirah Alatas, Faculty of Social Sciences and Humanities, Universiti Kebangsaan Malaysia, and Prof. Zaharom Naim, Professor of Media and Communication Studies, University of Nottingham, Malaysia.

Video of the conference is available on Youtube:

https://youtu.be/-sjSVN_XVyE]

Bakri Musa: The short and simple answer would be a definite and emphatic "Yes!" A more deliberate and meaningful response would be "Why?" and "How?" Most consequential of all would be, what if we do not revamp and the status quo were to prevail. I wrote my *An Education System Worthy of Malaysia* in 2003. Since then I have made periodic commentaries culminating in my 2020 book, *The Rot in Malaysian Education.* As the title suggests, things have only gotten worse.

The central criticism of not just Malaysian but all Asian universities is that they do not encourage much less teach critical thinking. This is especially true with Islamic education and education in general in Muslim countries, Malaysia included. Instead, indoctrination masquerades as education, more so with religious education. The American broad-based liberal education encourages critical thinking and, among other things, produces "T" (broad knowledge with deep understanding in a narrow field) versus "I" individuals. Malaysian (and Muslim) education in contrast erects mental silos.

Liberal education cultivates the mind and refines judgement. Few systems of higher education in the world offer this opportunity to indulge your intellectual curiosity, and to explore other disciplines unrelated to one's ultimate career choice during the early stages of one's undergraduate years. Liberal education is not embraced in much of Asia and Muslim countries, the Gulf States possibly excepted. There the presence of many branch campuses of major American universities helped change the intellectual climate. The National University of Singapore-Yale collaboration in that republic, erroneously acclaimed as the first liberal arts college in Asia, will close in 2024 and on less-than-amiable terms. The problem there is not with the reception by students or faculty, rather a political decision taken outside of academia. That reveals volumes on the state of academic and other freedoms in that republic and Asia generally.

Not all of Asia is thus blighted. Though political and other freedoms are severely constricted in the Gulf States, with enthusiastic state support they are embracing Western liberal education. That is an outlier in Asia as well as the greater Muslim world. It is an expensive proposition but thanks to their generous oil revenues, those states could afford it. Their enlightened leaders deemed it money well spent. As a result, today the region is attracting the brightest Arab minds, absorbing the values of liberal education in the comfort of their own familiar sociocultural ambience. It is not coincidental that the region is now a major financial center both for Islamic finance as well as traditional ones. Then consider this seemingly unrelated achievement. Of the top ten global airlines, three are from that region. I expect soon the leading Asian universities will be in this region. The American University in Cairo, established only in 1919, is today the college of choice for the Arab elite, far eclipsing Al Azhar University set up a millennium ago (Year 970). In nearby Lebanon despite the chaos, the American University in Beirut (AUB), its avowedly Christian origin notwithstanding, remains the crown jewel of Arab intellectual achievement.

Malaysian leaders and intellectuals endlessly lament the lack of critical thinking skills among their students, yet not a single local university, private or public, has a dedicated Department of Philosophy. When or where critical thinking is taught in Asia, the exercises and examples used are often alien to the students. Philosophy Professor Edward Omar Moad, an American Muslim, related his experience at Qatar University many years ago. The assigned text, chosen by the university president, a native Arab, was an American one. As such the examples were alien to the students. Thus they ended up merely regurgitating the views voiced by American commentators and pundits.

Instead Moad made his students read local publications for more relevant and meaningful examples. Further, as those issues had not previously been commented upon, his students were forced to think on their own. A few years later he had enough materials to publish his own textbook! That prompted me to publish (October 2021) my *Qur'an, Hadith, and Hikayat: Exercises in Critical Thinking* where I used examples familiar to Malaysians, at least Malays. I have used those exercises with both American students as well as Malaysians.

Back to the challenge at hand, Malaysia had her first university in 1962. Within the next dozen years four more were added. Then after a hiatus of a decade, the nation went on a building binge and added 15 more. With the liberalization of higher education in 1996, the private sector too joined in the spree. Within a few years then-Minister of Education Najib (yes, that same character of later 1MDB notoriety) approved nearly 600 applications! Most would collapse or remain as expensive glorified tuition centers above shop lots. Those are but blights of Malaysian education, stranding their students and quashing their and their families' dreams, not to mention draining their pockets. As an aside, Najib had no difficulty financing his expensive campaign to retain his Vice-Presidency of UMNO during those years, an early manifestation of his later 1MDB avarice.

The preamble to this program asserts, "Academia today, the scholars concede, have bowed down to the god of unfettered capitalism ... reduced to a production line [churning] out uncritical yet obedient workers to meet the needs of our ever-growing economy."

We have to be precise in our words, and with that, concepts. We should clarify first, the difference between capitalism versus big business; second, private versus public institutions; and third, cause versus effect. Meeting the needs of a growing economy means contributing to society, and thus serving the community, a worthy mission.

Malaysia today has 20 public universities and 91 private ones, but the definition between public and private is murky. Petronas University and Tenaga University are considered private, but their sponsors are government-linked corporations. Further, private Malaysian universities are profit-making enterprises. Foreign-sponsored private universities like the University of Nottingham Malaysia (UNM), while their parent institutions back home may be public (tax supported), their Malaysian branch campuses are private and proprietary, with shareholders and the distribution of dividends. UNM parent owner recently announced a "buy-out" of its local corporate partners, all so modern corporatism!

America has many public universities, funded at the federal (the various military academies), state (UCLA), and municipal levels (CUNY). Meanwhile the overwhelming majority of "private" universities (Duke, Harvard) are non-profit. They however too receive substantial public funding, directly through various research grants and indirectly from being spared many taxes including hefty property taxes. There are a few truly private or proprietary (meaning, profit-making) universities like DeVry and the University of Phoenix, but none highly regarded. They are also geared towards non-traditional students and working adults.

Anxieties about higher education are not unique unto Malaysians. New York University Business Professor Scott Galloway predicted that over half of American colleges would close or be "walking dead" within a decade. On-line teaching and the digital revolution have upended everything including college instructions. Covid-19 pandemic only exposes and accelerates the inevitable.

On the second concept, we should distinguish between capitalism (an efficient, responsive, and productive economic system) versus big business and its narrow short-term and self-interest. American big businesses are a threat not only to her universities but also all other American institutions, including and especially political. Consider that in America the highest paid and most powerful man (always a male) on campus is not the president or star professor, rather the football coach. As for the academics, right up to the week of Royal Bank of Scotland's spectacular collapse in the 2008 financial crisis, Harvard Business School professors were still extolling its business model. No surprise there as they were also the bank's highly paid consultants.

The current widespread opposition among Americans to Covid-19 vaccination reflects less an anti-science sentiment, more a distrust of big pharma's role in academia and medicine. Then consider the costs. If American healthcare is expensive, then her college tuition is extortionate. It is widely predicted that the next financial crisis would be the humongous student loans. By contrast, Malaysia does not have big business; instead, it has big, intrusive, and incompetent government.

The challenges of Malaysian universities are with both structure and mission. For structure, first the students, the primary component; second, faculty; and last, management. As for mission, the nation's first institution was less a University of Malaya, meaning, serving the nation's needs, rather a pathetic attempt to replicate a jungle version of Oxford and Cambridge, complete with their superficial trappings. Its leaders mistook scarcity and difficulty for quality and class. As such, the university insulated itself from local issues. It, like the rest of Malaysia, was caught flat-footed by the May 1969 disastrous racial riots triggered in part by the gross interracial inequities in education and elsewhere.

The University of Malaya then responded by starting its own *assasi* (foundation) classes to increase Malay enrolment in STEM, then the glaring problem and a major cause for the riot. That initiative was much needed. Though successful, the university has since failed to make enhancements to the program despite changing conditions. Today the program is redundant, expensive, and a drain on scarce campus resources. Those classes could be done better and cheaper elsewhere. Likewise with its copycat programs as with the Ministry of Education's extensive *matrikulasi*.

Nonetheless I give credit to the campus leadership for starting the *assasi* program. In truth, according to the late Tan Sri Majid Ismail, then Malaysia's Director-General of Health who was also Chairman of the University's governing board, he had to wring the neck of those academics to adopt his proposal. To the university, those matriculating offerings were beneath their academic dignity. Of note, many American universities too have the equivalent of foundation classes to increase the number of students from underrepresented minorities, but those were undertaken off-campus.

However, the success of *assasi* and *matrikulasi* emasculated Sixth Form, thus reducing secondary schools to but middle level. Malay College Kuala Kangsar (MCKK) abandoned its Sixth Form in the 1970s. Its students had to go elsewhere to matriculate. The introduction of IB a few years ago changed little. That program did not attract even MCKK's students. Elsewhere, IB is the crown jewel of a school, and its slots highly coveted, but not perversely at MCKK.

Students today have a mishmash of choices after their Sijil Persekutuan Malaysia (SPM – taken at Year 11), the *de facto* school terminal examination, to prepare themselves for university. However, according to Program for International School Assessment (PISA), Malaysian schools are at least 2-3 years behind those of advanced countries. Meaning, SPM is at best Form Three level elsewhere. This is also borne anecdotally. A Malaysian parent moved from Singapore and found that his son at Form IV was doing what he did in Form II earlier across the causeway.

SPM is conducted in December with the results not released until the following April. *Assasi* and *matrikulasi* however, begin in July. Students thus have over a six-month hiatus. Non-Malays enroll in the many excellent private classes right away in January; later they would apply to the much cheaper government's programs.

Years ago I gave a seminar to *assasi* students who ended up at American universities. One student who had read my book *The Malay Dilemma Revisited*, a critique of Mahathir's *The Malay Dilemma*, asked why in the class that he was in, of the group selected to go abroad early because of their superior mid-course scores, non-Malays were overrepresented despite the class being overwhelmingly Malays by design.

I immediately sensed his burden, what Stanford's Claude Steele referred to as "stereotype threat." Mahathir often asserted in his book that Malays are dumb, and lazy to boot. I inquired from that student what he did after his SPM Examination. Like thousands of other Malay students – nothing! In my earlier surveys of Malaysian students in America, almost all the non-Malays had enrolled in private foundation classes in January such that when they were admitted to the government-sponsored ones, they were already six months ahead of their Malay classmates who did "nothing." That is a significant advantage in what typically is a twelve to eighteen-month program. No wonder those non-Malays did well.

The relief on that Malay boy's face to my explanation was palpable. Imagine if he had not queried me, he would have carried that "stereotype threat" burden all his life. Worse, he would transmit those false destructive assumptions onto his children, and his students if he were to end up being a teacher or lecturer. Indeed that is the current destructive narrative propagated by the likes of those at Biro Tata Negara (National Civic Bureau).

In my Lower Form Six Class in 1961, a few of my classmates joined in April following their superior SPM results. Even with that much shorter three-month hiatus, they struggled to keep up with the rest of us. Imagine a six-month lag!

Get rid of *assasi* and *matrikulasi*. Universities should undertake only what could not be done elsewhere, that is, education at the undergraduate, graduate, and professional levels, together with the generation of new knowledge through research which can then be transferred vertically to the next generation or diffused laterally to the community through extension services. Leave matriculating programs to the schools. Resurrect and improve Sixth Form. That would be cheaper and more effective. It would also improve the academic standards of schools.

Make English and mathematics compulsory for all years right up to Form VI. Then you could dispense with MUET (Malaysian Universities English Test), except for foreign students. Mathematics enhances critical thinking. A recent British study compared those who continued taking mathematics at GCE-A level (Form Six) versus those who did not. With the appropriate control groups, the study found that those who continued with their mathematics studies had higher levels of neurotransmitters related with cognition and neuroplasticity, revealing a hitherto unappreciated relationship between education (specifically mathematical) and neurobiology. At the societal level, earning levels are correlated with superior mathematical achievements. Developed societies whether East or West share one commonality – the emphasis of mathematics (and STEM) in their curriculum.

Better-prepared secondary school students make good undergraduates. They in turn become superior graduates and would be able to serve the community better.

Enhancing The Faculty

This is more challenging. I hesitate to criticize Malaysian academics because invariably I would hurt the feelings of those dedicated, superbly qualified individuals toiling hard in the lecture halls, clinical wards, and science laboratories under very trying circumstances, their meager pay an insult. They are also often overlooked in promotions or being honored. I could not care less with such silly titles as Datuk and Tan Sri (after all crooks get honored in that system), rather the universities' own value system. Peruse the list of Professor Emeriti, dominated by "political" academics, overwhelmingly those in Malay and Islamic Studies. Few scientists or physicians are honored. To add insult, few professors in STEM and professional fields are invited to stay beyond retirement. What a waste!

The Professor of Chemistry in Tin Metallurgy at the University of Malaya retired many years ago and was grabbed by the National University of Singapore. No replacement; likewise, no expert on rubber chemistry. Malaysia desperately needs teachers of English, yet not a single university has a dedicated Department of English. Likewise, with a Department of Philosophy. There are many experts off campus at the various research institutes (Medical, Veterinary, Palm Oil) and industry. Few have adjunct faculty appointments. Another waste!

The market for academics is global. I salute the likes of Drs. Sharifah, Farouk, Ahmad Tajuddin, and others who stayed in local academia despite the lousy pay and other challenges. Malaysia cannot continue counting on their altruism alone.

Local academics are underpaid. An increase of 40-50 percent is much needed and would do wonders. Subsidized housing also helps. More significant would be to give automatic research grants to the tune of ten percent of the annual pay every year. My alma mater, the University of Alberta, secured top global talents by guaranteeing their research funds, thus sparing them from wasting precious hours and distracting efforts at writing for grants.

Malaysia has misplaced generosity to its staff. Professors travel first class, and campus ceremonies elaborate. Why not economy tickets and plenty left over to fund laptops and research? I was stunned to see full-page glossy pictures of the chancellors and top officials in a convocation program. Harvard's on recycled papers, and no glossy picture of its president!

In an earlier book *An Education System Worthy of Malaysia* (2003) I proposed "International Tract Appointments" with globally competitive salaries (in the range of RM250K annually) in such critical fields as STEM, English, and economics to serve as the nucleus and stimulus for excellence. There is little need for such appointments in Islamic or Malay

Studies not because those disciplines are not important rather that there is a glut of applicants in both fields.

If an annual pay of RM250K is unaffordable, consider this. Every year Malaysia sends thousands of students abroad at a cost of at least US $60K (RM250K) each per year. You could hire an American professor or a smart Malaysian from the private sector at that price. For the American, a good chunk of his pay would be spent on local taxes and living expenses. He would be lucky to save US $10K to repatriate at the end of the year. In terms of actual foreign exchange loss, importing six American professors would cost as much as sending one student abroad. Imagine how many more local students would benefit with the infusion of foreign talents, quite apart from the multiplier effects of their local spending.

Other ideas include special market allowances for those in badly needed disciplines allowing the faculty (with appropriate guidelines) to earn private income. The Professor of English could conduct writing classes for journalists at *Bernama* and *The New Straits Times*. God knows, they need that!

Today's headlines scream of the thousands of unemployed graduates, the overwhelming majority being Bumiputras. Yet there is little critical examination of the issue on campus. Are they unemployed because of their ethnicity, in which case the country has a very serious problem, or because of their chosen field of study? There are scarce data to clarify the issues. Most Malays gravitate to Malay and Islamic Studies, of little utility in the private sector. America with her broad-based liberal education, a religious study graduate would have skills (in particular, critical thinking skills and quantitative abilities) useful in the private sector.

This brings me to my third concept, the importance of discerning cause versus effect. While the leading universities are in the developed world, one could argue that because they are developed those countries could devote the necessary resources to creating great universities, versus the counter argument that the innovations and talents from those great institutions are instrumental to developing the nation.

The American University of Beirut, long the intellectual crown jewel of the Arab world, is no help to Lebanon, a nation perpetually divided along sectarian lines. Nehru's top priority was to set up a string of the elite Indian Institutes of Technology to rival Oxford and Cambridge as well as

Imperial College. That succeeded only in sending the brightest Indians to the West.

On the other end, the first thing Chairman Deng did when he took over from Mao was to seek President Carter's help in securing the admission of a few hundred of the brightest Chinese students into elite American universities. As a result, today Beijing and Tsing Hua Universities rival Harvard and Yale. Chinese scientists were the first to sequence the Covid-19 genome.

At the practical level, it is much easier and cheaper to develop your universities than it is the whole nation. Universities generate and transmit knowledge and then transfer it longitudinally to the next generation, the students, and laterally to the community through extension services. Such extension faculties also serve as routes for non-traditional students could to pursue a degree. Develop your universities and you develop your nation. It is not a guarantee of course, as India has demonstrated, but it would be a much surer and cheaper bet.

University Management – The Blight of Big Government

If American colleges are blighted by big business, then Malaysia's is with big, meddling, and incompetent government. The bureaucracy associated with education at all levels is expensive, expansive, and intrusive. It is also a major hindrance to campus innovation. Get rid of that massive bureaucracy and use the money to hire top faculty.

The government could exert far more influence if not control through intelligent use of its major levers of funding, as well as its power to appoint senior personnel, including and especially the universities' governing board members. Give these universities global annual budgets and then leave them alone. Those academics are far smarter than the bureaucrats in how to spend the money and resources on their respective campuses. California has many more state universities, yet it does not have a Ministry of Higher Education.

The late Ungku Aziz excepted, the tenure of local university heads is in the low single digit years. As such they do no acquire the necessary and unique experiences or be familiar with campus problems. Worse, most just aspire for the title, with the hope of a Tan Sri before retiring to the local masjid for their nightly *ratib* (religious chanting).

When in Malaysia in the mid-1970s, many of my colleagues were consumed in lobbying to be Departmental Heads, Deans, and Vice Chancellors to the detriment of their scholarly and professional developments. In a casual conversation with one blatantly pursuing the Vice-Chancellorship, I asked him what changes would he bring should he be successful in getting the position? He was dumbfounded. He had never thought of that. He was just interested in the title. That anecdote is emblematic of local campus leadership. In the end he did get the job. Today it would be difficult to ascertain the legacy of his tenure, if any.

In picking the Vice-Chancellor, the Minister should seek major input from the campus community. If not satisfied with the choice, make the reasons known and have the campus committee pick an alternate. Beyond that, the Vice-Chancellorship should be a terminal appointment. Meaning, you die, retire, or be fired from that position.

There is one other unacknowledged drag on as well as threat to local universities. I have to be extra cautious here lest I jeopardize the safety of our forum organizers! That is the oppressive, destructive influence of and in many cases control by the Islamists. By Islamists I mean those who exploit our great faith to further their political and other agenda. As per the wisdom of the late Nurcholish Madjid from Indonesia, "Islam, Yes! Islamic Party, No!" I would add, no Islamic politics on campus either.

Like Mao's Red Guards that destroyed Chinese universities, likewise today's Islamists in Malaysia. Nobody dares criticize much less restrain the Islamists. To them, indoctrination is education. They have trouble accommodating even fellow Muslims like the Shiites, much less non-Muslims! Shiite literature at the International Islamic University for example, is kept under lock and key. Should you inquire, you risk being reported to the Special Branch! Local public universities embrace this narrow, exclusive version of Islam, with campus leaders and community accepting this with no ruffles.

It is a toss-up whether the government or the Islamist is the more malignant influence on local public campuses. Make no mistake; both are. Unchecked, the Islamists would turn Malaysia into another Iran or Afghanistan, with no turning back.

Message of Hope

In their book *The Innovative University: Changing the DNA of Higher Education from the Inside Out*, Clayton Christensen and Henry Eyring traced the development of two American universities at the polar ends of the academic scale – Harvard and Brigham Young University Idaho. One accepts fewer than 4 percent of its applicants and is in a major city, a former religious institution but now secular, and proud of its diverse global student body and faculty. The other admits all applicants, located in rural America, with all its students Mormons. Yet both are successful because they respond to and serve the changing needs of their equally changing communities.

The communities that Malaysian universities must serve are many and diverse. Then there is the unique challenge of the dominant population – Malays. A nation and its universities cannot be stable much less thrive unless the special challenges of the majority population are met. That is true in America as in Malaysia. The current angst among rural white Americans to the influx of immigrants is an anxiety Malays could empathize.

Likewise with the challenges of the national language. If local universities had been responsive, there would not be a need for Dewan Bahasa dan Pustaka, the government's massive and expensive language and literary agency. Local academics should be doing the translating of major works into Malay, emulating the early Arabs with Greek philosophy.

Then consider the increasing racial polarization. Universities should be at the forefront in tackling that issue, as with having all freshmen live in integrated campus hostels. Instead local campuses, public and private, aggravate communal sentiments.

I do not need to belabor the point that local universities are far detached from their surrounding realities and the challenges. A sad commentary, and a major reason to revamp local universities.

The current obsession with ranking is misplaced. Improvements in ranking is the result of your innovations. Make the necessary changes to better serve your community and the ranking would take care of itself. Participating in these global ranking surveys is expensive and consume precious and scarce personnel's time and resources. Assume that no local institutions would make in the top one, two or even three hundred for the next generation or two. Quit participating in the surveys; divert the resources to enhancing the faculty and academic offerings. What is there to celebrate when your campus ascends from the 256th to the 334th ?

Problems with universities impact families directly especially those with potential university-bound children. For these parents I would advise them to be frugal and save furiously for your children's education. Prepare them for recognized certificates like IB, SAT, and GCE-A level. That is their passport out of the current intellectually constricting Malaysian system.

My suggestions are not cheap. That means Malay parents must defer or not undertake their umrah or Hajj, dispense with that luxury car, and not acquire a second or third wife. Instead, they should buy their children laptops and subscribe to a reliable 5G network. Guide them to use the Internet safely and productively. Having it is like having the Library of Congress at your fingertips, but the web could also lead you to the vilest sites. The Internet could also facilitate their learning English. There was a local sensation recently of a five-year old girl, Aishah London, whose mother let her listen only to the BBC channel. Just with that she could speak flawless English. She also acquired the critical and inquisitive traits of those superb BBC journalists.

We should impress upon the young that SPM (Malaysian schools' terminal examination taken at Year 11) is just the beginning, not the end, and that they should enroll themselves immediately in the many private Sixth Form and *assasi* classes as soon as their December vacation is over. Do that and you could not care less what happens to local universities. The whole wide world would then be open to your children They would then have choices.

Alas my proposals are beyond the reach of most Malaysians. As such, government programs from residential schools and university scholarships to *assasi* and *matrikulasi* should focus on them. A mark of distinction for local universities that would far overshadow global rankings would be to flout the percentage of their admittees who are the first in their family to go to university. That would be a distinction worthy of celebration. To get there, local universities must first collect the basic data on their undergraduates.

The central if not exclusive mission of Malaysian (if not all) universities is to serve the community they serve – meaning Malaysia and Malaysians, not to aspire to be a jungle version of Harvard or Oxford, nor be obsessed with scaling a few steps up the ranking scale. Living in Malaysia you are all very aware of the Malaysian problems. It would be presumptuous of me to elaborate on them except to highlight some central observations, as with the deepening polarization of society along identities.

I am sorry to end of such a low note. As a surgeon I often have to convey unwelcomed but truthful news to my patients. Never a pleasant or welcomed mission. However when I do, I would always accompany that with a message of hope together with a path towards remedying the problem. I hope I have done that with my presentation today.

Comments And Questions

Q1: Research at universities require funding, and these are usually underwritten by big business. Is that a problem?

Yes. There is for example the pernicious influence of big pharma on US campuses. The general (albeit minor) hostility towards the Covid-19 vaccine reflects this public mistrust. It is less an anti-science protest more the angst against big pharma. It is standard for institutions including where I work to have strict and explicit conflict of interest declarations. Nonetheless the problem remains. The issue is less over pressures on research with respect to your findings and conclusions rather on the very areas you would undertake the research.

Q2: Can you comment on the standard of local undergraduates?

Many years ago a local law professor lamented on social media that if she had her way she would fail over 95 percent of her students. However, she claimed that she was under tremendous pressure from the Administration to pass most of them. I do not know whether she was proud of being a 'tough' grader and demanding 'high' standards from her students or commenting on their quality.

Her observation was pathetic at so many levels. First, she could not have been an attentive or perceptive teacher if she found only towards the end of the year that her students had not understood what she had been teaching. When I was teaching medical students in Malaysia in 1970s, I knew after the first few lectures that what I was teaching went above their heads. As such I stopped everything and spent the next few weeks going over the basics. There was no point piling on. My efforts paid off.

Second, if what she said was true, she should have spent her first few weeks or even months on basic preparatory work. Many leading American professional schools have summer pre-law, pre-med, pre-MBA classes to better prepare their students. This again points to my earlier point of serving your community well as with adequately preparing your students.

Q3: You advocate liberal education and critical thinking. Can you elaborate on them?

The best definition of a liberal education is this: It cultivates the mind and refines judgment. Few systems of higher education in the world offer this opportunity to indulge your intellectual curiosity and explore disciplines that at this stage may seem unrelated to your ultimate career choice. I say 'at this stage,' for as you advance in your career you will find that you will fall back on the wisdom and insights you have gleaned from those apparently unrelated disciplines. I was privileged in that before embarking on my medical studies I had to take the humanities and social sciences. I believe I am a better physician for having been exposed to those disciplines. As for critical thinking, as someone observed, it is less answering the questions, more questioning the answers.

Q4: You mention that universities should serve the community that supports them. Can you translate that into campus research activities?

The University of Malaya should be the university for Malaya (or Malaysia). Meaning, it should focus (its teaching, research, and other activities) on the needs of the nation. You do not expect the University of Montana to be interested in tropical rainforests or mangrove swamps. Likewise the University of Malaya should focus on those areas as well as on local diseases like dengue. Local universities could not compete with rich Western universities on research in the immunology of kidney transplants for example, but we can on parasitic infections like malaria and amebiasis. Likewise local universities should be on the forefront of research on tin, rubber, and oil palms. Our engineering faculties should be engaged in intensive research on metal corrosion, a plague in our hot humid climate; likewise with solar technology as we are blessed with abundant sunshine. Often as was shown by local research on the Nipah virus, local findings have global implications and applications.

Q5: Universities are under pressure to produce employable graduates. Should big corporations dictate campus agenda?

Just because captains of industry like Jack Welch, Jeff Bezos, and Mark Zuckerberg had been to elite universities does not mean those institutions cater to big businesses. Rather those universities have equipped their graduates with skills that would benefit society. Those enterprises serve merely as their conduits. Again, we have to differentiate between cause and effect. No, big business should not dictate campus agenda, but campuses should be responsive to the needs of industry but not be beholden to them. That is a tough choice. Much of the public distrust with modern medicine today is that so much of medical research is industry funded. As one wag put it, 80 percent of medical research findings support their sponsor's agenda! Right up to just days before its collapse in the 2008 banking crises, Harvard Business School's professors we still singing high praises on Royal Bank of Scotland. Later it was exposed they had been the bank's consultants!

Yes, we should worry about big business dictating terms to universities. However, we should worry even more about big government doing the same to universities.

I make one big exception here, and that is the direct and pernicious role of athletics. Some universities are but farm schools for professional sports and where the highest paid official is not the President but the football coach. Malaysian campuses are fortunately spared that blight.

Q6. The government is using the public service KPI matrix to rate academics. Is that appropriate?

The best judges for you and your work are your peers. Hence peer reviews in my profession. KPI is developed for administrative purposes and are concerned with quantifiable output or metrics, less quality. If you use KPI in academia, then you would focus more on such things as the number of publications and less on their impact. The growth of predatory journals to cater to Third World academics is one negative consequence to the obsession with KPI. Many American colleges have student reviews of their lecturers. That too is a valid component for assessing quality and productivity.

A note of caution on imposing rigid criteria, more so on things that cannot be easily measured. Many years ago New York State published the complication rates and other data on the state's heart surgeons. After a few years the 'quality' of the state's surgeons 'improved,' as per those chosen criteria. However, the surgical complication rates of heart cases in neighboring Pennsylvania increased as New York surgeons were now referring their tough cases across the border so as to maintain their "superb" (low complication) standing. Beware of unintended consequences. Then there is the Hawthorne effect, where those being watched, scrutinized, or monitored become more productive.

Q7. Can you comment on the failure of local scholars to speak out on major issues?

That observation is less true today now that Malaysia has many private universities, thanks to the liberalization of higher education back in the late 1996. That was one of the few smart initiatives. However, its implementation was something else. Then Minister of Education Najib Razak approved no fewer than six hundred permits over a two-year time span. No surprise that he could finance his subsequent campaign to be one of UMNO Vice-Presidents with no difficulty. That was a prelude to his later 1MDB shenanigan as Prime Minister.

It is not a surprise that some of the more outspoken local academics and scholars like our fellow panelist Dr. Ahmad Tajuddin Rasdi are from by private universities. The other is Dr. Ahmad Farouk Musa. Nonetheless your observation is spot on. You can bet that neither

Tajuddin nor Farouk would make it into the National Professors Council anytime soon.

Q8: Can you comment on the acquisition of a second language, in particular the learning of English among Malaysians.

You mean among Malays, as most non-Malaysians are already functionally bilingual – their native tongue and Malay. Many are also trilingual, with English added. If not for the misguided influence of Malay leaders and language nationalists, Malays too would be bilingual, as with many in my generation. Contemporary Malay leaders actively discourage Malays to acquire a second language proficiency. Although English is taught in national schools it is being done perfunctorily, by teachers not trained or facile in the language. Consider that there is not a single English-medium Teachers' Training College. Likewise, no public university has a dedicated Department of English.

Malay leaders are misguided by the UNESCO Report purportedly recommending teaching pupils first in their mother tongue and only later to add a second language. Modern linguists however, supported by studies in the neurosciences, suggest that the younger we are exposed to a second language the better. Further, facility in a second language confers many cognitive advantages quite apart from increasing your utility in the marketplace.

That UNESCO study referred to those whose mother tongue is spoken by small communities, as with the many tribes in Papua New Guinea and South America. If their adherents are not encouraged to speak their native tongue, that language risks disappearing. Malay language however, is the *lingua franca* of over two hundred million people. There is minimal risk of it disappearing. Malays should be like Western Europeans. They are fluent English as well as in their mother tongue.

Earlier there was the question on doing locally relevant research. Malaysia with its plural society is a goldmine for such research on social "experiments of nature." Consider the learning of a second language, now very much a hot issue in many countries including and especially America. Malaysia has been doing it, formally and informally as well as implicitly and explicitly, for generations during colonial times. Study the results!

Appendix:

Harapan Dan Cabaran Teknoloji Digital (TD) Dalam Pembelajaran Talian

[Persembahan di webinar anjuran Islamic Renaissance Front, Sabtu Januari 31, 2021 bersama dengan ahli panelis Dato Dr. Madeline Berma dan moderator Shamshir Alam]

Harapan Dan Cabaran Teknoloji Digital (TD)

Kemajuan sesuatu negara atau masyarakat tergantung bukan atas kekayaan sumber alam atau suburnya tanah air, tetapi mutu insan nya, atau dalam Bahasa Ingeris, human capital. Itu pula berasaskan atas dua tiang—mutu pendidikan dan taraf kesihatan rakyat. Wabak Covid-19 mengoncangkan kedua dua asas itu. Taraf pendidikan Malaysia sudah merosot. Mengikut PISA, murid sekolah menengah Malaysia berkebelakangan dua ke tiga tahun bila di bandingkan dengan murid di Singapore dan Korea Selatan. Darjah kesihatan negara pula sudah ternayata rendah dan dimaklumkan dengan wabak Covid-19 yang masih belum terkawal dan negara belum lagi menyuntek penduduknya. Musim dan akibat wabak Covid-19 mendedahkan dengan nyata bukan juga kemunduran taraf pendidikan negara bahkan juga ketidakseimbangan antara murid bandar dan luar bandar, serta murid miskin dan mereka yang berupaya. Masaalah ini tidak terhad kepada Malaysia sahaja, bahkan seluruh dunia, termasuk negara maju seperti Amerika mengalaminya.

Saya akan meninjau cabaran dan harapan TD dari tiga segi. Pertama, peranan nya secara am; kedua, bagaimana sejarah menyelesaikan masaalah ketidakseimbangan dalam sesuatu masyarakat atau negara; dan ketiga, peranan TD bukan sahaja untuk meningkatan taraf pendidekkan negara tetapi juga untuk membina ekonomi dan pembangunan serta membebaskan fikiran rakyat. Saya akan bandingkan peranan TD dalam pendidikkan di Malaysia, khasnya di musim wabak Covid-19 ini, dengan pengalaman di luar negri.

Rakyat Malaysia sudah selesa dengan Teknoloji Digital (TD) melalui alat saperti Smart phone, computer, dan Internet. TD adalah satu rekaan yang tak terbatas hebat nya, lebih hebat lagi daripada rekaan roda atau elektrik. TD boleh meningkatkan dan dengan itu mengsamaratakan ke'adaan maanusia. Itulah kehebatan TD. Melalui TD, seorang anak miskin Orang Asli di hutan Gua Musang mempunyai peluang yang sama dengan anak hartawan di kondo mewah New York. Mereka berdua boleh menuntun wayang yang sama serta mendengar lagu yang sama. Mereka pun boleh berbual bersama melalui Skpe dan Zoom. TD menyentuh semua kegiatan maknusia bukan saja dalam pendidikan.

Merujuk kepada ketidaksamaan masyarakat, Professor Sejarah Stanford Walter Scheidel dalam bukunya, The Great Leveler: Violence And the History of Inequality (Pemsamarataan Yang Hebat–Keganasan Dan Tidak Keseimbangan Dalam Sejarah) menulis sepanjang sejarah apabila sesuatu masyarakat itu sudah jauh tidak seimbang keadaan nya, hanya empat cara sahaja yang boleh menukar atau meratakan keadaan itu. Pertama perang, kedua revolusi, ketiga wabak, dan keempat, keruntuhan pemerintahan negara yang mengakibatkan keadaan hura hara saperti semasa perang. Wabak Covid 19 mendedahkan serta meningkatkan ketidakseimbangan dalam masyarakat. Dengan nyata wabak Covid-19 ini mencabar pendapat Scheidel.

TD ialah unsur baru, yang kelima, untuk mensamaratakan masyarakat tetapi tanpa membawa maut dan kejahanaman saperti berlaku semasa perang, revolusi, dan keruntuhan pemerentahan. TD membolehkan masyarakat kebelakangan melompat, bahkan melebehi masyarakat yang maju. Sebaliknya, ketidakseimbangan digital (digital divide) yang kini mendalam akan menjadi gaung digital (digital chasm), dan dengan lebih cepat lagi mempisahkan negara yang maju daripada yang mundur.

Malaysia sekarang bernasib baik tidak mengalami peperangan atau revolusi. Tetapi kita seperti dunia luar, mengalami wabak Covid-19. Pemerentahan negara pula kurang cekap, tanpa kemahiran, raput dengan rasuah dan pecah amanah. Inilah masa nya untuk kita memuluk dan melebur dengan teguh TD dalam semua bidang negara, bukan sahaja dalam pendidikkan.

Dua unsur timbul dengan serta merta bila berbincang tentang TD. Pertama, peralatan atau hardware; kedua, software dan dengan itu, kandongan. Merujuk kepada peralatan, masaalahnya ialah harga. Membina satu menara 5G di Ulu Kelantan berkekehendaki infrastructure sokongan saperti elektrik and salurun internet. Di Amerika, satu Menara 5G berharga US\$50K. Itu belum masuk membina kuasa electric dan sebagainya. Di India, Sugata Mitra membina model "Hello Hubs" dan "School in the Clouds" dengan harga berhampiran US\$1 million.

Disini kita perlu teliti makna "harga" dan "mahal." Saya contohi dengan harga mesin mencuci baju. Harga membuat mesen pertama mungkin melebihi beberapa juta. Itu termasuk harga tapak tanah dan membangunkan kilang, engineer untok mengreka mesen itu, harga bahan, gaji pekerja, dan sebagainya. Tetapi sekarang selepas berjuta mesen di jual dan akibat pertandingan pasaranan, harga satu mesen tak sampai seribu ringgit pun.

Maksudnya, batasan harga boleh di ukur dan dinilai, atau dalam Bahasa Inggeris, quantifiable barrier. Kalau kita boleh beri nilai atau boleh diukur, maknanya masaalah itu boleh di batasi. Kusukaran yang susah di batasi ialah masaalah yang tidak dapat diberi angka. Tambahan pula jika kita buat tender terbuka dan jauhi syarikat berkaitan dengan Rosmah Mansor, kita boleh turunkan lagi harga membina Menara 5G dan peralatan DT yang lain. Kita boleh dan mesti memberi satu laptop kepada keluarga miskin di luar dan dalam bandar, serta memberikan laluan broadband yang percuma atau murah.

Kerajaan sekarang merancang dengan negara jiran untok membuat jaringan satelit mempayongi seluruh Tenggara Asia. Ini anggan2 Mat Jenin saja jika berkabung dengan semua negara ASEAN. Lebih baik berunding dengan Indonesia sahaja, dan jika hendak negara ketiga, Phillipines. Ketiga tiga negara ini mempunyai satu kesamaan alam, yaitu mereka semua negara kepulauan. Teknoliji wireless istemewa untuk negara kepulauan saperti Malaysia dan Indonesia. Kalau masuk campur Burma dan Thailand, itu akan menambah ragam dan masaalah.

Harga satellite serta melancarkannya sudah turun dan mungkin turun lagi. Malaysia sekarang sudah ada lima satelite. Tak mungkin semua keupayaan nya (capacity) sudah penuh di gunakan. Mungkin banyak lagi saluran yang kosong dan boleh diisi untuk memberi broadband ke luar bandar dan kawasan pendalam. Itu soalan engineering dan pentakbiran, khasnya undang undang negri, dan bukan soalan kos atau harga sebab setelite itu semua sudah di bayar dan ditanggung.

Harga boleh diturunkan lagi dengan membuka tender kesyarikat luar negri. Syarikat Cina Huawei boleh membina satelite untuk negara miskin di Afrika dan memberi computer kepada keluarga miskin. Bila kita bina sekolah kita tidak menyuroh ibubapa murid utuk membeli kerusi dan meja masing masing. Begitu juga untuk laptop. Pendek kata, masalah harga hardware boleh dan mesti di batasi. Jualkan Syarikat penerbangan MAS kalua taada duit.

Satu lagi sudut harga yang kita mesti telitikan. Yaitu berapa mahal lagi harga nya jika kita melalaikan atau menyangkar sebilangan besar masyarakat kita yang kebanyakkan nya terdiri dari kaum Bumiputra dari kemudahan TD? Sudah tentu nya tidak boleh diberi angka atas kerugian itu. Renungkan lagi, akibat kebelakangan itu akan berturun ke anak dan cucu mereka hingga tidak boleh di bela lagi.

Masaalah Kandongan

Masaalah kandongan, atau software dan isi, boleh dibatasi sebab sudah banyak yang sedia ada. Tiada gunanya kita membuang masa mengreka roda baru, hanya untuk mensuaii kandongan yang sedia untuk kehendak dan keadaan tempatan. Betul, lebih daripada 80 peratus kandongan Internet ialah dalam Bahasa Inggeris (BI), tetapi masaalah menterjemakan kandongan tidak timbul. Tinggikan sahaja kefasehan masyarakat kita dengan BI. Tambahan pula sekarang sudah ramai guru tempatan yang mengreka isi untuk murid mereka dan mengunakan Bahasa Melayu. Layari lah web Cikgu Norhailmi Abu Mutalib dan Samuel Isaiah di semenanjung. Kedua adalah finalist hadiah Global Teacher Prize. Di pendalaman Sarawak pula, ada Cikgu Nazmi bin Rosli, pemenang Golden Hearts Award. Ramai lagi guru guru yang mengambil kesempatan membuat kandongan yang menarik untuk murid mereka. Kita mesti hormati bakat tempatan dengan membiayi supaya keluaran mereka lebih meningkat dari segi mutu serta pengeluaran. Tidak payah menunggu mereka menerima pengiftaran dari luar negeri. Beri mereka grant duit; itu lebih bermakna.

Masyarakat kita mempunyai kelebehan yang sedia ada dan tidak terkira keistemewaannya. Iaitu kita mengunakan tulisan rumi. Itu menyenangkan kegunaan Internet. Kita tidak ada masaalah seperti apa yang di alami oleh masyarakat China, Thai, dan Tamil. Hanya kita tidak sedar kelebihan atau keistemewaan ini.

Batasan atau beban besar untuk murid kita islah mereka kurang fasih dalam BI sebab kita tidak memberatkan matapelajaran itu di sekolah. Kita salah faham mensifatkan kemahiran dalam BI atau apa Bahasa pun sebagai tidak mentarbatkan bahasa sendiri. Itu lah salah faham yang menjehanamkan sistem pendidikan negara dan juga bangsa Melayu.

Untuk menguasi Internet, murid kita mestilah fasih dalam BI. Inilah masaalah besar murid Melayu di luar bandar. Keadaan ini tidak mungkin semestinya. Dalam kajiannya dengan murid miskin di luar bandar India, Sugata Mitra mendapati bahawa dalam tempuh tak sampai dua bulan pun mereka boleh berbahath dan berbincang dalam BI melalui program Internet saperti "Grannny in the Cloud" dan "Schools in the Cloud."

Setahun dua dahulu ada cerita seorang budak Melayu berumur 7 tahun, Aisyah London, geleran nya. Dia fasih dalam BI, bukan BI rojak cara Malaysia, tetapi BBC atau "standard" English. Dia belum masuk sekolah pun! Macam mana ia mendapat kebolihan itu? Emak bapak nya membiarkan Aisyah mendengar siaran BBC serta membenarkan dia menenggok Youtube. Begitu juga murid luar bandar di India dengan computer membelajari BI.

Lebih baik kita membina 5G tower dan bilek computer di sekolah kampung daripada menghantar guru BI yang dilatih dengan cara culup dari kolej guru tempatan.

Pendidek Sugata Mitra membuat satu kajian dengan eksperimen "Hole in the Wall" di India. Dia letakkan sebuah computer di lubang dalam dinding. Lepas itu dia taruk videocamera di belakang untuk merakamkan perangai murid murid yang menyiasat nya. Tak sampai dua minggupun mereka dapat melayari Internet tanpa penerangan atau ajaran dari guru mereka. Bahkan guru mereka tidak tahu apa benda pun perihal computer. Experiment ini telah di buat di tempat lain. Pergilah kekampung. Berapa ramia yang sudah pandai mengunnakakn smart phone tanpa di ajar secara formal.

Keputusan pertama dari kajian Mitra ialah murid murid sama ada di India, Sweden, atau UK, boleh mengatur dan mengajar diri mereka dengan spontan untuk belajar dan mengajar antara mereka sendiri tanpa adanya arahan atau penolongan dari guru mereka. Akibat pemerhatian ini Mitra membuat program "Self Organizing Learning Environment" (SOLE) dan "Hello Hubs."

Balik ke simpulan saya yang pertama, masaalah harga "hardware" boleh dibatasi. Bahkan lebih mahal lagi jika kita abaikan cita cita murid kampung dengan tidak memberi mereka kesenangan TD. Masaalah kandongan tidak ada sebab kita bernasib baik kerana Bahasa Kebangsaan mengunakan tulisan rumi, selaras dengan Internet.

Tetapi ada satu lagi unsur terlebih penting yang kita ingkari. Saya berikan istilah budaya'an, atau culture-ware. Perkataan ini belum ada lagi dalam kamus Bahasa Melayu. Budaya'an ialah unsur unsur dalam budaya dan nilai masyarakat yang mendorong kita menyambut fikiran dan teknoloji baru, atau sebalik nya, menolak apa apa sahaja yang baru, kecuali kereta dan isteri.

Berbalek keatas, betul anak orang Asli dari Gua Musang boleh berbual dengan anak hartawan di New York melalaui Skype dan Zoom, tetapi mungkinkah ibubapa atau dan lebih luas lagi budaya dan masyarakat mereka membenarkan atau mengalakkan hubungan itu? Inilah unsur budayaan yang saya rujukkan sabentar tadi dan sukar di batasi. Mungkinkah masyarakat kita menerima apabila anak anak Melayu berfasih dengan BI sebab mereka ingin berlayar Internet? Begitu juga, mungkin kah pegawai JAKIM bersenang hati bila murid murid mendengar kuliah dan wacana diberi oleh Imam Syamsul Ali di New York atau Ilil Abdullah di Indonesia? Judy Garland pernah menyanyi lagu "How are you going to keep 'em on the farm once they have seen Gay Paree?" Terjemahan rengkas: Bagaimana nak balik kampung selepas melihat Bandar mewah Paris? Sekarang melalui Internet, Bandar Paris datang ke kampung! Inilah masaalah yang terkandung dalam istilah saya 'budayaan.'

Banyak kajian telah di buat apabila murid dapat melayari Internet dengan senang. Pertama kefasihan mereka dalam Bahasa Inggeris (BI) meningkat. Lebih endah lagi, BI yang di hafizkan mereka ialah gaya BBC, bukan bahasa rojak atau pidgin English saperti murid kita yang diajar oleh guru tempatan. Apabila penuntut menerima broadband dan memeluk TD, mereka cepat bertaraf sama dengan penuntut di negeri yang maju. Begitu juga taraf ekonomi masyarakat serta kecergasan kaum petani apabila mereka memeluk TD.

Disebaliknya, banyak unsur buruk dan kurang sehat malahkan jahat berkaitan dengan TD. Antaranya, berjudi online, isi lucah atau pornography, dan berbagai jenayah on-line. Teknoloji saperti "face recognition" (mengkenal muka) boleh digunakan untuk mencari kanak kanak yang hilang. Sebaliknya teknoloji itu juga membolehkan pemerentah yang kejam dan tidak adil memerhatihan rakyat dan memberkas kebebasan mereka saperti yang berlaku di negri China sekarang.

Inilah kebiasa'an sains serta rekaan maknusia yang lain, semuanya mempunyai dua sifat—baik dan jahat. Tenaga nuclear mengrengggankan beban maknusia dan membolehkan negara maju. Tetapi ia juga boleh menjehanamkan dunia. Begitu juga TD. Itu satu cabaran yang mesti di hadapkan.

Saperti disebut dahulu, TD menyentuhi semua bidang masyarakat, dari ekonomi, pertanian, dan perdagangan hingga ke pendidikan serta meninggikan dan membebaskan fikiran rakyat. Kita tidak boleh mengabaikan TD. Sebaliknya kita mesti memberi keutamaan kepadanya. TD ialah satu teknoloji yang membolehkan masyarakat melompat kehadapan untuk bukan sahaja bersamping dengan negara maju bahkan melebehi mereka.

Harapan Dan Cabaran Teknoloji Digital (TD) Dalam Pembelajaran Talian

Sungguh pun TD sudah luas digunakan dalam pendidikan diseluruh dunia dan disemua peringkat, tetapi buku terakhir tentang perkara ini belum lagi ditulis dan mungkin tidak dapat di tulis. Sebanya ialah model yang sesuai di satu negara tidak setentunya sesuai dengan yang lain. Perbedzaan juga berlaku di dalam negri. Masaalah dan cabaran di Kapit, Sarawak, tidak sama dengan di Gua Musang, Kelantan. Perbezaan juga berada di antara sekolah rendah, meneggah, dan perengkat universiti. Begitu juga dengan pendidekan khas dan matapelajaran istemewa seperti seni musik. Model "One Laptop Per Child" (OLPC–satu laptop, satu murid) kurang berjaya di Africa dan India, tetapi di Uruguay ia melompatkan pencapaian murid luar bandar dan mengurangkan ketidsamaan pencapaian antara mereka. OLPC seterusnya berjaya meninggikan pergunaan TD dalam masyarakat am akibat persebaran oleh murid kepada ibubapa mereka. Tetapi di Kenya, computer yang di beri ke murid terus hilang, dicuri, rosak, atau tidak diguna langsung!

Di Malaysia berita nya agak baik sedikit. Sekarang sudah muncul isi atau kandongan yang sesuai untuk keadaan tempatan. Tadi saya rujuk kepada sumbangan Cikgu Nazmi Rosli, Norhailim Mutalib dan Samuel Isaiah. Inilah endah nya TD. Tunas baru yang mungkin tidak di sangka akan timbul. Tanggung jawab kementerian ialah untuk menolong mereka bukan juga dengan hadiah tetapi dengan wang grant supaya boleh membesar dan meluaskan sumbangan mereka.

Ada tiga perhatian yang patut disedari. Pertama, di Lembah Silicon, California, Mekah TD, sekarang sudah muncul sekolah yang menarik, dimana komputer dan alat digital diharamkan dalam bilik darjah. TD hanya di gunakan untuk pentakbiran, bukan untuk pendidikan. Ibu bapa disini semua nya faham tentang peranan TD. Bahkan mereka bekerja dalam bidang itu, tetapi mereka tidak ingin anak mereka mengunakkan TD dalam pedidekkan. Sekali pandang ini mungkin pelik sedikit, menceritakan arus baru yang berlawanan dengan keadaan semasa. Tetapi tidak. Murid2 itu semua sudah fasih dan pintas menggunakan TD di rumah dan diluar bilik darjah.

Apa maknya bila di Mekah TD, guru dan ibu bapa tidak membenarkan computer dalam bilik darjah? Mereka balik keasal dengan cara lama. Iaitu, pendidikkan adalah satu perusahan antara seorang guru dengan murid nya, mengunakan kapur dan papan hitam saperti cara lama.

Ini ialah kecuali yang membuktikan kebenaran, the exception that proves the rule. Murid mereka semua sudah fasih dengan TD. Jadi guru mereka memberatkan benda atau unsur yang tidak boleh di ajar melalui TD, saperti budi bahasa dan bagaimana untuk berkerja bersama dan bantu membantu. Dalam musim ketatan Covid 19 ini, mereka dengan senang menyesuai dan menjalankan pengajian mereka melalui e-learning.

Perhatian kedua ialah di mana mana pun mungkin ada sekolah di mana guru enggan atau tidak berminat berkhidmat oleh sebab beberapa masaalah. Cara hendak menarik guru kesekolah serupa itu tidak tergantung atas ada atau tidak TD tetapi berlandasan unsur lain saperti gaji, elaun tambahan, dan beberapa galakkan yang lain. Saya yakin kalau kita naikkan gaji atau elaun mereka dan memberi kemudahan saperti rumah diam percuma, itu akan memberi kesanan yang lebih bermakna. Mungkin TD menyenangkan kerja guru tetapi itu dengan sendiri nya tidak akan menarik guru ke sekolah di Gua Musang atau Ulu Kapit.

Perhatian ketiga, sekolah yang disifatkan berjaya, sama ada di Malaysia, Finland, atau America, mempunyaii beberapa kesamaan. Antaranya ialah guru, ibubapa, dan masyarakat tempatan semua bersama aliran untuk menjunjung tinggi tujuan sekolah itu. Pendekkata, sukar untuk sekolah dan murid nya maju jika guru tidak dapat sokongan dari ibubapa dan masyarakat tempatan. TD tidak akan menukar kebenaran itu.

Malaysia bernasib baik sebab pendidikan adalah dibawah kerajaan pusat dan bukan kerajaan negri atau tempatan saperti di Amerika. Oleh sebab itu, ketidakseimbangan antara sekolah lebih senang di baikki. Ini adal masaalah terbesar di Amerika. Keadaan di Finland bersama dengan Malaysia tetapi di sana perbedaan tidak jauh jaraknya antara sekolah bercapaian tinggi dengan sekolah pencapaian rendah. Oleh sebab itu ibu bapa tidak heboh mencari sekolah yang baik untuk anak mereka. Mereka sebaliknya hanya memileh sekolah yang senang untuk mereka seperti yang dekat dari rumah. Di Malaysia ibu bapa heboh untuk memasokki anak mereka kesekolah bestari dan berasrama penuh dimana anak mereka akan ditanggung penuh oleh kerajaan. Sepatutnya sekolah berasrama dihadkan kepada anak B40 atau anak miskin.

Pencapaian dalam pendidikan, sama ada dizaman sebelum TD atau sekarang, berkaitan terus dengan kemajuan masyarakat, dan berkaitan songsang (inverse relationship) dengan kemiskinan. Ini pengalaman di seluruh dunia dan merujuk balik kepada nilai atau mutu insan yang saya sebutkan pada permulaan tadi. Mengikut kajian Muhammad Abduh Khalid, 100 peratus kanak kanak dirumah flat di KL dianggap dalam kumpulan kemiskinan; begitu juga di luar bandar. Kemiskinan meliputi di bandar dan luar bandar.

Pakar ekonomi Jomo menyatakan bahawa 90 peratus murid di Malaysia tidak dapat kemudahan TD. Itu angka yang saya rasa amat tinggi. Mengikut Yayasan Hasanah pula, hanya 37 peratus. Di Amerika, lebih kurang 15 peratus. Jomo mencadangkan membawa balik siaran pendidekan radio dan televisyen yang lama. Sekolah luar bandar boleh menerima siaran tersebut. Tetapi radio dan televisyen ialah teknolji lima pulohan. Untuk gunaan sementara atau stop-gap sahaja, itu saya setuju. Banyak kelemahan pendidikkan melalui radio dan televisyen yang cara lama itu. Anataranya, ia hanya satu arahan sahaja. Guru tidak dapat mengiktirafkan peneriman dari atau berbalas dengan murid. Murid luar bandar mesti menerima kemudahan yang seimbang dengan murid di bandar dan antarabangsa. Lebih baik lagi kalau di ubahsuaikan saluran televishyen untuk membawa signal internet seperti di Africa. Itu bukan masaalah engineering (itu boleh dibatasi) tetapi undang undang. Memberi kemudahan broadband di luar bandar, sama ada memileh cable, satellite, atau saluran telephone, adalah soalan engineering dan boleh di batasi mengambil latar belakang landskape (saperti lindungan gunung), keadaan physical (hutan), dan suasana masyarakat. Pilihan yang sesuai untuk rumah panjang di Ulu Kapit mungkin tidak di pantai Kemaman atau di hutan Gua Musang dan rumah pangsa di Kuala Lumpur.

Pilihan Yang Sesuai Untuk Malaysia

Apa saja model yang di pileh untuk sesuata tempat atau sekolah, kita mesti kaji dengan teliti masaalah serta kebaikkan nya supaya kita boleh membatasi kekurangan nya. Inilah kelemahan besar di Malaysia. Kita enggan mengkaji model kita. Kita bina dan lepas itu cabut dari kampung atau rumah panjang. Oleh sebab itu kita tidak dapat mempelajari dan membaikki kesilapan atau keburukan sesuatau model. Bandingkan dengan pengalaman Sugaro Mitra di India. Dia sentiasa membuat kajian dengan experiment nya "Hole in the Wall" yang di mulakannya pada tahun 1999. Tidak hairan jika ia boleh membaikki modelnya yang berikutan. Bandingkan di Malaysia. Berepa akitek melawat sekolah yang mereka rekabina dua atau tiga tahun kemudian untuk mempelajari dan membaikki kekurangan rekaan mereka? Sebulan sudah digunakkan, merata wire elektrik yang bergantung sebab arkitek tidak mensediakan banyak outlet electric di dinding.

Pada tahun 2003 saya melihat sekolah dikampung saya yang mana guru nya di beri sebuah laptop Apple yang mahal. Tetapi bila saya tanya, mereka tidak puas hati. Mereka terpaksa belajar mengunakkan computer di waktu sekolah sahaja. Habis sekolah laptop itu di kunci dalam almari di pejabat gurubesar. Mereka tidak ada masa untuk belajar meggunakan computer dimasa sekolah. Bandingkan pengalaman di Uruguay. Murid murid diberi computer yang mereka boleh bawa balik ke rumah dan digunakan untuk mengajar ibu bapa mereka untuk mengunakan nya dalam perniagaan mereka. Dengan itu taraf pergunaan Internet di masyarakat ikut meninggkat.

Banyak model yang sekarang sudah ada dan bolih kita contohi dan ubahsuaikan. Pertama, OLPC untuk murid supaya mereka boleh mengajar ibubapa untuk mengunakan dalam perniagaan mereka. Pak Din dengan warong goring pisangnya boleh mengunakan computer untuk menambah perniagaannya. Antara model Mitra yang amat sesuai untuk rumah panjang di Kapit ialah "Hello Hub."

Kesimpulan saya ialah pertama, semua murid dan sekolah mesti menyediakan broadband access. Ini mestilah dianggap satu kemestian seperti juga electricity dan bekalan air bersih. Jika tiap tiap sekolah luar bandar ada akses broadband, sekolah itu boleh menjadi pusat untuk penduduk sekelilingnya melayari Internet. Mereka akan mengunakannya untuk perusahan mereka. Kita mesti mensifatkan akses broadband itu satu kemestian atau keperluan. Pileh saja satu model untuk satu sekolah atau kawansan dan kaji dengan teliti impaknya. Model OLPC, Hello Hub dna Granny in the Cloud dan sebagainya.

Kedua, pendidikan melalaui talian TD semasa Covid-19 mesti lah dihadkan kepada mata pelarajan yang tidak boleh di ajar secara lain. Maknanya, hadkan kepada STEM dan BI. Mata pelajaran lain seperti ugama dan sejarah diketipan untuk sementara waktu. Ketiga, gunakan pendidikan melalui radio dan televisyen untuk sementarya sahaja. Keempat, kita mesti mencuba berbagai model dan belajar dengan teliti supaya kita boleh membaikki dan memberi tambahan kepada model itu. Tiap tiap sekolah mesti mengadakan satu atau dua orang "champion leader" yang memainkan peranan penting. Lateh serta beri mereka dana untuk mempelajari model lain. Kita mesti mengutip data supaya dapat mengubahsuai model kita dan membandingkan usaha kita dengan negara lain. Kelima, gunakan TD di semua tingkat termasuk ke universiti. Di zaman sekarang peranan guru sudah bertukar. Mereka bukan lagi disifatkan sebagai pendita di pentas, tetapi pemimpin di samping. Atau dalm BI, no longer a sage on the stage but a guide on the side.

Bibliography:

Abdullah Bin Abdul Kadir: *Cerita Kapal Asap*. Translated And With An Introduction by Annabell Teh Gallop. 2007.
https://www.tandfonline.com/doi/abs/10.1080/03062848908729700

Alima Joned: "The Awesome (Curious) Powers of the Registrar-General of Births and Deaths: Some Observations on the *Bin Abdullah* Case." *Journal of Malaysian and Comparative Law*, 47:1 2020

Ayu Utami: *Saman*. Kepustakaan Populer Gramedia, Jakarta, 2015.

Buhmann, D, and Barbara Trudell: Mother Tongue Matters: Local Language As A Key To Effective Learning. UNESCO, Paris, 2007.

Cagaptay, Soner: "'Islamist' or 'Islamic'? The Difference is Huge." Policy Analysis, Washingtoninstitue.org July 11, 2016.

Chandra Nair: "Malaysia's 'Malay First' Malaise," The Diplomat, March 4, 2020.
https://thediplomat.com/2020/03/malaysias-malay-first-malaise/

Christensen, Clayton M, Henry J Eyring: *The Innovative University. Changing the DNA of A University From Inside Out*. Josey-Bass, San Francisco, 2011.

De Soto, Hernando: *The Mystery of Capital. Why Capitalism Triumphs in the West and Fails Everywhere Else*. Basic Books, New York, 2000.

Feldman, Noah: *The Fall and Rise of the Islamic State*. Princeton U Press, Princeton, NJ, 2008.

Freire, Paulo: *Pedagogy of the Oppressed*. 30th Anniversary Edition. Translated by Myra Gergman Ramos, Bloomsbury, NY, 2000.

Galloway, Scott: *Post Corona: From Crisis To Opportunity*. Penguin Random House, New York, 2020.

Gomez, T G, K S Jomo: *Malaysia's Political Economy: Politics, Patronage and Profits*. Cambridge U Press, UK, 1997.

Gordon, Elijah: *The Real Cry of Syed Shaykh al-Hady*, Islamic Renaissance Front, Kuala Lumpur, 1999.

Hanna Alkaf: *The Weight Of Our Sky*. Salaam Read, New York, 2019.

Humphreys, Debra: "Making the Case For Liberal Education. Responding To Challenges." Association of American Colleges and Universities, Washington, DC, 2006.
(https://ge.ucmerced.edu/files/documents/Resources/making_the_case_for_libera_education_by_debra_humphreys.pdf)

Ibn 'Ata Allah Al-Iskandari: *The Book of Wisdoms: Kitab Al-Hikam – A Collection of Sufi Aphorism.* Translated by Victor Danner, The White Thread Press, London 2013. (themathesontrust.org)

E H Imrantski: "The Malaise of Malaysian Malays" (Newnaratif.com), March 8, 2018). https://newnaratif.com/malaise-malaysian-malays/

Islamicity Index: Latest 2021 Islamicity Index: Islamicity-index.org

M Kamal Hassan: *Corruption and Hypocrisy in Malay Muslim Politics.* Emir Publication, Kuala Lumpur, 2021.

Mahfouz, Naguib: *The Cairo Trilogy.* Everyman's Library, Alfred A Knopf, New York, 1957.

Kaseem, Suzy: *Rise Up and Salute the Sun.* An Awakened Press Original, 2011.

King, Martin L, Jr.,: "The Three Evils of Society." August 31, 1967. https://www.nwesd.org/ed-talks/equity/the-three-evils-of-society-address-martin-luther-king-jr/

Kiyosaki, Robert T: *Rich Dad Poor Dad: What the Rich Teach Their Kids About Money That the Poor and Middle Class Do Not.* Business Plus, 2000.

Kuru, Ahmet T: *Islam, Authoritarianism, And Underdevelopment: A Global And historical Perspective.* Cambridge University Press, Cambridge, UK, 2019.

Mahfouz, Naguib: *The Cairo Trilogy.* Everyman/Knopf, New York, 2001.

McGrady, Vanessa: *Rocks Need River: A Memoir Of A Very Open Adoption.* A Little, New York, 2019.

Muhammad Afifi Alkiti: *Defending The Transgressed By Condemning The Reckless Against The Killing of Civilians.* AQSA Press, UK, 2005

Muhammad Abul Khalid: *The Color of Inequality.* MPH Publishing, Kuala Lumpur, 2014.

Piketty, Thomas: *Capital in the Twenty-First Century.* Translated by Arthur Goldhammer. Belknap Press, Cambridge, MA, 2017

Piketty, Thomas: *Capital And Ideology.* Translated by Arthur Goldhammer. Belknap Press, Cambridge, MA, 2020.

Rosenblatt, Elizabeth M: *Literature As Exploration.* Heinemann, NY, 1970.

Muhammad Shahrour: *The Qur'an, Morality And Critical Reason. The Essential Muhammad Shahrour.* Translated, Edited and with an Introduction by Andreas Christmann. Brill, Leiden, Boston, 2009.

Scheidal, Walter: *The Great Leveler: Violence and the History of Inequality From the Stone Age to the Twenty-First Century.* Princeton U Press, Princeton, NJ, 2017.

Segran, Elizabeth: "The Malaysian Malaise. Letter From Kuala Lumpur." *Foreign Affairs*, October 10, 2013. https://www.foreignaffairs.com/articles/malaysia/2013-10-10/malaysian-malaise

Shahnon Ahmad: *Unggappan. In Seketul Hati Seorang Pemimpin*. Dewan Bahasa dan Pustaka, Kuala Lumpur 1989.

Talib, Nassim: *Black Swan: The Impact of the Highly Improbable*. Random House Inc, New York, 2007.

Tew, Yvonne: Stealth Theocracy. *Virginia J International Law*. 58:31, 2018.

Tolan, John V: *Faces Of Muhammad. Western Perception Of The Prophet Of Islam From The Middle Ages To Today*. Princeton U Press, Princeton, NJ, 2019.

Zainal Abidin Bin Ahmad (Za'aba): *Perangai Bergantung Pada Diri Sendiri*. Dewan Bahasa Dan Pustaka, Kuala Lumpur, 2007 (Reprint).

About The Author:

After over five decades of being a private practice surgeon, Bakri Musa now restricts his practice to managing, and where possible healing, chronic intractable wounds in a publicly operated hospital. Interspersed between his clinical and other responsibilities, he writes on developments, political and otherwise, in his native land – Malaysia. This is his 15th book.

His commentaries have appeared in the *New York Times*, *International Herald Tribune*, and the *Far Eastern Economic Review*, as well as in various Malaysian publications and on-line portals. He has given presentations on Malaysian affairs at Stanford's Shorenstein Asia-Pacific Research Center (APARC) and The Wilson Center in Washington, DC.

Born in Sri Menanti, Negri Sembilan, Bakri left the land of his birth on September 15, 1963, the eve of the formation of Malaysia, to attend the University of Alberta, Edmonton, Canada. He returned in January 1976 as a surgeon and was attached to the General Hospitals first in Kuala Lumpur and then Johor Baru. He left in May 1978 and has been in private surgical practice in California since 1981. In 2021 he closed his private surgical practice to join Santa Clara County's Health and Hospital System.

He has written two memoirs. First, *Cast From The Herd* recalls his days growing up in his matrilineal Minangkabau clan in Negri Sembilan, and his second, *The Son Has Not Returned*, his thirty months as a surgeon in Malaysia.

Apart from documenting his observations on his native land Malaysia, Bakri spends his time with his wife Karen on a ranch in Morgan Hill, California raising Katahdin sheep.